STRATEGIC SURVEY 1991-1992

Published by **Brassey's** for

**THE INTERNATIONAL
INSTITUTE FOR
STRATEGIC STUDIES**
23 Tavistock Street
London WC2E 7NQ

STRATEGIC SURVEY 1991–1992

Published by Brassey's for
The International Institute for Strategic Studies
23 Tavistock Street, London WC2E 7NQ

Director   Editor
François Heisbourg   Sidney Bearman

This publication has been prepared by the Director of the Institute and his Staff, who accept full responsibility for its contents, which describe and analyse events up to late March 1992. These do not, and indeed cannot, represent a consensus of views among the world-wide membership of the Institute as a whole.

First published May 1992

ISBN 0 08 041784 1
ISSN 0459-7230

Strategic Survey (ISSN 0459 7230) is published annually by Brassey's (UK) Ltd, 165 Great Dover Street, London SE1. All orders accompanied with payment should be sent directly to Turpin Distribution Services Ltd, Blackhorse Road, Letchworth, Herts SG6 1HN, UK. 1992 annual subscription rate is UK and overseas £17.00 single copy £20.00, North America $26.00, single copy $30.00. Airfreight and mailing in the USA by Publications Expediting Inc., 200 Meacham Avenue, Elmont, New York 11003, USA.
USA POSTMASTER: send address changes to Strategic Survey, Publications Expediting Inc., 200 Meacham Avenue, Elmont, New York 11003, USA. Application to mail at second-class postage is pending at Jamaica, New York 11431. All other despatches outside the UK by Printflow Air within Europe and Printflow Airsaver outside Europe.
PRINTED IN THE UK by The Friary Press, Dorchester.

CONTENTS

u
162

Perspectives

There are times when failure, rather than success, determines the course of events. For the Soviet Union it was a double failure. The fundamental one was the gradual inability of President Mikhail Gorbachev to achieve his probably impossible vision of a refurbished socialist country still under the control of a reformed Communist Party; the immediate one, however, was the rapid collapse of the *nomenklatura*-inspired coup in mid-August 1991. The cumulative weight of these failures not only destroyed the USSR, but changed the world as well.

As the Soviet Union sped to total disintegration in 1991, the European Community moved with deliberate speed towards partial integration. The climax for both came at the very end of the year, opening the door to a host of weighty questions to be answered in the months and years to come. When the Soviet empire sundered, its many parts immediately clamoured for association with, if not integration into, what will become a new Europe. Dealing with these desires is not made easier when the old Europe has not yet been able to complete its own adjustment. Before the question of how to align the various pieces into a new region can really be tackled, however, the relatively prosperous old democracies must determine how best to aid the new states to survive as new democracies. Both sides of the equation are filled with indeterminacies and multiple unknowns; it is little wonder that those struggling to find the correct solutions are floundering: beyond the failure of communism, the future place and role of the nation state in the international system is being redefined.

The Big Bang

It is a tribute to the tenacity of traditional thinking that the Western powers were so unprepared for the final demise. Despite Gorbachev's best efforts to hold the Soviet Union together, it had been clear for some time that the empire was unravelling. Yet President Bush, just a few months before the final disintegration, went to Kiev and chastised the Ukrainian nationalists who were tugging at the loose yarn, advising them that they should cease and desist. The President's stance was an attempt to assert tremulous hope over harsh reality.

Later that month, Gorbachev's conservative opponents had not made this mistake of refusing to recognize what was happening to the union. The abortive coup they mounted in August 1991 was intended to throw up an impenetrable barrier to a further slide into nationalist-driven independence by reasserting the absolute control of the centre. The mistakes they did make, however, were equally the result of a rigid mindset. They could not recognize that six years of *perestroika* and *glasnost* had so changed the structure of Soviet society that blind obedience to a positive assertion of authority, even if backed by what appeared to be strong armed force, could no longer be expected. The result was a triumph of heroic reality over false hopes.

One of the paradoxes in a year filled with paradox was that the failed coup precipitated what it had been designed to prevent. Gorbachev's vision of a renewed and strengthened socialist Soviet Union, guided by a reformed Communist Party, had failed because it destroyed an ill-functioning but existing economic system without being ready to replace it with market economics; and he failed because the instruments he used awoke forces that demanded more national and political freedom than he was willing to grant. The failure of the coup provided the opportunity and impetus for those forces to achieve their goals in double-quick time. With the collapse of the coup, the central organs of repression lost their last vestige of legitimacy along with their capability to inspire fear. The hollow union, with Gorbachev as its nominal head, then staggered briefly from one meaningless way-station to another, before collapsing completely.

The collapse was ordained when the republics refused to ratify a union which could enforce central control from Moscow. Instead, they created a Commonwealth of Independent States to act as a coordinating body in the transition from union to their full independence as governing states. The CIS was not intended to have, nor was it given, real sovereign power; it was only a useful instrument with which to handle the residual central responsibilities until the individual states could sort out how they planned to absorb them. It never looked like a stable body. Four months after its creation it had still not managed to become more than a debating society in which the ambitions of its individual units were imposing strains that could not be attenuated by its existence.

The future of the regions that used to compose the USSR thus remains wide open – in some respects dangerously open. Although some republics, most notably Russia, have embarked on a voyage to democracy and a free-market economy, totalitarian habits and outlooks are very much alive. Outside the Baltic republics there are hardly any democratic traditions upon which to build. The dangers are not only from the old reactionary left, but from a totalitarian right as well. Incipient Islamic fundamentalist movements and entrenched criminal organizations blur the picture. Furthermore, it cannot any longer be taken for granted that the average citizen, having now spent the forced savings accumulated under communist rule, can afford to wait patiently for things to improve. Empty stomachs are not only shameful; they are a security risk as well.

To its credit, the West, which was unprepared for the new challenges, has begun to move beyond stop-gap humanitarian aid. There is still a distinct risk, however, that it will pursue conflicting strategies, or that it will be unable to formulate a genuine strategy at all. Faced with the sheer magnitude of the problems at a time when its own citizens believe that dwindling resources can be better used at home, it may in frustration simply let matters drift. Nothing could be more dangerous.

The United States obviously considers Russia its most important partner. Not only its size and its nuclear arsenal, but the willingness of the present Russian government to play a constructive role in many fields, notably that of arms control, dictates such an approach. Should Russia slip into chaos, the other republics would probably follow. Yet the US approach has a built-in disability. The other states, concerned at the possibility of a revival of Russian dominance, might very easily jump to the conclusion that the US is no longer a disinterested honest broker. In particular, those republics holding strategic nuclear weapons might begin to feel that their bargaining position is strengthened – not weakened – if they cause problems and threaten to play up their nuisance value. The Ukraine is already edging in that dangerous direction.

Similarly, as an institution the EC, despite the close ties many of its members have with Russia, is bound to be particularly concerned with the new states (from the Baltics through Belarus to the Ukraine) bordering the recently resurrected Central European democracies. The EC is pushed in that direction because a membership for Russia cannot be a serious proposition for a long time to come, if ever – if only by virtue of Russia's sheer size – while varying degrees of integration into the concentric circles of the European economic area are, over time, feasible for the westernmost republics of the former USSR. To give in to these instincts, however, might shut Russia and Central Asia out, leave Turkey as the sole NATO country to look after the Caucasus, and create a new *cordon sanitaire* inside the former USSR.

On the other hand, NATO, out of a laudable desire to tie Central Asia to the European set of values and ideals, has opened the North Atlantic Cooperation Council to all successor states of the USSR. Yet, to keep its own identity distinct from that of the CSCE, it has refused to accept the neutral European nations. The latter will, therefore, not be tied into the international efforts to support positive change in key areas in the former Soviet Union. This is an odd conclusion for NATO to draw, as a glance at St Petersburg's juxtaposition to Finland indicates, unless NACC is destined to be an empty shell. The premature inflation of NATO's attempt to branch out may turn NACC into Groucho Marx's definition of a club not worth joining.

The risk is that the various institutions (to which can be added the OECD, the G-7, the WEU and the Council of Europe) will not divide the necessary tasks within a general framework. If each pursues an individual strategy in areas in which others are better qualified, the net result would not only be decreased efficiency but would open the way for those who seek support to play its potential providers off against each other. This has to be assiduously avoided. Close Western coordination and cooperation is called for, but the call has not yet been answered. Foreign Minister Genscher's vision of interlocking institutions is appropriate, but only if it isn't a euphemism for a hopeless muddle. Some institutions will eventually become subsidiaries of others (WEU *vis-à-vis* the EC); others (like NATO) will have to accept, as gracefully as possible, a less prominent role; while the EC, Europe's pivotal political and economic organization, will have to learn to devise security policies which will be more than the viewpoint of the most reluctant of its members.

Helping to create conditions that will ensure the viability of the states emerging from the ruins of the Soviet empire cannot be an end unto itself. The clear objective must be to build democratic institutions which respect human rights and will assure a fair chance for each individual to shape his own economic destiny. This means that Western support, beyond simple humanitarian aid, must be tied to conditions that reflect Western interests and values. Since these correspond to the aspirations of the vast majority of the people of the former USSR, such action will produce renewed hope for those struggling to attain these same ends. The alternative would be to produce despair – and despair is the breeding ground for totalitarianism and future insecurity.

The Nuclear Conundrum

The START Treaty, which had been laboriously negotiated over nine years, was signed by Presidents Bush and Gorbachev in Moscow in July 1991. In many respects it was a model of the arms controller's art. It called for a considerable reduction in strategic nuclear arms, and for significant and intrusive verification procedures. The achievement, at the end, was the result of a change in superpower relations from competition to cooperation. Yet this change also immediately made it an old-fashioned, out-of-date document.

Even before it has been ratified by the US Senate, and thus put formally into effect, START has been overtaken by a new form of arms control: reciprocal unilateral reductions. The first initiative was taken by President Bush, who promised in September to destroy all American ground-launched tactical nuclear weapons. President Gorbachev responded by promising to destroy all comparable Soviet systems and proposing deep cuts in strategic forces. Fears that these extraordinary advances would be lost when the Soviet Union disappeared were quickly put to rest by Russian President Boris Yeltsin who insisted that the CIS, which had assumed formal operational control of the Soviet nuclear arsenal, would adhere to all the arms-control commitments Gorbachev had made.

With these assurances Bush went a step further. In January 1992 he advanced new unilateral reductions, and offered even more if they were accepted by Russia, the Ukraine, Belarus and Kazakhstan, where the strategic nuclear weapons under Moscow's control were stationed.

Again speaking for the CIS, Yeltsin in February met this challenge, and then proposed yet more reductions of his own, if they were reciprocated by other nuclear armed states. This spiral of nuclear reductions has left the START Treaty limits far behind.

The encouraging progress that has been made in reducing arms has been tarnished, however, by the chaotic conditions that exist in the former USSR. The Ukraine, Belarus and Kazakhstan had all indicated in December and January that they intended to become nuclear-free states: they promised to transfer the nuclear arms on their own territory to Russia for destruction. Fears of Russian dominance, however, particularly in the Ukraine and to a lesser extent in Kazakhstan, have led to brinksmanship in handling relations with Yeltsin's government. As each former republic begins to build its own armed forces, while at the same time locking itself into increasingly tough rhetoric on nuclear weapons, it is no longer certain that any of them are prepared to give up their nuclear weapons wholesale. There is a disquieting possibility that in place of one nuclear power in the area, the world may soon face several.

Other problems in the nuclear weapons field arise from the potential of unattended nuclear weapons and floating nuclear scientists. It is no longer clear that sufficient controls remain to assure that neither can go astray. There are a number of rogue states throughout the world which are prepared to bid high for either. Both the ex-Soviet states and the West have recognized this clear danger; the latter has established a fund which will provide for the continuing employment of the scientists who might otherwise be open to offers of salaries so far beyond their present earnings that they could entice even those with the highest ideals. It would be folly not to recognize that those with a lower moral threshold might well agree to move their expertise to the bidding of less responsible dictators.

Non-Proliferation and Proliferation

The danger this poses is all the more acute because of the number of states which believe that either their goals can best be reached or their security can best be enhanced through the acquisition of nuclear weapons. What gives pause is that many are single-party totalitarian states, led by men whose judgement allows the world little reason for complacency. Some of them, such as North Korea, are demonstrably close to developing the bomb; others, such as Iraq, are only prevented from doing so by unusual outside supervision and control.

It is another of the paradoxes of 1991 that the world should find itself worried by nuclear proliferation just at a time when non-proliferation seemed to be gaining a secure position. On the one hand, since the 1960s, the only states that acknowledge their possession of nuclear weapons are the five permanent members of the UN Security Council. There had been some unacknowledged spread since then, but it had been regionally confined; Israel had become a nuclear state, perhaps as early as the 1960s, and India, although insisting that it had not built any bombs, had tested a nuclear device in 1974 and could construct weapons within a short time. Pakistan, following in India's footsteps, has a similar capability. But Brazil and Argentina, both at one time seriously moving towards a weapons' capability, signed a bilateral agreement in 1991 not to develop nuclear weapons. South Africa, a state with a powerful nuclear industry, signed the Nuclear Non-Proliferation Treaty in 1991, and France and China both joined the NPT as nuclear states in 1991 as well. In addition, the nuclear superpowers began to reduce their arsenals far below the levels they had maintained for so long, and were ready to play down the role of nuclear deterrence in ensuring international security.

On the other hand, some of the ex-Soviet Union's weapons may end up in the control of up to three states in addition to Russia. In the Middle East a number of states are working frantically to evade non-proliferation controls. Iraq has been prevented from doing so only because Saddam Hussein invaded Kuwait before constructing the nuclear weapons he was so close to completing. The overwhelming victory of the coalition over his depleted troops forced him to accept UN sanctions and the step-by-step dismantlement of his remaining nuclear weapons potential. Libya and Iran, however, have aroused sufficient suspicions about their intentions and capabilities to warrant grave concern. Syria's intentions, if not its capabilities, are also suspect.

Perhaps the most immediate proliferation danger involves North Korea. Overhead photography and other intelligence has made it clear that the North Koreans are not far from becoming a nuclear weapon state. The North Koreans deny this is their intention; their nuclear facilities, they claim, are purely for the production of much-needed nuclear energy. Much of the world, including China and Russia as well as South Korea, Japan and the United States, has been pressing the Pyongyang leadership to allow intrusive examination of their capability by the IAEA. Typically, Kim Il-sung has tried to appear accommodating, but it remains to be seen whether this isn't simply a way of putting off the day of reckoning.

These threshold states are rushing to complete programmes just as the nuclear weapons states are coming to the opinion that the weapons may have lost much of their political usefulness. It may be difficult to convince have-not nations, which believe that in the modern world non-possession of nuclear weapons somehow disqualifies a nation from great-power status, that there are better roads to international influence. There are useful models to the contrary, however, and not only in Japan and Germany, both powerful nations that have built their present positions on economic growth, rather than weapons acquisition: many of the OECD's members – the 24 most industrialized countries – could readily become nuclear powers but have deliberately refrained from doing so.

Whether the world will move towards a strengthening of the non-proliferation regime or rush to multiple nuclear armed states is a matter that may be determined within only a few years: in 1995, the 146 signatories of the NPT will decide the future of the Treaty. It may be time to look once again at some version of the Baruch Plan, which would indicate that nuclear power states are willing to vastly reduce their own armaments. Unless a way can be found to bring those states on the verge of proliferation back from the brink voluntarily, the major powers will have either to consider the use of military force or see the world threatened by a rapid increase in the number of those who can, through hubris or sheer stupidity, destroy much of what little civilization the world has thus far managed to acquire.

Building a New Order

The demise of communist control has opened the door to an era of greater cooperation than ever before. In many ways, glimmers of such a glowing vision of the future can already be seen. They are best discerned in a newly active, and more effective, United Nations, which has shed the Cold War antagonisms that hobbled it for the whole of its existence. Most telling, perhaps, is a willingness to consider intervening in what until now would have been considered a state's sovereign rights within its own borders.

The Security Council has stood firmly together against all Saddam Hussein's efforts to gain adherents for the view that UN sanctions, protection of the Iraqi Kurds, and destruction of Iraq's advanced weaponry contravened international law on the rights of sovereign states. The UN has begun to deploy a 14,000-man peace-keeping force, at a cost estimated to be over $600m, to the former state of Yugoslavia, despite the fact that there is still fighting there and no decisions have been made by the emerging states concerning ethnic enclaves or new borders. It has decided to dispatch a 22,000-man force to Cambodia, at a cost estimated to be over $2bn, not only to keep the peace, but to disarm and disband the opposing factions, and to run the country while it organizes elections for a new government. Although it has yet to find an effective way to stop the vicious civil war in the Sudan, it is reviewing the situation and has indicated that it may become involved there as well.

These actions, which go far beyond the narrow bounds of the self-imposed constraints of the recent past, are welcome indicators that there is indeed a possible new order developing on the international scene. They were joined in 1991 by the remarkable opening of talks between the Israeli government, on the one hand, and the Palestinians, Jordanians, Syrians and Lebanese, on the other. Thus far the talks are more procedural than substantive, and neither side has gone beyond rhetorical blustering, but neither has either side been willing to break the talks off. Much depends on the outcome of the elections to be held in Israel in July 1992; if a clearer mandate for compromise emerges from these elections the hopes of the adroit and determined US diplomacy which led to the dialogue may be met.

Another indication of the ability of the international community to foster change in a country's domestic arrangements was seen in the positive outcome of the referendum held in South Africa in March 1992. The white minority, who had for so long maintained a political stranglehold over the black majority, relinquished their grip by voting to continue the reforms which President de Klerk had begun. His courageous gamble owed much to their recognition that continued intransigence would only isolate their country further in an international system willing to maintain, if not increase, its broad array of sanctions.

Notwithstanding the remarkable stability of the Cold War world – at least in its European manifestation – the beginnings of this new, if still tentative, international system should be welcomed. There is a better, more secure environment to be gained, at a fraction of the cost of the armaments required in the past to ensure more dubious security. The technologically-advanced, democratic nations should be eager to support these efforts, willingly making the sacrifices necessary to assure forward movement. Compared to the sacrifices being demanded of the people of the former communist states as they struggle to attain the blessings of democracy and free-market economics, they fade to insignificance. Nowhere, however, is the challenge being met.

The UN is starved of funds. The effectiveness of its important new peace-keeping initiatives is jeopardized by the failure of many countries, most notably the United States, to make up their long-standing deficits, and to supply additional funds. The recently elected Secretary-General, Boutros Boutros Ghali, has moved smartly to restructure what had been a bureaucratically top-heavy organization; if not yet in fighting trim, it is certainly becoming leaner and fitter. Although the major countries are calling anxiously for the UN to do more, they seem unwilling to do more themselves. No new order can be built unless these countries are prepared to bear this burden, which appears financially insignificant in comparison to the monies spent on defence during the Cold War.

The United States

Americans have never been known for doing things by halves. At one time they were called on to bear any burden, and they responded. Now they are in retreat from international obligations, and they have a leader whose idea of how to lead is to follow the opinion polls. These polls show a people who believe that they have 'won' the Cold War, and like all victors, wish to reap whatever spoils are left. They no longer see an enemy out there against whom they must gird their loins, the enemy is within and the fight must be fought at home.

The United States has been accumulating domestic problems for many years and there is much justification in the cries that attention be paid to them. The economy is just groping its way out of recession; the budget deficit continues to mount; the inner cities rot a little more each year; infrastructures of all kinds are decaying; both the education and health systems need emergency repair. Money, however, is short. There is little enthusiasm for sending it abroad, whether to help those struggling to shake off the dark night of communist misrule or to improve the ability of the UN to first dampen, then tame the many conflicts that still poison the international atmosphere in more ways than one: there is also little US readiness to shoulder its share of reducing the emission of greenhouse gases, thus paving the way for a bruising confrontation with the EC and the Third World at the Rio Summit on the environment in June 1992.

Although they are on the brink of closing their eyes on external demands, however, Americans have not been put to sleep by the isolationist 'America First' lullaby sung by Pat Buchanan and others. Ex-President Richard Nixon was surely right when he pointed out in a trenchant speech in March 1992 that firm and decisive leadership is all that is needed to reawaken a realization that generosity abroad is needed to guarantee tranquillity at home. Both domestic and international burdens could be met if the administration were willing to work with, rather than against, those in Congress, like Senator Sam Nunn and Representative Les Aspin, who are trying to reallocate funds from the defence budget to meet other needs. The times call for such an effort.

The EC

The countries of Europe find themselves in much the same position. Their economies have slowed; each has pressing domestic concerns, notably with regard to immigration; and many ruling governments face unhappy electorates that show every sign of believing it is time for a change. As a result, they too have turned inwards.

Europe, however, has an extra reason for its present concern with itself. There is first the complex problem of unification, which was only partially addressed at the Maastricht summit in December 1991. Then there is the need to ratify the decisions reached at Maastricht; in some cases, notably France, ratification will require difficult constitutional change. Debate on these measures is growing fiercer, and second thoughts are mounting. Beyond this looms the question of enlargement. There are a clutch of countries which wish to move from EFTA to the EC, and there is a clamour from the countries formerly under communist grip which feel that their salvation can be reached more quickly and easily if they also are part of the EC. Grappling with these closer-to-home problems has left European leaders with little time, or scope, to lift their sights to wider horizons.

Germany and Japan

Despite unmatched generosity towards Central and South-eastern European countries and the former Soviet Union, even Germany, once the staunchest supporter of the principle of close integration in Europe, is now turning inward. The integration of the eastern *Länder* into the German Federation has proved a far more costly and difficult task than originally thought. Social tensions have arisen that do not make it any easier. Germans, from Chancellor Kohl downward, are no longer quite so certain that they wish to be constrained by tighter EC institutions, particularly in the monetary realm; the manipulation of recognition of Slovenia and Croatia through the exercise of German heft, despite the reluctance of other EC partners, was a harbinger of future friction. While the German economy is still basically strong, and by far the largest in Europe, it is suffering from the many burdens placed on it, not least the costs of integrating the former GDR.

Japan, too, is finding its ability to contribute to a new order adversely affected by changes in its economy. The leaders of the ruling LDP have been searching for many years for the proper role to play in international affairs. Because of the aversion of the Japanese people to the use of military personnel abroad, they saw their role best fulfilled in financial terms. The Japanese economy has slowed, however; while not yet in what others would consider a recession, the Japanese, accustomed to constant high growth, perceive it to be one. At the same time, a new series of scandals threatens to loosen the LDP's grip on power. The Japanese as well are now turning their gaze inwards.

Let's Not Lose the Peace

It is of course natural that the world's democracies have greeted the demise of the Soviet Union, and the end of any threat of communist control in most of the world, with a sigh of relief. These most welcome developments, however, do not allow the world's leaders to relax their vigilance. One set of problems has been solved; the solution, however, has exposed a wholly new set. It is easy to see how quickly the former communist states, if they are not nurtured with massive aid, can slide into other non-democratic traps. A stable, if unpleasant, world order has disappeared. The future promises far more pleasant vistas; the present, however, is rife with instability.

Stalin was fond of quoting Lenin (who knew he was paraphrasing Goethe) by proclaiming that ideology is grey, but the tree of life is ever green. He did not realize that life itself would condemn not the West, but the drawn-out Soviet experiment to the trashcan of history. History's trashcan is commodious, however. There will always be room in it for those who do not see reality clearly, and who thereby fail to rise to the challenges it sets.

Europe

THE END OF AN EMPIRE

The Soviet Union collapsed at the end of 1991. It was an event that had been long awaited, with gleeful anticipation by some and with dread by others. What triggered the final implosion was unexpected. Reactionary leaders of the most oppressive institutions in the Soviet Union mounted a coup in August 1991 which was intended to halt the economic reforms and the dissolution of the union, but which ironically had exactly the opposite effect. The swift and ignominious failure of the coup fatally weakened the institutions which had provided the foundations of central control. With these supporting pillars undermined the once awe-inspiring edifice crumbled.

The dust has not yet settled, and it will be years before anyone will be sure what kind of structures can be created out of the rubble. What does seem clear is that the pieces into which the Soviet Union has broken look anything but stable. The world has entered a new era which offers great opportunities, but complex and dangerous challenges as well. Balancing the risk and the promise presents a difficult test for statesmen both within the successor republics of the former Soviet Union and in the outside world.

Twilight of an Era

During the early years of his helmsmanship President Mikhail Gorbachev was able to occupy the middle ground between conservative and liberal forces – and to turn that position to his tactical advantage. Yet once the conservatives, whose core values and privileges were threatened, became more bitter and desperate, and liberal forces turned to nationalism to advance their cause, his room for manoeuvre dwindled. Gorbachev believed that the only way out of these perplexities was to strengthen his own formal position, thus concentrating in his hands the power needed to impose his views on the warring factions.

It was a dangerous game. Not only was opposition from the liberal and nationalist forces against a union presidency with extraordinary powers inevitable, but his move was a direct challenge to Boris Yeltsin. The Russian leader – once a rising star of the Party, then sacked from the Politburo when he became too outspoken – had lost any hope that the Communist Party, and the system which the USSR had inherited from Stalin and his successors, could be reformed. Fundamental, not superficial, change was needed. That meant not a strong union, or union presidency, but strong republics responding to the needs of their people and capable of doing so without interference from above. On that platform he won every election he entered. By the same token, Yeltsin was transformed from one of Gorbachev's closest allies into his most serious political rival. At a key meeting of the Central Committee in early February 1991, he was the only man with the courage to vote against the new and strengthened presidency.

Gorbachev's hopes, in fact, were in many respects closer to those of the liberals, but his fear that bold steps would provoke a disastrous conservative backlash made him shrink from decisions. This vacillation simply reinforced the liberals' swing towards nationalism, since the republican level remained the only one where substantial reforms still looked possible. This transformation confirmed Gorbachev's conviction that, in the short term, the liberals were his more dangerous problem. To ally himself with them would compromise the union, and without the union he could see no future for the USSR. From autumn 1990 Gorbachev gradually moved closer to the conservative camp. He had, after all, outwitted it many times in the past; he thought this temporary tactical move would not hold too many dangers. His plan, apparently, was to use the conservatives, who still held all the key positions in the traditional pillars of the state (the army, the internal security forces, the KGB and the Party) to stop the nationalist leanings of the liberals – and then, from a strengthened power base, to implement much of the liberal programme. In March 1991 he used his new powers to abolish Article 6 of the Soviet constitution (which provided the CPSU with a monopoly of power) and to define the transition towards a market economy as an eventual objective. His reasoning, however, turned out to be faulty.

By early 1991 the guns were in the hand of the conservatives – and they had been able to use them without any adverse reaction from Gorbachev in Lithuania. For them, Gorbachev was the man who had accepted the reunification of Germany, had thrown away the outer empire and might well throw away the union along with the power of the apparat. They despised Yeltsin and feared him at the same time – not only because of his political views, but also, and perhaps even more so, because he opposed the privileges of power and the *nomenklatura*. They considered Yeltsin a mortal danger; Gorbachev, however, seems to have appeared to them as weak, as a tactician, who would, if confronted with *faits accomplis* seek ways to live with them. Their strategy was thus first, to neutralize Yeltsin; second, to force Gorbachev to play their game, or neutralize him as well.

Conservatives in the Supreme Soviet of the Russian Republic hence pressed for an impeachment vote against Yeltsin, eventually scheduled for 28 March 1991. They clearly hoped that the brutal – and unpunished – use of force in the Baltics in January would intimidate many representatives. Yeltsin had been elected Chairman of the Supreme Soviet of the RSFSR only in the third ballot and with a very narrow margin. It would take only a few turncoats to sack him. That calculation turned out to be wrong too. At the crucial moment the conservatives could not even muster enough support to put the no-confidence vote against Yeltsin on the agenda of the meeting.

There were several reasons for this outcome. First, the liberal forces had been shocked by the resignation of Foreign Minister Eduard Shevardnadze in December 1990 and by the intervention in Lithuania in January 1991, but they had not been silenced. Above all, Boris Yeltsin refused to be intimidated. On 19 February he openly called for Gorbachev's resignation. People took to the streets of Moscow and other key cities, demanding fundamental economic reforms and opposing the return of dictatorship. Nor could these crowds be cowed. When a rally scheduled for 27 March, the eve of the vote in the Supreme Soviet, was prohibited and 50,000 troops were brought to Moscow to enforce the ban, no fewer than 100,000 protesters turned out. The conservatives were forced to recognize that getting rid of Yeltsin might induce large-scale riots.

Second, the miners went on strike in support of Yeltsin. Without them (and the transport workers, who were willing to join the strike), an economy already in free fall (industrial production declined in the first quarter of 1991 at an annual rate of 12% according to official figures) would collapse. Only Yeltsin had the credibility to deal with the exploding labour unrest. To sack him would be to sign the economy's death warrant.

Third, Gorbachev's hope of using a referendum to check the nationalist forces and hold the Union together had failed. Only nine of the 15 republics even participated in the 17 March poll that asked Soviet citizens to preserve the union. Although Gorbachev could claim that 70% of those voting had expressed their support for a renovated union, the referendum question had been so obscurely phrased that the results were ambiguous at best, and there had been negative majorities in Moscow, Leningrad and several other cities. Without Yeltsin's support there could be no hope for a new union treaty. The country might simply fall apart.

Finally, Gorbachev had to recognize that the conservatives (whose institutional power base he himself had continued to strengthen) could no longer be manipulated through clever tactics. Their attacks on him multiplied and increased in viciousness. Reactionary forces in the CPSU openly announced their intention to ask for his resignation as Party leader at the upcoming April Central Committee meeting. In June 1991, Prime Minister Valentin Pavlov even attempted a 'constitutional coup d'Etat' by requesting, unsuccessfully, that the Supreme Soviet grant him emergency powers to issue decrees without the approval of parliament. This was stymied, notably thanks to the belated recognition by Gorbachev that, for the time being at least, he needed to reach a *modus vivendi* with Yeltsin. On 23 April, on the eve of the Central Committee plenary, Gorbachev, Yeltsin and eight other republican leaders met at Novo Ogarevo, near Moscow. The meeting of the 'Nine plus One', as it became known, resulted in a joint declaration on urgent measures to stabilize the situation. Its key points were an agreement to conclude a new union treaty as quickly as possible, to adopt a new constitution for the USSR, and to call for democratic elections for the new state organs that would then be established.

It was an extraordinary meeting. The new body of the 'Nine plus One' stood outside all constitutional or Party structures. When it quickly turned into the only decision-making body with any remaining influence, the old structures of the union were rendered obsolete. Real power began to shift to the republics. In essence, Gorbachev gave up his claim to direct the destiny of the country and agreed to share power. Significantly, the six republics which had refused to participate in the 17 March referendum (i.e., the three Baltic republics, Georgia, Moldova and Armenia) were not invited to the meeting.

'Nine plus One' might have had a reasonable chance of solving the perplexities of the decaying USSR had it reflected a genuine intention by the republics to tackle the country's problems together. That will, however, no longer existed. In the end, the meeting simply hastened the inevitable collapse of the USSR. Instead of filling a power vacuum, it only highlighted it. Gorbachev and Yeltsin had teamed up in hopes of achieving their own goals, but their relationship was still one marked more by rivalry than partnership.

Yeltsin proved the shrewder tactician. On 12 June he was elected President of Russia, accruing 57.3% of the votes (his closest competitor received only 16.9%). Sworn in on 1 July, Yeltsin immediately made it clear that he was determined to get things moving, whether Gorbachev and the republics agreed or not. He announced his determination to move Russia quickly towards a free-market system. On 3 August he crossed an important threshold by prohibiting all activities of the CPSU in Russia. In effect, he declared war on the old system and on the privileges of the *nomenklatura*. His move clearly reflected the mood in the country. Russia seemed determined to go its own way, with little regard for anything the new union treaty would say.

Gorbachev, on the other hand, still dithered. He again made concessions to the conservatives, whose mood now bordered on panic. He tried to appease them by suggesting changes to the text of the new union treaty, scheduled for signing on 20 August. Almost to the very end he seemed not to recognize that none of this mattered. The conservatives and Yeltsin, by 3 August at the latest, had begun a power struggle in which the details of legal texts no longer had any meaning. Yeltsin was convinced that Russia would have to insist on its own sovereignty; the conservatives knew all too well that there would be no room for them in such a Russia. The country was on the brink of a revolution which the conservatives could not hope to survive. On 18 August, in desperation, they struck back.

The Coup

Shortly after 6am (Moscow time) on 19 August 1991, the USSR – and the world – were awakened by an announcement from TASS and Radio

Moscow that Gorbachev had fallen 'ill' and was no longer capable of fulfilling his functions. Vice-President Gennady Yanaev, a well-known conservative, assumed power as acting president. A state of emergency was declared for a period of six months; an eight-man 'State Committee for the State of Emergency', headed by Yanaev, would supervise it. Its members also included Defence Minister Dimitry Yasov, KGB Chairman Vladimir Kryuchkov, Soviet Prime Minister Valentin Pavlov, Soviet Interior Minister Boris Pugo, and First Deputy Chairman of the USSR Defence Council Oleg Baklanov. The USSR was declared to be in 'mortal danger'. In order to overcome 'chaos and anarchy', 16 measures were decreed – including a ban on all strikes, demonstrations and rallies, activities of political parties and mass movements that would prevent 'the normalization of the situation', and the imposition of press censorship. Security organs were ordered to restore law and order. The Soviet constitution and union laws were declared to have supremacy over every other legislation. The world was assured that the new leadership would honour all Soviet international obligations, treaties and agreements. These declarations, repeated every hour over the Soviet media, were underlined by the deployment of troops to the streets of Moscow.

The effort to take over the country had begun the evening before when unannounced visitors arrived at the President's Crimean *dacha* and demanded an audience. Sensing danger, Gorbachev tried to call Moscow – only to find that all his telephone lines had been disconnected and his villa surrounded by KGB troops. When he finally received the plotters he was confronted with an ultimatum: either join the coup or hand over power to Yanaev. Gorbachev refused both options and was placed under house arrest. For the first time the eternal tactician had refused to accept a *fait accompli*. This decision was probably a distinct surprise to the plotters; it was the first of many shoals on which the coup was soon to founder.

The second was in Moscow. Yeltsin, who had not spent the night at his home, was awakened in the early hours of 19 August by a telephone call, warning him that he was about to be arrested (dozens of people were indeed rounded up in Moscow that morning). He was spirited by car to the White House, the seat of the Russian government and parliament in the heart of Moscow, on the way crossing the path of the security forces sent to arrest him.

Throughout much of that day, the situation hung in precarious balance. It has become fashionable to state that the coup never had a chance and was conducted in an amateurish fashion. The sober reality on that Monday morning was quite different. Official (though not private) telephone lines had been cut throughout Moscow and its inhabitants were in profound shock. By 10am no more than a few dozen people had gathered outside the White House – and none elsewhere. A company of armoured cars had drawn up in front of the building. The republics were anxious, but except for the Baltics, initially remained largely neutral. Had Yeltsin been arrested during these critical hours, the coup might have succeeded, at least temporarily.

The turning-point came when an outwardly relaxed Yeltsin emerged for some minutes from the White House, shook the hands of the bewildered troops, used the confusion of the moment to mount an armoured car, and, filmed by CNN and other news organizations that would beam these pictures around the world, declared all orders of the Emergency Committee null and void, called for a general strike and announced democratic Russia's active resistance to the coup. It was at this moment, on Monday, 19 August at 12.55pm local time, that the coup lost its driving force.

It had been a venture based on wrong assumptions. The conservatives had believed that they would meet little resistance from Gorbachev. Equally wrongly, they had also assumed that a demonstration of power would cow most of the populace. There might be a few deaths (as there had been in Vilnius in January), but they could not visualize any strong resistance to the coup either at home or abroad. Least of all did they believe that for the coup to succeed it would be necessary to use on a large scale the power that, in their eyes, was so visibly theirs: international telecommunications continued to function, as did the airports; by holding a live televised press conference the plotters inadvertently allowed the whole country to learn of Yeltsin's call for a general strike. These were the classic mistakes of lifelong *apparatchiks* who craved nothing but power and who could not understand that others might put greater weight on other values – such as freedom. It was also a measure of their failure to grasp that although Gorbachev's reforms had been ineffective in some regards, in others they had altered the Soviet Union beyond recall. Indeed, the plotters would have found it difficult to give decisive, shoot-to-kill orders to less than unquestioning soldiers.

The initiative flowed rapidly away from Yanaev and his accomplices. From hundreds of people milling about the White House in the morning, the mass rose to a solid wall of perhaps 50,000. Some commanders and troops openly defected to the Russian side. Inside the White House, Yeltsin had managed to gain access to a private telephone line, and had established contact with other centres of resistance around the country and with the West. British Prime Minister John Major and US President Bush began an intensive, and ultimately effective, drive to organize international opposition to the plotters.

By midday on 20 August the tide had clearly turned. The miners were out on strike. Hundreds of thousands of people were on the streets of Moscow and St Petersburg. The armed forces would not obey orders from the Emergency Committee and at best would stay neutral, and several newspapers and radio stations ignored the censorship and called for resistance. By now most of the republics had swung behind Yeltsin. Seizing the moment, Yeltsin went on the offensive. He issued an ultimatum to the coup leaders, demanded to meet Gorbachev within 24 hours, and insisted on the immediate withdrawal of all troops from Moscow and St Petersburg.

Faced by such defiance, the plotters – or at least some of them – decided to use force against the White House. A curfew was declared in Moscow, but the people would not leave the streets, nor was any army or KGB combat formation prepared to carry out the order to attack. The Emergency Committee consequently panicked. Yanaev assured Yeltsin that he would not permit any assault on the Russian parliament building. Pavlov fell 'ill'. Rumours begun to circulate that Yasov and/or Kryuchkov might have resigned. Communications between the coup leaders and the White House, which had never been broken off, became frantic. The plotters began to look for ways to save their skins.

On 21 August, Yeltsin called an emergency session of the Russian parliament and announced that the plotters had accepted his demand that a delegation of the Russian government could meet with Gorbachev. Yeltsin ordered the immediate arrest of the members of the Emergency Committee and within hours that order was executed and other arrests had begun. The presidium of the USSR Supreme Soviet, meeting in an emergency session, declared the coup attempt illegal and restored Gorbachev to power. On 22 August the President returned to Moscow, looking haggard, but in good health. The coup was over.

The End of the Soviet Union

The end of the coup signalled the end for the CPSU and the USSR as well. The positions of Russia and of Boris Yeltsin had been profoundly strengthened. The CPSU and all central institutions had been irrevocably discredited. The Russian government took *de facto* control; Russian Prime Minister Ivan Silaev formally took over the union premiership on 28 August. Activities of the CPSU were at first only suspended, but on 6 November the Party was officially banned. Under such circumstances, any attempt to restore central authority would have been seen by the republics as a bid for Russian predominance. None would have it. In the midst of the coup the Baltic states had already declared their full independence, a step rapidly acknowledged by the West and by the dissolving USSR on 6 September. The other republics would soon go their own way as well.

None of this seemed to be fully understood by Mikhail Gorbachev when he gave his first press conference immediately after his return to Moscow. While his account of his personal ordeal awakened sympathy, his refusal to resign as Secretary-General of the CPSU, and his pleas not to engage in 'witch hunts' and to continue on a 'socialist path', simply illustrated how profoundly out of touch he had become. He had clearly changed and would continue to change (he resigned as CPSU Secretary-General only two days later), but the country had changed even more fundamentally and was evolving much more quickly than he could. From the outset, Gorbachev had no chance to restore even a semblance of a real power base. The fact that Yeltsin did his best to assure this, humiliating him in front of television cameras in both the Russian parliament and the Soviet Supreme Soviet, hardly mattered. At the end, Gorbachev became a living incarnation of his own dictum that history will punish those who act too late.

It was a sad exit for a leader who had profoundly altered world history. Gorbachev had not only recognized that the survival of the Soviet Union depended on fundamental reforms, but had actually initiated them. It was his policy of *glasnost* that had created the men and the mood which ensured that the conservative coup, when it eventually came, would founder. He embarked on a path that would end the Cold War, free Eastern Europe, bring about German unity and profoundly change East–West relations. The world owes much to Gorbachev.

Yeltsin and democratic Russia celebrated their victory with high hopes for a new beginning. One after the other, the old, discredited institutions of the union dissolved – starting with the Supreme Soviet and the Congress of People's Deputies. Negotiations on a new union treaty continued, but the time for such an initiative had passed. The republics had tasted freedom and would not surrender it again. They also feared Russian preponderance and were determined not to simply replace Soviet with Russian rule. Yeltsin, endowed with extraordinary powers by the Russian parliament on 1 November, did little to allay these fears. His statement on 27 August that republics seceding from the union might have to face territorial claims by Russia and the prospect of conflict, was an amazing blunder. Although immediately revoked, it would not be easily forgotten.

The first session of the new Supreme Soviet, opening on 21 October, was attended by delegates from only seven republics. Among those absent was the Ukraine. The political centre of gravity had indeed shifted elsewhere: to an evolving set of direct negotiations between the republics. Russia, no longer believing in the union, had taken the lead. On 29 August, it concluded a bilateral treaty with the Ukraine. The major significance of the agreement was that neither party treated the other as part of the USSR, but as sovereign states. The next day a similar agreement between Russia and Kazakhstan was reached, and Yeltsin invited all other republics to join in this treaty network. By 1 September Gorbachev was obliged to acknowledge that the country's future might lie in a confederation rather than a union.

Although 13 republics joined in a preparatory meeting in Alma Ata, only eight of them concluded a treaty on economic cooperation on 18 October. The Ukraine refused to join. On 14 November, the Soviet constitution was abrogated. The republics had by now adopted their own constitutions as supreme and were no longer willing to cooperate in the drafting of a new one at the union level. The following day seven republics (but again not the Ukraine) agreed to work towards the creation of a Union of Sovereign States to replace the old USSR. More reasonably, the new entity was to be a confederation, but even that soon proved too ambitious. On 25 November the proposed treaty of this new union was rejected by the leaders of the seven republics. Without the Ukraine the new construction seemed doomed – and the Ukraine, fearing Russian dominance, would no longer join any union, whether it was a confederation or not.

The pace of dissolution picked up. On 1 December an overwhelming majority of the Ukrainian population voted for independence. On 8 December the leaders of Russia, the Ukraine and Byelorussia (now named Belarus) met in Minsk to create a Commonwealth of Independent States. The charter stated that the USSR 'as a subject of international law and geopolitical reality is ceasing its existence'. On 13 December the five Central Asian republics declared their willingness to join, and on 22 December the CIS expanded to a grouping of 11 sovereign states, tied together only by a few, and very ill-defined, joint organs, while the CIS itself did not become a subject of international law. Georgia and the three Baltic states remained aloof, and Russia took over the USSR's seat as a permanent member of the UN Security Council. All attempts by Gorbachev to ward off the inevitable had failed. On 30 December he resigned. The Soviet Union had ceased to exist; the Russian flag replaced the Red flag over the Kremlin.

A Sea of Troubles

It is difficult to determine whether the CIS is going to survive or not, and, if so, under what guise. There are good reasons for believing though, that the CIS, at least in its current form, will prove to be only a transitional structure, helpful in managing a divorce, but not able to maintain even a semblance of central or military 'union'.

The 14 articles of the Minsk agreement were supposed to form a code of conduct for the successor states of the USSR. The members of the Commonwealth recognized their respective borders; national minorities in all member states were guaranteed 'equal rights and freedoms in accordance with common international norms on human rights'; agreement was reached on the joint control of the strategic, nuclear and space arsenal of the former USSR; coordination, including corresponding joint institutions, were to be established for foreign policy, economic policies, transport and communications, ecology, migration and the war against crime; and all international obligations, treaties and agreements concluded by the former USSR were guaranteed by its successor states. Minsk was declared the location 'to station the coordinating organs' of the CIS. There is no question but that in a disintegrating union these fundamental issues had to be settled, and quickly, if chaos was to be prevented. The only problem with the agreement was that it remained far from clear whether it truly settled any of them.

Nuclear Weapons

The nuclear issue remains wide open. It is essentially composed of four different problems: control over strategic nuclear weapons; the problem of tactical nuclear weapons, of which there are an estimated 17,000 (most in operational service and undisclosed thousands in deep storage); the danger that Soviet weapons experts might be lured by lucrative offers into the services of Third World dictators; and control over nuclear fissile material and the production plants for such materials.

Both Yeltsin and Gorbachev responded immediately and positively to President Bush's offer in early September 1991 to destroy all ground-launched tactical nuclear weapons. All the new states supported this decision, and accepted that these weapons should be moved to Russian soil before July 1992, before being dismantled. By March 1992, tactical nuclear weapons continued to be stationed only in Belarus, Russia and the Ukraine. However, the Ukraine changed its stance in March and sought to prevent the transfer of some 2,200 remaining tactical nuclear weapons to Russia.

Aside from the uncertainty concerning the Ukraine's intentions, the key problems in this area remain the continuing uncertainty about the number of weapons that actually exist, and the fact that existing dismantling facilities are inadequate to do the job quickly. Western financial and technical assistance will be needed to overcome this obstacle.

Strategic nuclear weapons (at least 12,000 deployed warheads) present a more complex problem. Their numbers will be substantially reduced under the START Treaty if it is implemented; like the US, Russia has clearly signalled a willingness to go even further. Genuine co-operation has replaced confrontation in this relationship. The attitude of the other three successor states with strategic nuclear weapons (the Ukraine, Belarus and Kazakhstan) continues to shift, however, and hence is more difficult to fathom. The Ukraine, still suffering from the consequences of Chernobyl, officially states that it intends to become a nuclear-free country, and has announced that it would eliminate all strategic nuclear weapons from Ukrainian soil by the end of 1994, plenty of time for vacillation. Belarus gives the impression of being an interested onlooker to these debates. The situation is particularly alarming in Kazakhstan, where 104 SS-18s can launch a number of warheads compared to the combined totals of China, France and the UK. Although Alma Ata may simply be seeking to improve its bargaining position, official statements have been increasingly ambiguous, suggesting that nuclear disarmament could be linked to that of the recognized nuclear powers.

CIS summits held in Minsk on 14 February and in Kiev on 20 March failed to resolve the issue of the future of these nuclear weapons. Although Russia's President and the CIS Minister of Defence appear to have joint control of the nuclear button, prospects are far from encouraging.

Even more worrying is that there appears to be little hope of ensuring that either nuclear expertise or fissile material can be kept out of the wrong hands. Soviet nuclear scientists currently earn around 900 roubles per month, an insignificant sum compared to what their expertise could bring them on the world market. Several Third World countries have reportedly offered hundreds of thousands of dollars for such experts. The US and Japan have agreed to provide $75m to establish a scientific technical institute that would give these scientists meaningful work and satisfactory salaries. Although most of these scientists will undoubtedly conduct themselves responsibly, there is no guarantee that all of them will. In all probability, at least a few will be tempted to sell their skills to outside powers.

Nor is there any certainty that the secretive and compartmentalized ex-USSR maintained a comprehensive centralized inventory of all special nuclear materials, or that those who continue to produce weapons-grade material are incorruptible. (Before it was stopped, Tajikistan, with an almost charming naiveté, was offering to sell enriched uranium on a commercial basis.) The international community – and, equally important, the leaders of the republics most directly involved – have recognized these problems and are actively seeking remedies. To hope that leakage can be completely prevented, however, would be folly. The break-up of the Soviet Union has added to the urgency for vigorous, internationally co-ordinated and effective policies to control nuclear proliferation.

Other Armed Forces

A problem closely linked to the nuclear issue is that of the future of Soviet and republican conventional forces, arms stockpiles and exports. Again, several problems need to be considered: the fate of existing arsenals; the problems posed by existing armed forces and the issue of the future conventional forces of the various republics; export policies and the problem of defence conversion.

Existing weapons stockpiles are enormous. It appears far from certain that the necessary facilities exist to reduce them to the levels agreed upon in CFE, let alone to lower levels. It must be taken for granted that large quantities of weapons continue to be sold on both the open and the black market. It is equally obvious that the conversion of the military–industrial complex towards civilian production has not yet seriously started – and will prove a formidable challenge given that the defence industry represented some 25% of the USSR's industrial activity. In February, Yeltsin and others were saying that production and sales of conventional arms would continue because it was impossible to shift to civilian production and the hard currency that could be acquired in this way was essential.

The most alarming aspect of all this is that the collapse of the USSR has transformed the former Soviet armed forces into an army without a state. Soldiers are badly paid and fed, if paid and fed at all, housed in overcrowded barracks, and have not the slightest idea what will become of them. They are led by hundreds of thousands of officers who, only a few years ago, were the elite of the nation and are now left with few professional prospects. While the members of the CIS argue about the future of the former Soviet forces under joint command and the establishment of national forces, the sober reality is that at least parts of the armed forces (in the Baltics, in the Far East or in Moldova) have shaken off all political control. It is a more than troublesome prospect that the one segment of society with the bleakest future is precisely the one which controls the guns.

A Rising Nationalist Tide

The two key components of the problem of nationalism are minorities and borders. With the collapse of the USSR there is no remaining central authority capable or willing to protect national minorities outside the key Slavic republics. The bloody civil strife in Georgia is as much evidence of this as is Azerbaijan's attempt to solve the Nagorno-Karabakh issue by force. Fearing a repetition of the situation in Afghanistan, in early March Yeltsin pulled out the last of the former Soviet army troops that had formed a barrier, albeit an ineffective one, to a total war between Armenians and Azeris, rather than reinforcing them in hopes of maintaining peace.

National minorities along the borders of the former empire are now arming in hopes of fending for themselves. The most sadly picturesque example in this context is perhaps the 'Dniester Republic', a region with a population of Ukrainian background which Stalin had attached to Moldova. It not only declared its independence, but took over the 14th Army that had been stationed on its territory – and appointed the army commander its 'defence minister'.

Nor, despite the Minsk declaration, should borders be considered a settled issue. The Minsk agreement only guaranteed them 'in the framework of the Commonwealth', thus implying that secession from the CIS or a break-up of the Commonwealth could reopen the issue. There is a serious chance that at least the Ukraine might opt for such a step. The dispute between Kiev and Moscow about control of the Black Sea Fleet is not only a dispute about ships, but – more profoundly – one about the Crimea (taken away from Russia in 1954 and given to the Ukraine by Khrushchev).

Other flash-points include the relationship between the Ukraine and Moldova, particularly if the latter should decide on reunification with Romania, the 'Dniester Republic' and the Russian area of Kaliningrad, now separated from Russia's territory by Lithuania and Belarus. The borders between the Ukraine and the Central European democracies, and the numerous autonomous regions within the Russian Federation and other successor states must also be considered, in the longer perspective, at least as potential trouble spots. The internal administrative borders of the USSR had been drawn by Stalin as arbitrarily as those of Africa by its colonial masters. Whether the newly independent states will recognize, as the African states did in the 1960s, that any attempt to correct borders will open a Pandora's box, remains to be seen.

Economic Disaster

Finally, all these interlinked problems are overshadowed, and amplified, by the desperate economic situation. According to the last official Soviet figures, the GNP had shrunk (at an annual rate) in the first nine months of 1991 by 12%, industrial production by 6.5%, agriculture by 10% (with an expected grain harvest of some 180m tons), oil production by 9%, that of coal by 11%, and foreign trade by 38%. At the same time, foreign net debt increased to around $80bn and inflation rates have soared to three-digit figures. These figures paint a grim picture, but the reality is even – and ever – worse.

Except for barter deals, trade between the republics has to a large degree simply stopped. The Ukraine, for example, no longer delivers grain to Russia – and Russia no longer supplies oil and petrol to the Ukraine. One of the legacies of 74 years of communist dictatorship and economic mismanagement is that the successor states are left with an absurdly specialized economic structure. In the highly centralized and integrated Soviet command economy everyone produced at least something virtually exclusively.

This translates into a situation in which each state (with the possible exception of Russia) is desperately lacking most goods – and is hence all the more determined not to sell, but only to barter, its own specialized commodities. To reintegrate these economies on a barter basis is, however, simply impossible. To illustrate the point, one has to visualize that in order to repair broken TV sets in Kiev, the Ukraine would have to negotiate a specific barter arrangement with Lithuania which produces the spare parts. The only way out of this quagmire would be a transition towards a genuine market economy, based on hard and convertible currencies and open borders. Yet that would require on the one hand a clear understanding of the way market economies work and what needs to be done, and on the other a willingness to accept further hardship, including major unemployment, on the part of the population. Neither of these essential preconditions exists.

On 3 January Russia and other republics 'freed' prices. Because there is no private production capability that could be triggered into action, and since state enterprises have not the slightest idea what their products actually cost, this step was largely meaningless. In many cases, it simply further increased prices and the tendency to hoard. Similarly, the Ukraine introduced a second temporary currency, the 'coupon', instead of the rouble, but because there was nothing behind it, it was immediately as worthless as the rouble had been. The situation is made even more dramatic by exploding budget deficits that are financed everywhere simply by printing more money, a process slowed only by the limited capacity of the printing presses. Russia's political prospects can only be seen as sombre against this backdrop of economic chaos and social disorganization; under these circumstances even the most well-intentioned shock therapy would resemble open-heart surgery without anaesthetic.

Clapping with One Hand

The collapse of the Soviet Union is an historic political and military watershed. The world has witnessed the disintegration of a nuclear superpower ruled by an incompetent but dangerous communist ideology. This is reason to rejoice, but there is also reason to be cautious. The USSR belongs to the past; the problems, tensions and contradictions on which it foundered, however, have not only all survived, but have even been amplified. This poses a formidable challenge to the successor states of the USSR – and to the international community – for they will continue to be a determining factor for the future security of its European and Asian neighbours, as well as for global security. The end of the Cold War, the Warsaw Pact and the Soviet empire have not brought the end of history, but the return of history – and history in full unimpeded flow.

CENTRAL EUROPE'S STRUGGLING STATES

With the disintegration of the Soviet Union and its two imperial pillars in Central Europe, COMECON and the Warsaw Pact, Hungary, Poland and Czechoslovakia found themselves in 1991 in an entirely new strategic setting. New states emerged on their eastern borders, all seeking democracy and admittance to the European framework of cooperation. They themselves concluded association agreements with the European Community, and together with other East European states joined the North Atlantic Cooperation Council at its creation.

Two or three years ago this could only have occurred in pleasant dreams. Central Europeans are far from celebrating, however. Instead, there is growing disappointment and bitterness. This paradox was well expressed by Czechoslovakia's President, Vaclav Havel, in his 1992 New Year address:

> Why, at a time when no other power threatens us or interferes in our affairs and, for the first time in centuries, for us as a state and as citizens our fate is really in our own hands, why do we have hardly any reason for joyful happiness? What are the roots of our nervousness, confusion, impatience and often even of hopelessness?

The questions are, of course, purely rhetorical. The roots of public frustration are well known to Havel and other Central European leaders. They can be found in the tragic state of their economies, in their

fragile and ineffective political structures, and in the unstable international environment. Despite many efforts undertaken both by Central European and Western governments in 1991, none of these problems were even close to resolution.

Sources of Instability

A sharp drop in production, rising unemployment and falling real wages
represent the most striking manifestation of the continuing economic
trauma in Poland, Hungary and Czechoslovakia. It is true that some
grim statistics are misleading, as they only paint a part of the picture
and tend to ignore the growth of private businesses and the relative
abundance of goods now available for purchase. Yet hopes for a quick
and smooth transition to a market economy have faded, and there is
growing unease in all three countries about the social price of reforms.
The privatization of thousands of monopoly enterprises which used old
technology, but nevertheless supported entire communities, proved
extremely difficult. And the collapse of both COMECON and the Soviet
market left many businesses in a state of bankruptcy. The World Bank
now predicts that output per head in Eastern Europe may not recover to
the level of 1989 until 1996 or later.

This is of little comfort to Central European politicians facing
increased labour unrest, financial and banking scandals, and a loss of
public consensus about the merit of economic change. The situation
looks especially grim in Poland, where the radical economic reforms of
the first two post-communist governments went well beyond the willingness of the people and mainstream politicians to endure the sacrifices
necessary to bring them about. The third post-communist government of
Jan Olszewski has decided to slow the pace of reforms, and has promised
to stimulate the economy through tax cuts, subsidies for state-owned
enterprises, and combating financial swindlers. Experts fear, however,
that this policy will only produce hyperinflation, prolong the life of
inefficient enterprises, and discourage Western bankers and investors; in
effect, Poland would follow the path of pre-1991 Argentina.

To be sure, Central Europe's economic prospects cannot be
measured by Poland's standards only. Last year, Hungary's hard currency exports increased by 41%, and the country attracted about half
the total foreign capital (about $1.5bn) earmarked for the Soviet Union
and Eastern Europe. But even in Hungary, most of the large industries
are still not privatized, foreign debt remains high (some $20bn), and
unemployment rose consistently, reaching 8.15% by early 1992.

That the economies remain anchored in the doldrums continues to
threaten the stability of the region; so too does the lack of political
vitality. Although all three countries now have democratically-elected
parliaments, and their governments are free of communists even in the
police and the army sector, 1991 brought further fragmentation rather
than consolidation of major democratic political forces. For example,

no less than 29 parties are now represented in Poland's parliament, and none received more than 13% of the vote in the October 1991 elections.

The balance of power between the legislature, the judiciary and the executive has still not crystallized, due to prolonged battles about the new shape of national constitutions, and the tone of successive political debates resembles more a Persian bazaar than any model of constitutional democracy. Thus far, Hungary appears the most stable country of the three. Even there, however, President Arpad Goencz used harsh words to describe Hungary's realities:

> The political forces attack each other with wolf-like passions and sometimes social emotions also flare up, the unaccustomed submission, resignation and hardship create mistrust and discord . . . After hardly a year, our unity is threadbare and the fight is faltering.

The rise of ethnic conflicts also undermines stability. After more than a year of constitutional squabbling, Czechs and Slovaks are still without a compromise that would create a workable federal or confederal system. An eventual split between Czechs and Slovaks would probably involve little or no violence, but a division of Czechoslovakia would create a security vacuum that might be exploited by adversative forces in the region. Leaders of the Hungarian minority in Slovakia have already made it clear that they would press for the secession of the Hungarian areas of Slovakia if the latter were to leave the federation. This in turn would create a serious dilemma for Budapest, which in 1991 was also confronted with the problem of its Magyar minorities in Romania's Transylvania, and in Yugoslavia's Vojvodina. Poland, for its part, was involved in a conflict with Lithuania concerning the treatment of the Polish minority in parts of the country. Nor were any solutions in sight to the problems of Poland's own Byelorussian and German minorities.

While the ethnic, economic and political problems of the three Central European countries are less acute than those of their neighbours, this provides little comfort for governments which are increasingly confronted with an unstable international environment. The war in Yugoslavia has driven more than 40,000 refugees, including deserters from the Yugoslav federal army, as well as many members of the Magyar minority, to Hungary. Hungarian airspace was repeatedly violated by Yugoslav army planes, which also dropped a scatter bomb on the Hungarian village of Barcs. In addition, Budapest and Belgrade were engaged in a constant war of words over Hungarian deliveries of weapons to Croatia (some admitted and some only alleged), as well as over the legal status of the Yugoslav province of Vojvodina. The war in Yugoslavia also deprived Hungary of oil deliveries from the Middle East via the Adria pipeline.

The process of disintegration of the former Soviet Union is also a matter of concern. Governments in Central Europe fear, in particular, a massive influx of refugees and other migrants from their new eastern neighbours. They also fear a proliferation of nuclear weapons, especially in the Ukraine and Belarus. They are alarmed that a possible war between the former Soviet republics may result in armies outside political control, attempting to use the territory of Central European states for their operations. A possible rise in the hegemonial aspirations of Russia or the Ukraine is also being taken seriously by the Hungarian, Polish and Czechoslovak governments.

Although not all these fears will prove justified in the coming years, the present combination of domestic instabilities and international uncertainties represents a formidable challenge to the inexperienced security elites in all three countries.

Security Policies

By 1992 the defence and foreign policies of the three had matured beyond those of the immediate aftermath of the democratic revolutions of 1989. Dramatic statements and overambitious pan-European initiatives were replaced by detailed negotiations with both West and East European partners. A further distancing from the Soviet/Russian sphere of influence and integration in European and Western structures continued to represent the ultimate aim of the three. In 1991 they also took the first serious steps aimed at coordinating foreign and defence policy within the triangle.

Despite these improvements, however, Central European efforts were only partially successful. Although the association agreements reached with the EC in 1991 will gradually dismantle trade barriers between the three countries and the Community over the next ten years and will establish channels for regular political dialogue among top officials, they stopped short of creating a clear prospect for admitting the three to this organization. Moreover, the agreements envisage slower and less extensive trade liberalization measures than Central European countries had hoped. The restrictions are especially painful in the areas where the export capacities of the three are at their best: agriculture, steel and textiles. Nor have the three been very successful on subsidiary issues, such as increased rights for their citizens to work in the EC.

Central Europeans also hoped for preferential treatment by NATO, if not eventual membership, but instead NATO created the NACC, which initially attempted to provide both an organization for cooperation with former adversaries, and a framework to address Central Europe's feeling of being left out of the West's security structures. The latter objective was in effect dropped when the NACC was opened to all republics of the former Soviet Union, which are treated on equal terms as the Central European countries. The Council offered its Eastern members a 'security dialogue' rather than the 'security guarantees' that they had requested. Nor was the response of the WEU encouraging; the WEU special memorandum suggested that it should give 'assurances of

support' to Central European countries, but ruled out an enlargement of
the Union, and warned that the utmost caution is necessary in giving
'formal guarantees'.

Nor did Central European efforts to strengthen and further insti-
tutionalize the CSCE Helsinki framework produce many results. During
the January 1992 CSCE foreign ministers' meeting in Prague, President
Havel produced a proposal to give the CSCE documents a 'more pronounced character of international agreements whose observance can
be monitored and whose breach would result in sanctions'. He also
suggested the creation within the CSCE of a body similar to the UN
Security Council. But Havel's ideas evoked little enthusiasm among most
of the CSCE's members, of which there were 51 by March 1992.

Bilateral diplomacy among the three produced a strange mixture of
hope and frustration. In the autumn of 1991, after protracted and
difficult negotiations, they were finally ready to sign their new treaties
on cooperation with the Soviet Union just before that country finally
disintegrated. They then had no choice but to adapt to a new and rather
uncertain situation. The Russian Federation proved a reliable partner
in the field of politics, but not in the field of economics. Ukrainian diplomacy has been very friendly, especially towards Poland and
Hungary, but the establishment of a Ukrainian army raises fears in all
Central European countries. Czechoslovakia and Poland also concluded treaties of friendship and good neighbourliness with Germany.
In both cases, however, the treaties caused political ructions: from the
left in Poland and Czechoslovakia, and from the right in Germany.

There was, however, clear progress during 1991 in one important
area: cooperation in the Czechoslovak, Polish and Hungarian triangle. The
idea of such cooperation was born during the Višegrad summit of February 1991, and reinforced during the October 1991 summit in Cracow.
The most pronounced aspect of the triangular cooperation is the coordination of efforts aimed at joining Western institutions such as the EC,
NATO and the WEU. Yet the development of various practical forms of
consultation and mutual assistance between the three in the fields of trade,
security or migration might also prove extremely important.

The three signed military cooperation agreements with each other
designed to help them deal with their common problems, such as the
depoliticization of their armed forces, the joint management of their
airspace, and the rationalization of their arms production and procurement in the face of a shortage of funds. None of the three countries
wish to create the impression that they are forming a security alliance
against anybody in the region, and all three are afraid that strengthening
trilateral economic cooperation would provide the West with an excuse
to deprive Central Europe of easy access to its markets. Both in economic and security terms, they still give unequivocal priority to their
integration with the West, and claim that any development of trilateral
cooperation should be seen as a means towards this goal, rather than as
a goal in itself. Nevertheless, their threeway cooperation will

increasingly cover those areas in which the West is reluctant to become involved. It will also mitigate unnecessary competition between the three for access to Western institutions, and will help to alleviate historical stereotypes and national animosities still present in the region.

Western Dilemmas

With the disintegration of the Soviet superpower, and the democratization of its residual parts, the West has fewer strategic reasons to treat Central European states any differently than the Ukraine, the Baltic states or the Russian Federation. The three are no longer a unique bastion of democracy and anti-communism in Eastern Europe. They no longer require any special protection against the imperial Soviet threat. Instead, the West is now confronted with more acute security problems in Yugoslavia and the former Soviet Union, which have lessened its concern about the relatively stable countries of Central Europe.

Nevertheless, a policy of benign neglect towards Central Europe will not serve Western interests either. Any Western design for security in the former Eastern Europe should first prove its worth in those countries with the most advanced democratic systems. If chaos and bullying politics were to prevail in Central Europe, there would be few chances for stability in the rest of the post-communist world. Moreover, keeping Germany firm within Western structures will best be helped by active Western involvement in Central Europe as well. Germany's geographical location, economic interests and ethnic realities raise a barrier to its turning its back on problems in Poland, Hungary and Czechoslovakia. In addition, any major instability in the former Soviet Union will first spill over to Central Europe before eventually reaching the West. Enhancing the security of the three is surely in the West's interest.

Today the key to security in Central Europe is neither in formal defence guarantees nor in widening the old alliance structure. Potential sources of conflict in the region are primarily of an economic and political nature, and should be treated accordingly. Progressively greater integration with the European Union would be the optimal solution that would help prevent their situation from turning dangerously desperate.

TURMOIL IN THE BALKANS

The initial phase of post-communist reconstruction in the Balkans both suffered from, and created, predictable political instability: a polarization between left and right on the transition towards market economies, and, particularly in the case of Yugoslavia, the emergence of virulent nationalism. The period from late 1989 to early 1991 sharpened the distinction which had emerged between the countries of Central Europe and the Balkans. The relative order in the former contrasted sharply with political practices to the south, which was dominated by a lack of tolerance in the fledgling democracies, mass agitation and disruption, and the use of mobs by both governments and opposition as a method of dealing with political problems. True to form, the Balkan peoples largely continued in this vein in 1991 and early 1992. Most serious, however, was the outbreak of war within the Yugoslav federation.

The Balkans

(—— · —— · —— Borders of CSCE member states as of 31 March 1992)

Cry Havoc

The dogs of war were loosed in Yugoslavia towards the end of June 1991. During the previous year there was still some hope that the ever-deepening crisis would not spiral into a conflict: despite fanning the flames of nationalism, the leaders of the six federal republics kept alive the prospect that an overall political solution could be hammered out for the country. This was always an illusion. The constituent parts of Yugoslavia were on a collision course, with Slovenia and Croatia insisting on the confederal model as the maximum of coexistence, while Serbia and Montenegro defended the federal model. There was no room for compromise, as was shown when Bosnia-Herzegovina and Macedonia unsuccessfully offered one that was constructed on a hybrid of federal and confederal systems.

There was a sense, however, in which the constitutional wrangle merely clouded the essential issues in the Yugoslav crisis. Most

Yugoslavs had already decided that coexistence was no longer desirable. The secession of some republics was already conceded; in principle it was not opposed even by Serbia, the republic seen as the staunchest supporter of central authority. The problem related more to the modalities of secession, and in particular to the question of ethnic territories and borders. Who could invoke the right of self-determination? Was it the republics within their existing borders or the nations within as-yet-to-be defined confines? Thus, in the case of Croatia, the government in Zagreb at the start of 1991 was facing an open revolt of ethnic Serbs in large tracts of Croatia's republican territory. Those Serbs did not see themselves as a minority, and had no wish whatsoever to live under any Croatian authority, let alone one that ruled an independent Croatia. The view that they were manipulated from Belgrade was mistaken, although Belgrade did indeed insist on their right to self-determination.

Slobodan Milosevic, the President of Serbia, whose nationalist policies were widely perceived as the chief catalyst in the Yugoslav crisis, appeared in March 1991 to be on the brink of losing power. Large-scale demonstrations organized by the opposition (a group as nationalist-minded as the ruling party) brought chaos and violence to Belgrade, forcing the government to deploy troops on the streets. Milosevic, though badly shaken, survived. This event coincided with the intensification of the conflict between Serbs and Croats in Croatia. This was not quite a war, but a series of sporadic and increasingly more serious armed clashes. By this time the army, acting as a buffer between the two groups, had become entangled in the affair. The nationalist Croats, however, saw the federal forces as an army of occupation. The army was a conservative institution *par excellence:* almost entirely officered by Serbian communists, it was the last bastion of Titoism. However much it insisted on its neutrality, the Croats were bound to perceive it as a hostile force. Thus the clashes in Croatia in spring 1991 inevitably pushed the army into Serbia's hands.

The crisis in Yugoslavia reached a new height in May, when Stipe Mesic, the Croat representative on the federal collective presidency, was prevented by Serbia from routinely assuming the rotational post of head of the collective presidency. Although inter-republican talks continued on the ensuing crisis, this action was the deciding factor for Slovenia and Croatia: on 25 June they both unilaterally declared their independence, with the Croats being somewhat more cautious in their formulation. The federal Prime Minister ordered federal troops to take control of Slovenia's international frontiers. An unexpectedly well-trained and well-armed Slovene territorial defence force, some 35,000-strong, resisted effectively, and Yugoslavia was at war. The EC took on the task of conflict-management and brokered an agreement whereby the army would withdraw to barracks, while Slovenia and Croatia would suspend further independence moves for three months.

This was merely a prelude to much more serious developments in Croatia. The involvement of the federal army in Slovenia had been distinguished by its lack of commitment: the Serbs in particular had no interest in stopping the Slovenes from seceding. The difference in Croatia was that its ethnic Serbs wanted to stay in Yugoslavia. During July and August, armed incidents in Croatia multiplied and spread. The EC, which arranged one cease-fire after another, was powerless to prevent them being broken at will.

Believing that only outside recognition would halt the fighting, some EC members, notably Germany, agitated from the beginning for the diplomatic recognition of the breakaway republics. This became a distinct possibility in September, when an EC-sponsored peace conference on Yugoslavia convened in The Hague. Lord Carrington, the Chairman, proposed the establishment of 'sovereign and independent Republics with international personality for those who wish it', with the proviso of 'special status for certain groups and areas'. Of the six republics, only Serbia rejected the plan, for it would have meant the loss of Serbian enclaves in Croatia – the issue at the very heart of the war. The peace conference accordingly collapsed.

Militarily, the war was being won by the Serbs who had the crucial support of what by now were remnants of the federal army. About 30% of Croatia was in their hands. The problem for Milosevic was how to stop the war, which had become increasingly unpopular in Serbia, and yet to keep the Serbian enclaves from falling under Croatian sovereignty. By September he had concluded that UN involvement in Croatia would be the solution. Having previously rejected any notion of European peace-keeping troops, he turned to the UN for precisely that reason. His intentions were to use the UN troops not so much to keep the peace as to keep the enclaves out of the hands of the Croats. In December an agreement with Cyrus Vance, the special UN emissary, was in the making. Croatia, too, wanted peace, and pinned its hopes on the UN as a way of regaining its lost territories. By the beginning of 1992 a true cease-fire was finally holding on the battlefields. Germany had recognized Slovenia and Croatia shortly before Christmas, and the rest of the EC, in some cases very reluctantly, agreed to follow suit in mid-January 1992.

The EC had also offered to recognize other Yugoslav republics, provided it was satisfied that human rights and the rights of minorities were adequately respected. This put enormous pressure on Macedonia and Bosnia-Herzegovina to seek recognition. A commission, under the Head of the French Constitutional Council, Robert Badinter, was entrusted with the task of assessing whether the candidates for recognition met the EC's conditions in terms of the human rights and the minorities situation. Both Slovenia and Macedonia were considered by the commission as meeting these criteria, with judgement reserved in the case of Croatia and Bosnia-Herzegovina. Macedonia had already held a referendum on independence in September 1991, with the majority in favour. It therefore applied for recognition, but agreement was blocked by Greece which refused to accept the name 'Macedonia' for a state on its northern border for fear that such a state would demand reintegration of the Greek province of Macedonia. The question was still being debated in the EC at the end of March 1992. Bulgaria, however, rushed to recognize Macedonia. Bosnia-Herzegovina also held a referendum at the end of February, and a majority voted for independence, but those in favour were the republic's Muslim Slavs and Croats; its Serbian population had boycotted the referendum. By the end of March 1992, the mixed population had established a *de facto* territorial partition.

After months of warfare only the position of Slovenia was beyond dispute. Advance parties of UN troops entered the former Yugoslavia in March 1992, with the rest of the planned 14,000-man main force poised for deployment in April. A snapshot of the disintegrating Yugoslavia at this time revealed a long-term problem of the Serbian enclaves in Croatia, a most precarious situation in Bosnia-Herzegovina, the internationally difficult question of Macedonia, and a host of other problems, including the long-simmering, unresolved question of the large Albanian enclave of Kosovo, within Serbia itself, as well as potential problems in the Muslim Novi Pazar region of Serbia. There is a pause for review, but a solution is still far off.

Romania: The Beginnings of Improvement

Romania had been saddled with a poor international image in 1990 and 1991. The government of the National Salvation Front, made up of ex-communists and overwhelmingly triumphant in the country's elections, had lurched from crisis from crisis, while employing heavy-handed methods in dealing with the opposition. It was widely felt that despite the removal of Nicolae Ceauşescu, Romania was still governed by a dictatorship, or at best was a one-party state. The embittered opposition's slogan became 'the stolen revolution'. Western financial organizations and the EC identified with these sentiments and tended to ignore Romania's pleas for much-needed economic and financial aid. Subsequent government reforms and the introduction of further austerity measures, however, won the all-important support of the IMF, which early in 1991 granted Romania a stand-by loan facility.

Placating the West on the economic front was a tactic laden with risk for the NSF on the home front. Throughout 1991 some of the familiar scenes (anti-government demonstrators blocking traffic in the city, with the riot police responding violently) continued to be seen in Bucharest and other cities. In general, the transition to a market economy in Romania showed unmistakable signs that it was going to be every bit as painful as in the rest of Eastern Europe: soaring prices led to a series of damaging strikes; there was falling production, rising unemployment, and social and political tensions; and an absence of structures to make the market work. The NSF could take some solace at the end of January 1991 when the G-24 aid donors announced that Romania would also be included in its programme.

It was not surprising that the facade of government unity began to crumble in the face of these difficulties. In March 1991, following another push for price liberalization, several NSF ministers offered to resign on the grounds that the measures did not go far enough. President Ion Iliescu, on the other hand, had directly intervened to curtail the reform process because he feared social unrest. This was not out of character: the NSF had won votes in the election partially because it had promised to adopt a cautious approach. It had not been elected to shock the economy into life. Prime Minister Petre Roman, himself a reformist, could ride out the crisis because there appeared no viable alternative to his government, either from the conservative wing in the NSF, or from the fragmented opposition. Roman appeared to have a firm grip on the NSF, while the opposition offered no convincing programme of its own: its least incoherent demand was for the return of the ex-King Michael.

Internationally, the EC as well as the IMF were by now backing the Roman government. In April 1991 President Mitterrand paid a visit to Romania, thereby taking an important step towards bringing the country out of isolation. Relations with Hungary remained strained in the light of the continuing problem of the ethnic Hungarian minority in Romania, but a bilateral version of the then prospective 'open skies' agreement at least promoted cooperation between the two countries on the military level. Romania also concluded a controversial security pact with the USSR, which barred the signatories from participating in 'offensive' alliances against the other.

Romania's main fixation in foreign affairs, however, was on building up links with the neighbouring, mainly ethnic Romanian, Soviet republic of Moldova. In late August, when the republic declared its independence from Moscow, the dream of reunification began to appear as a distinct possibility. The declaration of independence by the Ukraine in December threw up the prospect of a clash with Romania, since this former Soviet republic also incorporated Romanian territory lost after the 1939 Hitler–Stalin Pact.

Nevertheless, in the second half of 1991 the economy remained the biggest headache for the government. There were not yet sufficient financial injections from the IMF and the EC, and the image foreigners had of Romania proved an effective brake on large-scale Western investment. Labour unrest was chronic, yet the embattled government did not flinch from its declared aim of establishing a market economy. In mid-August it legislated for an ambitious programme of privatizing state industry.

Such schemes, however, were going to take a long time to become effective, and the patience of the long-suffering citizens was wearing thin. In an ironic twist, the coal-miners who had defended the NSF in the streets of Bucharest in 1990 returned to the capital in September 1991 to firebomb government buildings in protest against declining living standards. Troops were deployed to restore order, but not before the riots toppled the government of Petre Roman. His reforms had been resisted by conservatives in the NSF, but the workers themselves (described by Roman as 'lumpen proletariat') were not ready to swallow the bitter medicine. The events may have constituted, as Roman claimed, a 'communist putsch from below', but it was all too easy to start. President Iliescu, once again, survived.

Paradoxically, Teodor Stolojan, a radical reformer in the Petre Roman mould and not an NSF member, was named prime minister. This reflected Iliescu's strategy of hiding behind, and manipulating, a government of technocrats with little political power of their own. Stolojan announced a coalition cabinet which for the first time gave smaller parties a share in power. He pushed on with the privatization programme and took steps towards making the currency convertible. In November the parliament adopted a new constitution which defined Romania as a presidential, multiparty republic, but at the same time invested the President with sweeping powers. Opposed by the monarchists and the Hungarian minority, the constitution was endorsed by a referendum the following month.

Iliescu's triumph on this score, however, was offset elsewhere. Early in 1992, Stolojan threatened to resign if his reforms were delayed. At the same time, 14 of the largest opposition parties united under the umbrella title of the Democratic Convention, while the NSF had by now split more or less openly into conservative and reformist factions. In the February 1992 local elections Romania finally began to change. The opposition took control of many cities, including Bucharest, and thus dealt a telling, and perhaps decisive, blow to the two-year-old domination of Romania's affairs by an increasingly divided NSF.

Bulgaria: Muddling Through

During 1991 Bulgaria was the quiet man of the Balkans. The outcome of the political struggles in the previous year, often fought in the streets, was the formation of a coalition government which for the first time brought opposition parties into power along with the (ex-communist) Bulgarian Socialist Party. In terms of progress towards a market economy, many months had simply been wasted.

At the beginning of 1991, the government, headed by non-party technocrat Dimitur Popov, faced acute food and energy shortages, and pinned its hopes on IMF support. Moving swiftly, Popov announced a packet of reform measures, including a painful price thaw, reductions in state subsidies and increasing interest rates. In many ways, Bulgaria appeared hopelessly ill-prepared to adjust to new economic realities: it was perhaps the hardest hit by the collapse of the COMECON trading bloc; it was bankrupt, unable to service its large ($10.5bn) foreign loan inherited from the communist past; and it suffered from a negative 'Balkan' image in the eyes of potential Western investors.

The political climate in the country, however, had improved dramatically since the formation of the Popov government. The government repeatedly pointed to the country's new-found stability to impress investors, who nevertheless remained unimpressed. The government did, however, succeed in gaining agreement from the Paris Club of creditors for rescheduling some of Bulgaria's loans. A gradual shift in perceptions of Bulgaria began to take hold abroad.

The crucial factor was that the population was not revolting despite savage change in the economy. Popov was introducing measures as radical as anywhere else in the former Soviet bloc, and yet he was able to do so in cooperation with the trade unions, which had accepted wage increases as a modest cushion against some of the attacks on the workers' standards of living. In August, the World Bank approved a $250-m loan, while the US granted Bulgaria MFN status later in the year; these were small but symbolically significant international steps in recognition of Bulgaria's efforts.

The key domestic development of 1991 was the general election on 13 October. This had been preceded in July by the adoption of a new constitution. The election itself was again fought between the two chief protagonists, the Bulgarian Socialist Party and the umbrella opposition coalition of the Union of Democratic Forces. As in 1990, the Socialists held sway in the countryside and in state and local bureaucracies, while the UDF drew urban support. The ensuing UDF victory, however, was too narrow to enable the formation of a single-party government. Much against its instincts, the UDF entered into a coalition with the Movement for Rights and Freedoms, the ethnic Turkish party which emerged as the third-largest force in Bulgarian politics.

Although the Turks did not get a cabinet post in the new government headed by the UDF leader Filip Dimitrov, the hostility felt by many Bulgarians against anything Turkish played into the hands of the Socialists who had monopolized the nationalist vote. This issue proved to be of some importance in the January 1992 presidential elections when the widely respected Zhelyu Zhelev of the UDF stood for re-election. His major opponent was the nationalist Velko Vulkanov, who had secured the backing of the Socialist establishment. The fact that Zhelev was forced to go to the second round in the election before emerging as the winner, showed that the strength of nationalism in Bulgaria could not be underestimated. Nevertheless, the UDF now had a government and a newly-elected president committed to radical economic reform.

Whatever the degree of internal accord reached in Bulgaria, the country found itself in a highly unstable regional environment, brought about in particular by the break-up of Yugoslavia. Bulgarian foreign policy, however, was a mix of wishful thinking and overhasty, high-risk diplomacy. Attempts to extract NATO security guarantees, for example, fell into the former category. More seriously, relations with Greece, which had steadily improved in 1990–91, were severely strained as a result of Bulgaria's prompt recognition of Macedonia in early 1992. Sofia had viewed the agony of Yugoslavia with scarcely concealed delight, and its historic interest in (not to say designs on) Macedonia overrode all other regional considerations. Relations with Belgrade, always bad, grew worse. Thus a Sofia–Athens axis has inevitably been replaced by a Belgrade–Athens axis.

Albania: The Invalid State

The process of controlled change which the Albanian communist regime of Ramiz Alia had tried to pursue in 1990 resulted in little change, but a loss of control. By early 1991 Albania was a sinking ship, being abandoned by thousands who fled to Italy, Greece and Yugoslavia. Yet in the first free elections in March 1991, the old communist apparatus proved sturdy enough to pull the ruling Party of Labour to the fore. As elsewhere in the Balkans, the communists won largely on the strength of their support in rural areas. It was significant, however, that the opposition Democratic Party showed enough self-confidence to turn down an offer to join a coalition government. Gramoz Pashko, a leader of the Democrats, asserted that the communists were 'finished', and that 'in two months they will be in pieces'.

The latter part of this prediction turned out to be correct almost to the day. A manifold drama was developing: post-election violence; an economic situation bordering on collapse; the prospect of famine; and a general strike ordered by independent trade unions in May. By the beginning of June the general strike, which had led to violent clashes in the capital, Tirana, brought down the government. Once again, street pressure in the Balkans was paying heavy dividends. The DP, eager to push for early new elections, then agreed to join in an interim government. Pashko, as a Deputy Prime Minister, described it as a 'kamikaze government', but added that someone had to take the responsibility. However, widespread scepticism among the Albanians was reflected in the continuing exodus. It was a sad, if apt, comment on the state of Albania when a delirious crowd, said by some to be 300,000 strong (one-tenth of the country's population), welcomed US Secretary of State James Baker on 23 June as if he were some extraterrestrial saviour.

The problem in Albania was simply that the old communist economic structures had ceased to exist and that nothing had been created to replace them. New legislation was slow, ineffective or ignored. Elements in the Party of Labour, now renamed the Socialist Party, continued to obstruct change. Turbulence in the population was inevitable. In August, wretched, desperate Albanian 'boat people' poured across the Adriatic to southern Italy, only to face the tear gas and the

batons of the *carabinieri*. In September, an exasperated Italian government sent 500 troops to Albania to manage an emergency food programme. The DP, increasingly embarrassed by the inability of the
coalition government to reverse the slide into chaos, was banking on
new elections, which it hoped could be staged at the start of 1992.
When its demand was not met, it withdrew from the government in
December. A caretaker administration took over with widespread
unrest, food riots and a crime wave sweeping the country.

During 1991 Albania had on paper become a normal member of
the international community. It restored diplomatic ties with the US
and the UK, and joined the CSCE and the IMF. None of this provided
any comfort. Even the war in neighbouring Yugoslavia could in no
way overshadow the anarchy at home. When the elections were held at
the end of March 1992, they produced a victory for the DP, so doing
away with the protracted period of communist rule. Albania was at last
entering a new era, but in the grimmest of circumstances.

A New Pattern of Stability?

Despite extraordinary turmoil in the Balkans during 1991, there were
some hopeful signs that the countries in the region, with the significant
exception of fractured Yugoslavia, were settling down to the serious
business of economic reconstruction after an orgy of political activity.
By the spring of 1992, they had reached the stage at which the principle, if not yet the modalities, of accelerated transition towards market economies was no longer in question. The political forces emerging in Romania, Bulgaria and Albania at last expressed popular
feeling and confidence. The difficulties and sacrifices inherent in the
move to free markets were widely recognized, but at least the political
elites in these countries had popular backing for their policies. In light
of this, the scope for further political conflict appeared much reduced.

Yugoslavia, however, was a different picture. There were many
reasons, both internal and regional, for pessimism. The international
community had proved unable to manage, let alone prevent, a widely
predicted internal conflict. The Yugoslavs themselves eventually
decided to embrace the UN peace mechanism, but the fundamental
question in the war – the issue of self-determination – was still present
in the Serbian enclaves of Croatia, and had surfaced in many other
areas in Yugoslavia. The war had not spilled across to the territories of
Yugoslavia's neighbours, but, if fighting returned, there was a serious
possibility that it might. Against this must be put the growing aversion
of all sides in Yugoslavia to a continuing war, combined with economic exhaustion, and in some cases almost complete collapse. These
factors provided a slim hope that the many ethnic factions in the country would forego the systematic use of force and rely on political
methods to advance their interests.

EUROPEAN INTEGRATION: ON THE HORIZON

When historians look back on 1991, they are likely to conclude that the year marked a watershed in Europe's development. From the vantage point of 1992, however, whether they view it as a decisive step forward towards European integration, or a muddled opportunity remains an open question; that the ratification process of the recently signed Maastricht Treaty will be fraught with significant difficulties in several European countries is symptomatic of the uncertainties still in the way of European integration. The year began auspiciously, with the opening on 15 December 1990 of two EC intergovernmental conferences – one on political union, the second on economic and monetary union. When the dust settled at Maastricht in December 1991, the EC heads of state and government had produced two draft treaties and a score of declarations and protocols. Their mighty, but often contentious labours, however, left open more questions than they resolved.

The impetus towards 'ever closer union' came from many quarters. Its roots lie in the lofty visions of Jean Monnet, Robert Schuman, Konrad Adenauer and Alcide de Gasperi, whose goals for a united Europe remained alive despite the often disappointing reality of postwar European politics. The process gained a new burst of energy in 1985, with the commitment to the Single Market Programme, scheduled to culminate in a barrier-free Europe for people, goods, capital and services. The decisive push, however, came from the cataclysmic political changes that shook Europe beginning in 1989, which opened the door to a profound debate over Europe's future.

The collapse of the Soviet empire, and the dissolution of the Soviet Union itself fundamentally altered the European landscape. In many ways, the bipolar division of Europe provided a clear, albeit confined, context for the growth of European integration through the EC. It defined the relevant universe of participants – Western democracies that shared a common security problem and commitment which gave NATO a pivotal role. Of the EC countries, only neutral Ireland is not a member of NATO, while a handful of European NATO members remain outside the EC, either by choice (Iceland) or because the EC membership questions their 'Europeanness' (Turkey). It allowed the Community to focus on economic integration, and in a sense compelled Europe to avoid a political union, with NATO providing the security umbrella. It provided the impetus for restoring (West) Germany's sovereignty, driven by the need for an economically vibrant, militarily capable Federal Republic as a cornerstone of the West's defence against the Soviet Union and its East European satellites. It suppressed historic rivalries among West European states in face of the need to preserve solidarity against a common enemy. It assured continuing US involvement in Europe, which also helped mediate West European quarrels, while enabling the US, through its security role, to play a major political role. It contributed to the US posture of supporting West European integration.

The framework crumbled almost as quickly as the Berlin Wall in the autumn of 1989, raising fundamental questions about Europe's future. Will 'Europe' and its regions replace the nation state? Who is now eligible for the Community's Europe? What role should the Community play in foreign and security policy, when, as seems inevitable, the US presence diminishes dramatically and new sources of instability emerge on Europe's periphery? How should Europe respond to a newly united, increasingly powerful economic and political Germany? Would traditional rivalries re-emerge with the disappearance of the common, unifying external threat?

The debate over these issues throughout 1991 revealed much about the underlying political objective of Europe's major actors. For Germany, the goal was to carve out a role that recognized its growing economic and political clout, while remaining faithful to Thomas Mann's oft-repeated maxim that Germany should seek a European Germany, not a German Europe. France sought to structure European policy to retain France's influence (and hem in Germany) in a world where the post-Yalta assumptions of France's Gaullist policies had dissolved beneath its feet. With Margaret Thatcher's departure, the UK seemed ready to play a more engaged role in Europe's construction, but the core of Britain's vision of the Community – a loose-knit association of sovereign countries committed primarily to advancing free markets – remained apparently intact. The Community's poorer members sought to advance a structure that would continue the process of 'levelling up' their standard of living to that of their richer neighbours. On the Community's outskirts, would-be members (in both EFTA and the new democracies of Eastern Europe) sought a share of the economic largesse and political stability through close association with the Community.

The Community's leaders had to face these difficult challenges at a time when the pressure of domestic and international events threatened to swamp their capacity to cope: a large-scale conflict in the Persian Gulf, the outbreak of civil war in Yugoslavia, the final collapse of the Soviet Union, economic hardship in Eastern Europe and recession in Western Europe, the fear of a tidal wave of refugees fleeing political and economic chaos in the East and South. Simply organizing ministers' diaries for the literally hundreds of high-level meetings of the EC, WEU, NATO, NACC, CSCE, UN and G-7 pushed the process to breaking point. The year's accomplishments (and failures) must be judged in light of the mind-boggling magnitude of the problem that Europe faced.

Economic and Monetary Union

When seen from the relative calm of early 1989, the principal task on the Community's agenda was economic and monetary union. Long a Community goal, the momentum generated by the Single Market Programme led a number of EC states to push for a single European currency and more coordinated fiscal policies. As with most crucial policy debates in the Community's history, the issue was framed in terms of sovereignty. For some countries, led by the UK, a single currency and common central bank represented (in the words of Margaret Thatcher): 'the biggest transfer of sovereignty we've ever had'. For others, notably France, EMU represented an opportunity to regain some say in macroeconomic policy previously lost through the European Monetary System, which, in their eyes, had turned Europe *de facto* into a 'Deutschmark zone', forcing Germany's EC partners to follow, often against their better judgement, the Bundesbank's dictates with no say in its decisions.

The path to an EMU agreement was strewn with political and policy land-mines. Germany insisted that a new European Central Bank mirror the Bundesbank's perceived virtues: independence from government and an iron-clad commitment to price stability. The Community's poorer countries resisted any plan that would create a two-speed monetary Europe where the fiscally healthy members moved to a single currency, leaving the others to join at an uncertain date in the future. France aimed to enhance the role of governments in setting broad economic policy to guide the ECB's activities, and to create a mechanism that would produce unstoppable momentum to the move to EMU, reducing the possibility that Germany would get cold feet before it could be implemented. John Major, in the face of strong pressure from his Conservative Party, insisted that he could not tie the hands of a future parliament by committing the UK in advance to a single currency.

Predictably, the result at Maastricht in mid-December was a little something for everyone. The Central Bank's charter bore the Bundesbank's strong imprint. The Community set forth stringent criteria for 'convergence' in its members' economic policies as a precondition to creating the single currency, but, in a bow to the fiscally troubled states, gave future Community leaders some flexibility in deciding whether a country meets the criteria. Under the agreement, the Community will implement a single currency in 1997 if a majority of the members meet the convergence standards, but (in deference to France), there will be a single currency for qualifying states by 1999, regardless of how many countries pass the test. Prime Minister Major wrested a special clause that reserved the United Kingdom's right to have a separate parliamentary vote on acceding to a single currency (a prerogative that in the end will likely prove of little but symbolic value), but he was unsuccessful in his attempt to have the 'opt in' clause apply to all EC members.

Political Union

As early as 1990, progress towards EMU was tied to parallel progress on 'political union': reforming the Community's institutions to improve their efficacy and democratic accountability. Germany played a leading role in linking the two issues, insisting that the EC agree to more 'democratic' procedures (primarily a strengthened role for the European Parliament) and expanded 'communitarian' jurisdiction over issues such as workers' rights, immigration and environment as the price for relinquishing national control over the Deutschmark.

These issues quickly took a back seat to the debate over whether and in what form the Community should pursue a common foreign and security policy (CFSP), and the need for a military arm of the union. Here German policy was caught in a squeeze between France, which placed a premium on enhancing Europe's security identity, and the US, which continued to insist on the primacy of NATO. Chancellor Helmut Kohl and Foreign Minister Hans-Dietrich Genscher walked a narrow line, attempting to please everybody, at the risk of pleasing nobody. The debate turned on two principal items of contention: whether the Community would allow majority voting for the CFSP, and the WEU's relationship with NATO and the EC. Britain and Italy laid down a marker in early October 1991, proposing to strengthen the WEU for out-of-area operations, but limit its activities to supporting NATO in Europe. In response, Germany leaned decisively towards the French model: Kohl and French President Mitterrand outlined a scheme for gradually developing the WEU as the defence arm of the union, and a Franco-German corps (as the core of a hoped-for European corps) to give the union military muscle.

The final result in Maastricht was a typical stew of compromise and temporizing. In the field of security, the EC leaders agreed to pursue CFSP, but it will remain an intergovernmental process, outside the communitarian structures, with qualified majority voting. On the crucial question of a defence role for the EC, the Community could only manage a maybe: CFSP will include 'eventually the framing of a common defence policy, which might in time lead to a common defence'. The WEU will retain links to both NATO and the union. At least rhetorically, however, the ties to the Community will be closer: the WEU will become an 'integral part' of the union, with membership open to all EC members but only associate status for European states that are members of NATO but not the Community. Progress on strengthening the European Parliament's role was limited; the EP did gain the right of co-decision in some areas but not for security policy. Immigration and police issues, like security policy, will remain mostly outside the Rome Treaty framework, though Germany did gain a small victory with the decision to allow communitarian policy on visas. Spain failed in its efforts to get the Community to adopt an automatic compensation mechanism to aid the EC's poorer states, but did receive assurances of increased funding as part of a new EC budget agreement which must be hammered out in 1992.

In the end, the most dramatic and contentious issue at Maastricht was the Community's role in social policy (workers' rights, occupational safety and employment conditions and standards). The summit produced a rather startling result: in the face of British intransigence, the leaders of the other 11 EC nations decided to go it alone and create a separate treaty, which will nonetheless be administered by Community institutions. This solution allowed John Major to take home an important political token of firmness in the face of the continental welfare states, but it may have the rather longer-lasting effect of opening the way for multiple geometries in which member states can pick and choose in the Community's restaurant; this may have particularly important consequences for the Community's capability to handle the pressures of 'enlargement'.

How Big is Europe?

One of the most consequential issues facing the Community – the question of enlargement – was sidestepped at Maastricht, but it was not far from the minds of the Community's leaders. The pressure for enlargement comes from two directions: the prosperous, neutral nations of EFTA (three of whose members, Austria, Sweden and Finland, have already applied for membership, and others, notably Norway, can be expected to follow), and the new democracies of Central Europe. Ironically, the EFTA countries' interest in joining the Community may have been inadvertently accelerated by the attempt by EC President Jacques Delors to head off EFTA pressure for EC membership by proposing that the EC and EFTA create a European Economic Area, giving EFTA nations a limited say in the economic aspects of Community policy. However, the long and difficult negotiations over EEA convinced many EFTA members that without the full benefits of membership they would be subject to EC rules and economic burdens without adequate means to protect their interests. In a similar vein, at the end of 1991 the Community finally signed enhanced association agreements with Poland, Hungary and Czechoslovakia (after dealing with French objections that East European agriculture imports would harm EC farmers), but these moves, while welcomed, merely whetted the East Europeans' appetite for full membership. The problem is further complicated by the applications of states such as Turkey, Malta and Cyprus.

The prospect of a Community with 18 or 24 or even more members raises fundamental questions about its future. No one doubts that the institutions and procedures of the Rome Treaty, already strained at 12, will require major revision to accommodate a Europe which wanted to admit more than two or three new members. There appear to be two radically different options: a looser, more confederal Europe that focuses on free trade, or stronger federal institutions in Brussels to break the decision-making log-jam that is certain to arise with a more diverse (politically and economically) membership.

The lines were thus beginning to be drawn in 1991. The UK in its familiar role of championing a free-trade Europe, saw nothing but good in expanding the Community's membership, thus perhaps ending, for all time, the possibility that the Community will move towards a single foreign and defence policy and the risk that Germany will dominate European affairs willy-nilly, unfettered by EC discipline; France, eager to build the Community's security role and preserve its own influence, looked anxiously at the prospect of broadening. Once again, Germany was caught in the middle: with geographic, political, economic and cultural ties to the East and many EFTA members, it is drawn into advocating early expansion, but it must reconcile this wish with its avowed commitment to a 'deeper' Community and the heavy financial demands which new EC members from the East would place on the Community. By 1992, shifts had begun to occur, as it became apparent that enlargement could become a convenient lever for those determined to further the process of federalization.

The Community agreed at Maastricht to study the issue, but it cannot delay for long: it has agreed to take up Sweden and Austrian applications in 1992, and it is difficult to imagine that they will be denied. Malta's and Finland's applications are also on the table, soon to be followed by Norway's, not to mention the long-standing Turkish candidacy. The only question is how fast the enlargement process will go, and whether the current members can find a consensus on the institutional reform to accommodate them. This is no easy task, and as soon as the Maastricht treaty is ratified, institutional reform to accommodate enlargement will become the highest priority. Although the treaty is due to be ratified by the end of 1992, the process may not be as clean as planned: for a variety of reasons, ratification will be drawn out and contentious, notably in France, where it will entail constitutional amendment in politically difficult circumstances.

NATO: Searching for a Role

Throughout 1991 NATO struggled to adapt to the dramatic pace of change in Europe and the world. The unexpectedly rapid collapse of the Soviet Union, following closely on the heels of the dissolution of the Warsaw Pact and the ongoing withdrawal of Soviet troops from Eastern Europe, left NATO in search of a new *raison d'être*. At the same time, the Gulf War demonstrated NATO's value in new dimensions, through the logistical and administrative support NATO quietly lent to the allied war effort, and the long habit of cooperation that helped the allies fight together effectively.

As the year began, NATO leaders recognized that the preliminary steps taken in their 1990 London summit were insufficient to reorient NATO to its new environment and maintain its viability. What was needed was a new 'strategic concept' to replace the doctrines of Forward Defence and Flexible Response (developed in 1967) and new force structures to match. The objective was fourfold: to streamline NATO's structures in response to the diminished threat; to increase flexibility to meet new, unforeseen challenges; to sustain the integrated approach to planning and operations in order to prevent the re-nationalization of Europe's, and especially Germany's, defence; and to provide a basis for a continued US military presence in Europe, a goal supported by all of America's allies, including France, as a means of assuring a continuing US commitment to European security and stability.

Although France, somewhat surprisingly, agreed to participate in the strategy review, the road to agreement proved difficult. Much of the controversy centred around the creation of a NATO Rapid Reaction Corps, to replace NATO's traditional 'layer-cake' defence of Central Europe; a proposal that was put forward even before the strategy review had been completed. Although the details are still being developed, the RRC will consist of four to five divisions (about 70,000–100,000 troops) from European NATO countries, supported by American aircraft and helicopters. The RRC was designed to provide the Alliance with the ability to respond promptly (the Corps is expected to be deployable in five to seven days) and to assure the continued integration of NATO forces, as well as to increase the flexibility and mobility of NATO operations. The RRC is to be backed up by six or seven corps (all but one multinational) as the 'Main Force', reinforced in turn by 'Augmentational Forces' (drawn primarily from US reserves and European territorial forces). A small, 5,000-troop immediate reaction brigade rounds out the new NATO force structure.

The negotiations over the new force structure revealed divergent national interests which strained relations within NATO. The government of the UK was convinced that the only way to maintain the British Army of the Rhine was through British leadership of the RRC. This put the UK squarely at odds with Germany, which believed that the size of its contribution earned it a greater role in the definition of the forces, as well as in their composition and command. France was convinced that the RRC was a thinly disguised ploy to short-circuit its efforts to create a distinctive European defence identity which would assume the principal responsibility for European security. In military circles there was grumbling that the movement towards multinational forces was a response to political imperatives without adequate military rationale.

NATO defence ministers approved the plan for the RRC at their half-yearly meeting in the spring, but deep disagreements over the political rationale for the new reorganization and the role of nuclear weapons led NATO leaders to postpone their planned summit from June until November. An important breakthrough on the nuclear issue came in September in the wake of the failed Soviet coup, when President Bush announced the US decision to withdraw unilaterally all US short-range, ground-delivered nuclear weapons (*Lance* missiles and nuclear artillery shells). The US move was soon followed by a NATO decision to cut in half the number of gravity bombs deployed with Alliance forces. This decision mooted the effort (led by Germany) to seek arms-control negotiations on short-range nuclear weapons, but left open the still controversial question of the need to modernize air-delivered systems, as well as the issue of whether NATO should adopt a policy of 'no first use'.

Finally, after months of wrangling, NATO leaders endorsed a new strategic concept at their meeting in Rome on 7–8 November. They reiterated their commitment to NATO's four 'core' functions which had been set out at the Copenhagen meeting of NATO foreign ministers in June: to provide one of the foundations of European stability; to serve as a forum for transatlantic political consultations; to deter and defend against attacks on member states; and to preserve the strategic balance in Europe. They formally acknowledged that the threat of a 'simultaneous, full scale attack on all of NATO's European fronts' had disappeared, and in its place NATO faced 'multi-faceted and multidirectional risks', arising from the 'serious economic, social and political difficulties, including ethnic rivalries and territorial disputes' in Central and Eastern Europe, as well as the proliferation of weapons of mass destruction and ballistic missiles on Europe's periphery. In light of the new environment, the Alliance leaders placed particular emphasis on preventive diplomacy and crisis management as a centrepiece of NATO's new role.

The Rome summit took an important step towards recognizing the emergence of a distinct European defence identity. NATO leaders accepted that 'integrated and multinational European structures' could have a role to play in parallel with NATO integrated military forces, while pledging to develop 'practical arrangements . . . to ensure the necessary mutual transparency and complementarity between the European security and defence identity and the Alliance'.

As NATO debated its own future force structure and missions, it was under increasing pressure from East European nations to respond to their perceived security needs, through membership in NATO or other forms of association. Czechoslovak President Vaclav Havel travelled to Brussels in February 1991 to press the case for his country's joining NATO, but was turned away with vague promises of increased 'diplomatic liaison and high level contacts'. As the situation in the East evolved, however, NATO's leaders convinced themselves that they needed to do more. In May, US Secretary of State Baker and German Foreign Minister Genscher issued a statement calling for 'more intensive contacts between NATO and the former Warsaw Pact countries', and at their Copenhagen meeting, NATO's foreign ministers stated that 'our own security is inseparably linked to that of all other states in Europe'.

These steps culminated at the November NATO summit in the decision to create a North Atlantic Cooperation Council embracing the former members of the Warsaw Pact. At its first meeting in December 1991, participants included the five former non-Soviet Warsaw Pact countries, the three Baltic states, and the USSR. The latter's representative, however, indicated before the close of proceedings that he was henceforth participating in the name of Russia. Subsequently, apparently at Germany's suggestion, the NACC's membership was opened to all republics of the former USSR. This created a new problem, since a club including states such as Turkmenistan or Tajikistan was unlikely to cater to the security concerns of Poland, Hungary and Czechoslovakia, which was one of the reasons that had led to the creation of the Council in the first place.

This episode highlighted NATO's continuing dilemma. Despite the new strategic concept and the enunciation of NATO's core functions, NATO's role in the new Europe remains ambiguous. There is still no consensus on whether NATO should assume a military role beyond defending the 16 member nations' territory (i.e., 'out of area'). NATO's diffident approach to the conflict in Yugoslavia left many wondering just what role (military or political) the Alliance intends to play in responding to ethnic and national conflict on its borders. It is difficult to imagine that humanitarian activities will be sufficient to justify NATO's continued existence. The continuing reduction of US forces in Europe and conflicts between the US and Europe over economic issues have led many to wonder whether the US Congress will continue to support a substantial number of stationed US troops in the future. And the Maastricht EC summit represented a new (although tentative) step towards Europe assuming responsibility for its own security.

Yet in view of the prevailing uncertainties to the East and the South, not to mention the difficulties faced by Europe in reaching agreement on its own security role, none of NATO's governments are yet prepared to see it disbanded. NATO thus seems destined to remain an important element of the European security landscape for some time to come. Its chances of securing a longer-term role imply that it does not lose its way in territory better covered by other institutions (UN, CSCE, EC) and that it manages to focus on what it does best: organizing the security and defence relationship between North America and Western Europe. This relationship could become increasingly bilateral as Western Europe moves towards a common security policy and as Canada, by withdrawing all its forces from Europe, appears to be removing itself from the mainstream of Euro-American relations.

Is There an Architect in the House?

The Community's efforts to prepare for an uncertain future cannot be seen in isolation from the broader play of political forces and institutional development in Europe. In 1991 it became clear that one of Europe's most pressing challenges was to address the growing political, economic and cultural turmoil arising from the Soviet Union's collapse and instability in the Middle East and North Africa.

There was no lack of candidates for that role. At its November 1991 summit, NATO had at last begun to adapt to the new realities by shedding its military preoccupation with countering the Soviet threat. The CSCE continued on its path of institutionalization, setting up a Conflict

Prevention Centre in Vienna, an Office for Free Elections in Warsaw, and a secretariat in Prague, as well as convening the first meeting of the CSCE Council in Berlin in June. The EC not only negotiated new association agreements with several Central European countries, but also continued to serve as the focus for economic assistance to the East, and coordinating its members' response first to the Baltic states' declarations of independence, and later to the political change in the remaining Soviet republics. The CSCE's membership grew rapidly, moving from 35 members in mid-1991 to 51 less than a year later.

Yugoslavia was the real test of fire, however, and that crisis illustrated how far Europe has yet to go, in whatever format one chooses to define it, be it from San Francisco to Vladivostok or the EC Twelve. While Euro-champions pointed with pride to the EC's activism (in organizing economic sanctions and a peace conference) and blamed the failure to halt the fighting on the underdeveloped state of European foreign-policy and security mechanisms, the prospects remain troubling. The CSCE proved of little value in moderating the conflict. The debate over whether to recognize Slovenia and Croatia, as Germany advocated, caused tensions, which were exacerbated at the year's end by Germany's threat to recognize them unilaterally, thus confirming in some minds the risk of go-it-alone German assertiveness in the wake of unification. On several occasions, Europeans canvassed the options for military involvement as peace-keepers or even peacemakers through the WEU, but the will, agreed objectives and the means were all lacking. NATO stood resolutely silent on the sidelines. In the end, Europe, and Serbia, turned to the United Nations, in the hope that, emboldened by its successful role in the Iraqi crisis, it could succeed where European and Atlantic institutions had failed.

It is understandable that Europe's latest revolution should produce a period of uncertainty and experimentation. The architects' neat visions of 1989 have given way to the hard reality of politics and the pressure of unfolding events. New crises loom on the horizon – the conflict in Yugoslavia will not end at the borders of Croatia and Serbia, and could (through Macedonia and Kosovo) spill over to engulf the entire Balkan region. Czechoslovakia's future as a unitary state is in doubt, and conflict in many parts of the former Soviet Union seems certain. Germany, preoccupied with the social and economic challenge of unification, is still in the midst of a wrenching internal debate over its own role in Europe and beyond, and the anxieties of its neighbours could ironically produce the very result they fear the most – a slowing down of West European integration and a re-nationalization of economic and security policy. The events in Eastern and Southern Europe have shown that old-style nationalism and the quest for the ethnically defined state is not yet dead; without strong leadership and a greater willingness to seek consensus, there is a risk that Western Europe could slide back in that direction as well.

The Americas

The peoples and governments of the Americas turned their faces inwards in 1991. The heavy emphasis on internationalist cooperation that had marked the last six months of 1990 reached its climax with the coalition victory over Iraq and the proclamation by President George Bush of the dawn of a new world order. It had hardly been floated before it sank unmourned beneath a wave of concern about domestic economic and political problems.

In the United States, President Bush faces an election year with his personal popularity plunging from the highest point ever reached by an incumbent president to well below 50%. The electorate is making it clear that it is more concerned with a raft of domestic problems which in its view he had been ignoring, than with an enhanced international role. In these circumstances, the administration will spend no more than the minimum amount of time possible on foreign problems.

In Canada, Prime Minister Brian Mulroney also found himself buffeted by an economic downturn which stubbornly refuses to right itself, and a consequent loss of popularity. A clear indication of the extent of the trend to emphasize domestic problems came when the Canadian government announced that it would withdraw all its troops from NATO and Europe. In Latin America, political and economic pressures dictated that governments concentrated heavily on their domestic problems, as well as on regional trade agreements. At a time when the extraordinary changes on the international political and security scene required more than passing interest and effort, the governments of the Americas seemed poised to move away in 1992 from the internationalism that characterized the Cold War era to the home-grown or regional tasks in which their people were now far more interested.

THE US LOOKS INWARDS

What a difference a year makes. At the end of February 1991, US President George Bush was riding high. He was being hailed for the adroit diplomacy that led to the creation of a coalition of forces in the Persian Gulf and UN authorization of military action against Iraq. The coalition itself, led by American field commanders and soldiers, had just completed a stunningly successful military campaign. Bush's approval ratings reached 91%, the highest level ever recorded for an American president; this led almost everyone to conclude that he was certain to be re-elected in 1992. Some observers speculated that the diplomatic and military prowess on display in the Gulf represented the beginning of a new era, an era in which the United States, the world's only remaining superpower, would serve as the policeman of a new world order.

By the end of February 1992, however, Bush was struggling to convince voters that he deserved a second term as president. The military victory in the Gulf had been tainted by political indecisiveness and timidity in the White House; thousands of Kurds were slaughtered or driven to die in the mountains of northern Iraq and Turkey by surviving Iraqi forces in March 1991 while Bush fretted over what to do. Saddam Hussein was still in power in Baghdad, and UN inspectors subsequently discovered that his nuclear weapons programme had been missed by the coalition's aerial assault. The President supported Mikhail Gorbachev long after the balance of power in Moscow had tipped decisively in favour of Boris Yeltsin and the republics. Bush's trip to Japan in January 1992 was nothing short of a humiliation, less because of an ill-timed attack of gastroenteritis, than because the President reduced himself to the role of an ineffective car salesman. As far as the American people were concerned, though, Bush's greatest failing was his apparent neglect of pressing domestic issues in general and the economic recession in particular. By March 1992, his approval ratings had dropped to 45%.

As the 1992 electoral campaign unfolded in the first few months of 1992, the American political debate became increasingly parochial. Voters seemed to care little about foreign policy, except when it impinged on domestic issues such as unemployment and trade. The leading presidential candidates – including Bush, an avowed internationalist – pandered to this point of view. Given the self-involved mood of the country, the idea that the American military might function as a 'globo-cop' was simply laughable. The United States was turning inwards; the only question was how far this process would go.

The Changing Context of American Foreign Policy

In 1991, American foreign policy was transformed by two developments: the collapse of the Soviet Union and the economic recession at home. The break-up of the USSR deprived American foreign policy of its overarching purpose. For 45 years, it had been driven by the need to contain Soviet military power and political influence: alliances were formed, frequently with unsavoury regimes; conventional forces were sustained at levels unprecedented for peacetime; nuclear weapons were developed and deployed in large numbers; expensive military and economic assistance programmes were instituted.

Now both the ends and means of American foreign and defence policy had to be reassessed. What were America's core national interests and goals in the post-Cold War world? What kind of political and military commitments should the United States make to secure these interests and further these goals? How much of the national treasure should be devoted to defence and foreign assistance programmes? The domestic debate over these questions intensified sharply after the failed coup in Moscow in August 1991, and the dissolution of the Soviet Union itself in December.

The other development that galvanized and shaped this debate was the economic recession in the United States. When the effects of the recession extended into late 1991 and early 1992, many Americans began to wonder if decades of international activism were responsible for the country's economic woes. The federal budget deficits seemed out of control (the federal deficit was expected to reach $400bn in FY 1992); unemployment was on the rise, notably in the hitherto unscathed service sector; and the symbolically, as well as substantively, important automobile industry was being savaged by Japanese competition. At the same time, many Americans were troubled by pressing social problems – horrifically expensive and ill-distributed health care, a faltering educational system, inner-city decay, crime and drugs – that only seemed to be getting worse.

A minority viewpoint, but one which received a disproportionate share of attention from the media in the US and around the world, was staunchly isolationist in character. Most forcefully expressed by Pat Buchanan, the right-wing candidate for the Republican presidential nomination, the isolationist manifesto held that because the US faced few threats to its core interests internationally, it should disengage itself from military and economic commitments almost everywhere. Isolationists maintained that the United States should withdraw all American troops from Europe and East Asia, cut off all payments to the UN, the IMF and the World Bank, and eliminate most foreign aid programmes. They believed that by spending less money on defence and foreign aid and by putting 'America first', the country's economic and social problems could be solved and its economic competitiveness restored.

A second school of thought was internationalist in character. This line of thinking was best represented by the Bush administration, which felt that the United States continued to have a wide range of global interests and that it therefore needed to be actively engaged on many diplomatic fronts. This implied that the US needed to maintain large military forces capable of extending American power around the world. One indication of the administration's commitment to the internationalist agenda was its January 1992 proposal to lower defence spending by only $10bn in FY 1993. This internationalist stance had multilateralist 'new world order' and unilateralist variants, the latter best exemplified by a leaked Pentagon planning draft which posited the prevention of the rise of any other power to a position which could challenge that of the US as the basic goal of US international policy.

As the domestic debate over America's role in world affairs heated up in late 1991 and early 1992, a third school of thought moved to the fore. Moderate commentators suggested that, although the US continued to have political and economic interests around the world, these interests were not as wide-ranging or important as they once were, due to the disappearance of the Soviet Union as a global adversary. They also maintained that the country could afford far deeper cuts in defence spending than the current 25% compromise struck in February 1991 for the 1991–5 period. The most serious threat to the country's long-term position in world affairs, they insisted, was its deteriorating economy. The origins of this threat were said to be both internal (a growing federal deficit, declining economic productivity, weak savings and investment rates, inadequate research and development) and external (unfair trading policies, primarily in Japan).

Public opinion polls in late 1991 and early 1992 showed that many Americans were beginning to embrace this point of view: 44% believed that no country posed a serious military threat to the United States; 49% believed that the United States should not serve as the world's policeman; most believed that economic competitiveness was a 'vital' issue and that big defence budgets were hurting the economy; 70% would rather spend more money on problems in the United States than on economic aid to the former Soviet Union; 72% believed that Japan, not the former Soviet Union, posed the greatest threat to the future of the United States.

By early 1992, most Americans felt that the country's leaders needed to devote more time and money to domestic and economic problems, and less to foreign and defence issues. Inevitably, these views affected the tone of the presidential campaign as well as American relations with the former Soviet Union and with its allies around the world.

Relations with the Former Soviet Union

The Bush administration's handling of relations with the former Soviet Union in 1991 and early 1992 was characterized by conservatism, slow-footedness and tight-fistedness. As a result, the administration rarely played a leading role in Western efforts to deal with the cascade of events that took place in Russia and the other republics.

Throughout 1991, Bush looked for every opportunity to keep US–Soviet relations on familiar terrain. Although many in the administration questioned Gorbachev's commitment to structural reform, fear of the unknown and the prospect of chaos in the Soviet Union led Bush to embrace Gorbachev in a futile attempt to prop up the centre.

One of Bush's most embarrassing miscues followed the Moscow summit with Gorbachev on 31 July and 1 August 1991. After signing the long-awaited START Treaty, Bush travelled to Kiev, the Ukrainian capital, where nationalist sentiments were surging. Astonishingly, the President took this opportunity to warn the Ukrainian people of the dangers of 'suicidal nationalism', and he noted that his administration intended to 'maintain the strongest possible relationship with the Soviet government of Mikhail Gorbachev'. This statement became known as the 'chicken Kiev' speech.

Bush's immediate reaction to the news that a coup had taken place in Moscow on 19 August was typically faint-hearted: rather than denounce the plotters and insist that Gorbachev be returned to power, Bush indicated that he expected Moscow to live up to its international commitments. He later came out more forcefully against the putschists, but only after British Prime Minister John Major and US Senator Sam Nunn had done so and after it had begun to appear that the reformers might be able to withstand the plotters after all.

When the coup failed and Gorbachev returned to Moscow, Bush had kind words for Yeltsin's courageous actions, but he once again threw his weight behind the known quantity: Gorbachev. Bush still hoped that Yeltsin's challenge to Gorbachev's political authority could be contained and that the centrifugal forces building in the republics could be dampened. He consequently withheld diplomatic recognition of the breakaway Baltic republics – even though the United States had never accepted Stalin's annexation of them – until 2 September, some time after most European capitals had extended recognition.

Bush was on firmer ground in dealing with arms-control issues, long the centrepiece of US–Soviet relations. On 27 September he proposed sweeping changes in the US and Soviet nuclear arsenals. The rationale behind his far-reaching initiatives was clear: given the growing instability in the Soviet Union, it was in the West's interest to eliminate the estimated 17,000 tactical nuclear weapons in the Soviet arsenal; the only way to make this politically palatable in Moscow was for the United States to do the same. Although Gorbachev reciprocated with extensive unilateral cuts of his own, he was unable to implement his disarmament decisions in the few weeks he had left in the Kremlin.

Although Bush professed to be concerned about developments in the Soviet Union, he was unwilling to spend much money on looming problems there. Sam Nunn, the Chairman of the Senate Armed Services Committee, and Les Aspin, the Chairman of the House Armed Services Committee, took the lead in September 1991. They tried to shift $1bn from the US defence budget to create a Soviet economic assistance fund. Their effort failed: both Congress and the administration were unwilling to run the risk of antagonizing public opinion. A scaled-down version of the Nunn-Aspin proposal, one that called for $400m to be spent on the deactivation of Soviet nuclear weapons and $100m on humanitarian assistance, was ultimately approved by Congress in December. This, too, was a Congressional initiative.

Although the Soviet Union was on the verge of dissolution in December, the Bush administration continued to act as if some sort of central authority could be preserved in Moscow and some sort of political role could be found for Gorbachev. When this proved impossible, and Gorbachev announced his resignation on 25 December, Bush declared that the United States would establish full diplomatic relations with six of the republics of the former Soviet Union: Russia, the Ukraine, Belarus, Armenia, Kazakhstan and Kyrgyzstan. Full relations would be established with the other republics when they demonstrated their commitment to democratic and economic reforms, minority rights guarantees, and international agreements that had been made by Moscow.

The administration became somewhat more energetic about helping the republics in January, after Yeltsin instituted a series of radical economic reforms. Bush and Secretary of State James Baker hosted a 47-nation conference in Washington on 22–23 January that was intended to help coordinate Western assistance efforts. In opening the conference, Bush announced that he would ask Congress for $645m in humanitarian and technical assistance for the republics, to be spent over two years. Baker announced that the American airlift of emergency aid to the republics would be expanded. This brought US assistance pledges to $5.2bn, no small sum given the prevailing domestic attitudes, but most of this aid came in the form of credit guarantees for the purchase of US grain and would therefore have direct domestic benefits as well.

The week after the coordinating conference ended, Bush announced yet another series of defence cuts and arms-control proposals. In his 28 January State of the Union address, the President suggested that the US and the republics cut their strategic nuclear arsenals to around 4,700 weapons each; this would represent a 50% reduction in post-START forces. Yeltsin went even further the next day, proposing a reduction in strategic forces to 2,500 weapons on each side. The nature of US–Russian relations was changing in fundamental ways. The two countries seemed to be moving in the direction of establishing a security relationship based more on partnership than confrontation.

Bush and Yeltsin met at Camp David on 2 February for a mini-summit, but no major substantive agreements were reached. In fact, none were anticipated: the purpose of the meeting was to strengthen personal ties between the two leaders and to set out their joint agenda for the immediate future. Bush finally gave Yeltsin his full and unequivocal support, noting that the Russian leader was 'totally committed to democratic reform'. The two presidents agreed to meet at least twice more in 1992.

Although the Bush administration was beginning to pursue a more vigorous policy towards the republics in the first few months of 1992, many commentators maintained that it was doing 'too little, too late'. Some critics maintained that the Bush administration's failure to take advantage of an historic opportunity to help consolidate democratic and economic reforms in Russia and the other republics would ultimately have profound implications for Western security. Whether the President was being short-sighted or realistic about what the United States could do to influence events in the republics was an open question in the spring of 1992.

Relations with Europe

On the surface, the American role in European security affairs seemed to be healthy. American relations with its West European allies were generally cordial, and Bush received very high marks from his European counterparts for his September 1991 and January 1992 arms-control initiatives; the German reaction was especially laudatory. Refinements in NATO doctrine and force structure policy were reached at the Rome summit in November 1991 without significant incident; the main bone of contention in the run-up to the summit, a Franco-German proposal to create an independent European army, was successfully finessed for the time being.

American leaders did not interpret the results of the EC's December 1991 Maastricht summit, which took steps towards greater political and economic union and issued a statement of interest in developing a common EC foreign and defence policy, as an immediate threat to American interests or transatlantic relations. There was some grumbling in Paris and Bonn when Baker announced in December that the United States would host a coordinating conference on aid to the republics of the former Soviet Union; some felt that the Bush administration was trying to take credit for Western relief efforts when most of the hard cash for the republics was coming from European capitals. This mini-crisis soon blew over, however; Bush was gracious in praising European relief efforts in his opening remarks at the conference, and it was agreed that a second conference would be organized by the EC and held in Lisbon.

What was only dimly perceived by policy-makers was that the premises of US–European security relations had changed in fundamental ways in 1991. For over four decades, a strong American military presence was needed in Western Europe to offset Soviet power and most Americans appreciated that this requirement existed. They believed that their country could afford to maintain large and robust military forces in and around Europe. By 1992, neither of these propositions was valid.

With the collapse of the Soviet Union and the Russian economy, Moscow no longer posed a clear and present military danger to West European security. Although West European and American officials repeatedly stated that it was nonetheless important for the US to maintain a meaningful military presence in Europe, they were unable to provide a jointly agreed and compelling strategic rationale for doing so. In any event, European efforts to develop a common defence policy – however faltering – implied that in many contingencies American military efforts would not be needed and might not be wanted. Officials on both sides of the Atlantic protested that this was not so, but many Americans felt that European actions spoke for themselves.

Although American officials repeatedly stated that a small military force in Europe, of the size of a single army corps, need not be expensive, many Americans believed that the country could not afford to spend any money on non-essential activities. At the same time, Americans were increasingly inclined to let European capitals handle – or not handle – residual European security problems; this attitude was reflected in Washington's decision to wash its hands of the Yugoslav crisis in the summer of 1991.

In all probability, these underlying developments will affect policy only slowly. For years to come, some American troops will be deployed on European soil; current plans call for 150,000 troops to be stationed in Europe, but this target will inevitably be lowered to under 100,000. The rationale for such a force, rather than resting on tangible intra-European military conditions, could well rely on out-of-area convenience – the Gulf is close to Europe – and on the lessons of twentieth century history: once removed, it is not easy to reintroduce forces when and if they are needed. In future, NATO will perform a variety of tasks, although of an increasingly inconsequential nature, while policy-makers will try to devise convincing rationales for preserving arrangements inherited from the Cold War. But unless a new basis can be found for the transatlantic security compact, historians may well look back on 1991–2 as the time when the United States and Europe began to go their separate ways on security issues.

Relations with East Asia

Relations between the United States and Japan deteriorated sharply over the course of 1991–2, at the public, if not the official, level.

The collapse of the Soviet military threat allowed latent tensions in the US–Japan relationship to surge to the surface, and the lingering recession in the United States led many Americans to blame unfair Japanese trading practices for economic difficulties at home. Although the US trade deficit with Japan had improved in recent years, from $60bn in 1987 to $43bn in 1991, it was still unacceptably high. American critics maintained that the problem was not the quality or price of US goods; the United States, after all, had a $16-bn trade surplus with the EC in 1991. The problem, they insisted, was Japanese barriers to imports: Japan ran a trade surplus with most of the industrialized world.

Mounting frustration with the recession and with Japan led some in the United States to call for retaliatory protectionist legislation; only a recognition that this course would be self-defeating in the long run kept it from gaining widespread support. Others favoured informal retaliatory measures: boycotts of Japanese goods and 'buy American' campaigns were started in parts of the United States, and the Los Angeles County Transit Commission cancelled a $122m contract with the Sumitomo Corporation on nationalistic grounds. In addition, harsh words were spoken on both sides of the Pacific; 'Japan bashing' and 'America bashing' became more commonplace. The speaker of the lower house of the Japanese parliament, Yoshio Sakurauchi, aggravated the situation when he referred to the United

States as 'Japan's subcontractor' and declared that the problem with American workers was that they 'can't read' and 'don't want to work'.

President Bush's trip to Japan in January 1992 only made matters worse. The trip was originally scheduled for November 1991, but Bush cancelled it when domestic critics accused him of spending too much of his time on foreign policy. This disturbed many in Japan, who had hoped that Bush would use his trip to promote a US–Japan strategic partnership in world affairs. When Bush rescheduled the trip, he lowered his sights; pandering to domestic concerns he shifted the focus to the bilateral economic problems. Taking along the overpaid chiefs of the three largest US auto manufacturers, hardly the cream of American industry, further undermined his credibility as an economic partner and his stature as a statesman. With elections looming in 1992 in both the United States and Japan, the best that could be said about the state of relations between the two countries was that they were in turmoil.

Relations between the United States and China, on the other hand, stayed on a steady if cool course in 1991 and early 1992. Washington welcomed the constructive role that Beijing played in the Cambodian peace settlement and its decision to sign the NPT. At the same time, American leaders remained critical of China's political repression and human rights abuses. Washington opposed Beijing's plans to sell missiles to Syria and Pakistan, and nuclear reactor components to Iran and Algeria. It also complained about China's refusal to respect US patents and copyrights, especially with respect to computer software.

All of these issues were on the agenda when Secretary Baker travelled to Beijing in November 1991; this was the first time a member of the US cabinet had visited China since the Tiananmen Square massacre of June 1989. Baker and the Chinese leadership reached a number of agreements: China agreed to constrain its nuclear exports and put pressure on North Korea to curtail its nuclear weapons programme, a major American concern; it also agreed to adhere to the guidelines of the Missile Technology Control Regime and to do a better job in the area of copyright protection. But significant areas of disagreement remained, mainly in the area of human rights, which Beijing insisted was an internal matter.

Although the Bush administration sought to nurture a constructive relationship with Beijing, many in Congress remained highly critical of China's political and economic transgressions. Congress consequently attached a number of conditions (mainly relating to human rights, arms sales and trade issues) to the annual bill that extends China's MFN trading status with the US. Although Bush's veto was sustained in the Senate after failing in the House, it was clear that many in the United States were still dissatisfied with China's domestic and international activities – and with the administration's accommodating posture towards Beijing.

Defence Posture

The American people witnessed a paradoxical spectacle in early 1992. On the one hand, Secretary of Defense Dick Cheney acknowledged that the threats to national security had changed in fundamental ways in 1991. On the other, he insisted that the US defence budget could be cut by only $9bn – from $276bn to $267bn – in the new fiscal year. In the weeks that followed, several Pentagon planning documents were leaked, all of which sought to justify high levels of defence spending and powerful force structures. Cheney was particularly adamant about retaining 1.6 million troops in uniform, even though this target had been set before the Soviet Union fell apart.

The Bush administration did make some concessions to strategic and political reality, however. In September 1991, Bush announced that, in addition to destroying and redeploying large numbers of tactical nuclear weapons, he would cancel the mobile basing schemes for the MX and SICBM missiles; he also cancelled the SRAM programme. Sceptics noted, though, that the air force had never been particularly interested in mobile basing, and that cancellation of the SRAM strengthened the case for the B-2 bomber, which the air force and administration were keen to build. In January 1992, Bush cancelled the SICBM programme altogether; stopped production of warheads for the D-5 SLBM, of the advanced cruise missile, and of additional MX missiles; cancelled the *Seawolf* submarine programme; and proposed ending B-2 production after only 20 bombers had been built. Finally, Bush planned to reduce defence spending by $50bn over five years. Many in Congress wanted to go much further. The House, for example, was unlikely to provide funds for any B-2s beyond the 16 that had either been built or were under construction.

Many in Congress challenged the administration's interest in developing and deploying a strategic defence system that would require renegotiation of the ABM Treaty and would cost, according to the Congressional Budget Office, $87.5bn. Furthermore, critics questioned the rationale for having 1.6 million in the armed services, given that the strategic landscape had changed radically since this force was first designed. They also maintained that defence spending should be cut more sharply. Aspin, the knowledgeable and influential leader of the House debate, maintained that the defence budget could be cut by an additional $50–120bn. In late March, Senator Sam Nunn suggested that the cut should be about $85bn.

The US defence debate was just beginning to play out in the first few months of 1992, but it was clear even then that the Bush administration would be hard-pressed to justify its proposals, given that important elements of its plans remained unchanged by the cataclysmic events of 1991. With Bush facing an electorate which wanted a shift from heavy defence to domestic social spending, it would be no surprise if it didn't even try.

NORTH AMERICAN FREE TRADE AREA IN TROUBLE

Since the US Congress in May 1991 granted the Bush administration fast-track authority for negotiating a free-trade accord with Mexico, US Trade Representative Carla Hills and other officials have repeatedly characterized the project as a 'win-win-win' proposition for all three participating countries: the United States, Canada and Mexico. The essence of a free-trade area is to remove all tariffs and non-tariff barriers, which would allow goods and services to be produced by the most efficient companies in member countries, thus raising the GNP of each. The North American Free Trade Agreement (NAFTA) would create a massive market, with annual production in excess of $6 trillion and with almost 370 million consumers. Of that, the US economy represents $5.5 trillion, and Mexico's $150bn.

Since Mexican President Carlos Salinas de Gortari first proposed the idea of a free-trade accord between his country and the US, Mexican officials have been in the forefront of those urging that such a move is needed if North America is to compete effectively with Europe and Asia. The latter two regions have gone much further than North America in integrating their economies, so that these countries can achieve economies of scale in producing the goods and services in which they have a comparative advantage.

The US and Canada reached agreement on a free-trade accord (FTA) that went into effect in 1989. There was some fear among Canadians that FTA would lead to US domination of Canada's economy, but despite a recession that economists ascribe to domestic Canadian causes, the FTA has thus far not created significant disadvantages for Canada. Some US critics charge that Canada is not complying with local-content rules (50% North American content is required for duty-free treatment) intended to keep third countries, notably Japan, from using Canadian production locations to enter the US market. In early March 1992, Washington decided to deny duty-free access to Honda cars assembled in Ontario and imposed a large duty on lumber shipments from Canada on the basis that they were subsidized by low tree-cutting charges in provincially-owned forests. Prime Minister Mulroney, in an interview with the *Financial Times* in early March, made it clear that Canada would consider retaliatory action, but noted that Ottawa would refer the issues to settlement panels established under the FTA. Pointing out that this avenue of redress would not exist but for the FTA, Mulroney said that Canada remained committed to NAFTA so as to protect the gains it felt it had made in the FTA.

Although there have been some objections in Congress, the FTA was not particularly controversial in the US since both countries are at similar levels of economic development and have similar social and political institutions. The same is not true with regard to Mexico. In the short term, Mexico, which has already reduced its tariffs to an average of 10%, would be the major beneficiary of NAFTA. US pro-

ducers would move south and Mexican exports to the US would
increase, creating more jobs in Mexico. Over time, this growth would
spur an increase in demand for American imports, thus buoying US
GNP. According to Washington, about 25,000 new jobs are created in
the US for every additional $1bn in net exports.

Growing Unease

At present Mexico is the third-largest US trade partner, with a total
two-way trade of $52bn. Two-thirds of Mexico's imports come from
the United States. In the short-term, however, the US will suffer job
losses as plants relocate to Mexico. Mexico argues that if they do not
do so, they will go to Asia instead. US Department of Labor studies of
the assembly (*maquiladora*) plants in Mexico support this assertion,
showing that if the *maquiladora* plants shut down, the jobs of 76,000
US workers who supplied them, and some $2.6bn in GNP, would be
lost. To ease the transition to NAFTA, the Bush administration has
promised retraining and other assistance to US workers affected by
plant closures.

US labour unions, and especially the United Auto Workers
(UAW), are dubious that these commitments will be met, and some
Democratic presidential candidates have argued that the US should
stem the flow of its manufacturing base to other countries.
Congressmen, including the powerful House Majority Leader Richard
Gephardt, doubt that a Republican administration will take seriously
the need to help workers who lose their jobs. Gephardt has bluntly
warned the administration that Congress could reject an accord that
does not address a range of domestic concerns. One possibility
looming is an amendment proposed by Democratic Senator Don
Riegle, backed by the UAW, that would give the Senate the right to
consider individual components of the international agreement that
fast-track negotiations would not currently allow.

In addition, the administration has promised to ensure that Mexican standards for labour safety and environmental protection are
improved, to lessen the incentive for US businesses to move to Mexico
to escape domestic regulations. The administration undertook a review
of the environmental issues at stake in 1991, and in Congressional testimony on 9 December, Deputy Assistant US Trade Representative
Charles Ries outlined the following conclusions of the review:

> First our findings indicate that a NAFTA should not lead to system-
> atic shifts in investment from the United States to Mexico based
> on expected differences in pollution abatement costs. Second, it is
> quite possible that removal of trade barriers through a free trade
> agreement would reinforce the recent tendency of maquiladora-type
> plants to locate in the less congested, less expensive Mexican
> interior, modestly reducing future environmental stress on the bor-
> der. And third, it is clear that over the long term a NAFTA will con-

tribute to the generation of additional resources that may be of great importance to Mexico in achieving improved environmental protection particularly in the border area.

Those recommendations are deemed far too sanguine by a number of US Congressmen, who want more aggressive measures to strengthen Mexico's environmental protection regulations, and especially enforcement of those standards. Representative Sam Gejdenson disagrees with the administration's optimistic outlook and warns that it will affect votes in Congress on approving NAFTA.

Growing Mexican Concerns

Formal negotiations on NAFTA began in 1991, but the US recession and rising protectionist sentiment led the Bush administration to postpone completion of the accord until after the 1992 presidential elections, or at least not to present it to Congress. Although the administration remained a staunch defender of the merit of a free-trade accord, by early 1992 the prospects for completion and approval of NAFTA were dim. Mexican officials privately acknowledged the exigencies of the American political climate, noting that a postponed NAFTA was better than one voted down by a Congress under heavy pressure from constituents and lobby groups.

Even though a delay in the completion and ratification of the accord seemed all but certain, negotiations on NAFTA continued in 1992. The negotiators ran into disagreements over issues such as the local-content rules. The Mexican interest is in encouraging investment from all countries, while the US is concerned with preventing Japan from using Mexico as a back-door into the US market.

The impact of a delay in NAFTA on Mexico could be serious. The free-trade accord has been touted by the Salinas government as the keystone of its sweeping programme of economic reform. In order to lift per capita income, Mexico has set a target for economic growth of 6%, but this will be difficult to achieve in the best of circumstances, given its 2% population growth rate and the fact that during the 1980s its standard of living dropped by 45%. To achieve that growth rate, Mexico is counting heavily on foreign investment, and NAFTA is the intended mechanism for attracting that capital.

Postponing the Agreement is not only likely to delay the expected investment inflow, but could cause a crisis of confidence in Mexico if investors fear that NAFTA might not be concluded. At present, 75% of foreign investors have put their money into easily liquidated portfolio investments, rather than fixed investments. If Salinas is unable to reassure current and potential investors that a NAFTA is only a matter of time, much of that capital inflow could be reversed.

Such a scenario could also damage the work Salinas has done to resurrect the image of the governing Institutional Revolutionary Party (PRI), which narrowly won the last presidential elections. To boost the political fortunes of the PRI, the Salinas administration intended to have NAFTA in place by the next election.

The worst-case scenario, from the Mexican point of view, is that President Bush will lose the presidential election. Most Democratic candidates harbour misgivings about NAFTA, and would, at a minimum, be more responsive to the complaints of US opponents of the accord. A Democratic victory would, at the least, slow down NAFTA further, possibly requiring another vote in Congress to renew the fast-track negotiating authority which expires in 1993. If the US economy continues to be weak, protectionist pressures might derail the NAFTA project altogether.

Wider Considerations

Yet despite domestic political pressures, many in the US are convinced that the global trend towards regional trading blocs requires the United States to move forward with NAFTA sooner or later. With such an Agreement, three large trading units might dominate the world's commerce: North America, Asia and the European Community (EC), which in 1992 is working towards the completion of a common market, an even closer integration than NAFTA entails.

The impact of NAFTA on the rest of the world could be negative if it leads to a 'fortress' mentality. Although NAFTA negotiators repeatedly stress that the intent is not to keep foreigners out of the market, the debates over local-content rules have revealed US fears of being dominated by Japanese trade and investment. To the extent that NAFTA halts the decline of the US motor industry, Japan's increase in US market share could be halted or even reversed. But by and large, NAFTA should have positive effects on the rest of the world. The fundamental premise of NAFTA, increasing GNP of member countries, will stimulate demand for imports from countries beyond the area.

The main impact that NAFTA will have is likely to be in Latin America. The Bush administration has offered, as part of its 'Enterprise for the Americas' Initiative, to expand the US–Mexico free-trade area to encompass the rest of the hemisphere. Many Latin American countries fear that they will be left behind, and that Mexico will reap the benefits of being the first partner. They justifiably fear that Mexico will capture the bulk of US foreign investment, as well as US markets in product sectors that are also key sectors of their economies.

In an effort to position themselves to take advantage of the creation of NAFTA, Latin American countries during 1990 and 1991 began to form subregional trading areas, (see p. 70). Yet trade among Latin American countries has always been minimal, in part because they produce many of the same products, and the United States has been the principal supplier of manufactured goods. The efforts to dismantle trade barriers will stimulate intra-regional trade to some extent; however, the rush to form subregional trade pacts is intended primarily to make the Latin American countries desirable trade partners for the US. By lowering tariff barriers, these countries will then be in a stronger position to request early inclusion in NAFTA. If NAFTA becomes the victim of an ailing US economy, growing protectionist sentiment and the dynamics of the US presidential election, however, these efforts will have been in vain.

LATIN AMERICA: ORTHODOXY AND UNCERTAINTY

Governments throughout Latin America appeared to have finally found a formula to ensure stable economic growth in 1991, but the slow progress in political reform left the future of the region uncertain. As 1992 began, all Latin American countries, except for Cuba and Haiti, could boast elected civilian governments. Yet ineffective parliaments and weak judiciaries, poor tax collection systems, corruption and restive armed forces continued to undermine democratic political arrangements. Over the course of 1991, more countries were hit by the social, political and international effects of the spreading drug industry and the cholera epidemic. Among the brighter, if inconclusive, developments in the region were increased bilateral and international agreements on trade, nuclear non-proliferation, frontier disputes and the resolution of the civil war in El Salvador.

The New Economic Orthodoxy Takes Hold

In 1991, almost all of the 37 nations of Latin America and the Caribbean embraced policies to tame inflation, to reduce public spending, to privatize markets and to promote exports. Although many elements of these programmes have been implemented before, there had never before been such a widespread consensus in favour of such a systematic drive of economic liberalism. Performance indicators in 1991 reinforced this consensus. After three years of stagnation regional economies grew by an average of 3%. Chile and Mexico were still well ahead in the effort to pull the economy out of the tentacles of state control, but the recently-elected leaders of Bolivia, Uruguay, Peru, Venezuela, Colombia, many of the Central American countries, and most recently Argentina, enacted similar 'free-market' policies. Even Brazil's President Fernando Collor de Mello had been elected in 1990 on a free-trade platform but his administration has failed to follow much of the neo-liberal recipe.

Since 1985 Chile has pursued sustained classic neo-liberal policies which have reduced inflation and regenerated growth. In 1991 President Patricio Aylwin, elected in the autumn of 1990 on a centre-left platform, continued with the model designed under the previous military regime to curb government spending, maintain a cautious monetary course and promote international trade. His administration was rewarded with a 5.5% growth rate and inflation under 20% for the year. Mexico began its third year of market reforms in 1992, having recorded a 4.8% growth rate and 20% inflation in 1991. President Carlos Salinas de Gortari, midway through his six-year term of office, received strong public support for his stabilization and adjustment policies, the fruits of which were negotiations on a free-trade agreement with the United States (see p. 63 *passim*).

Argentina garnered the most dramatic results from its market-oriented, anti-inflationary policies during 1991. In April, President Carlos Menem's newly-appointed Finance Minister Domingo Cavallo announced a programme limiting government money creation by pegging the currency to the US dollar. Inflation, after topping 6,000% in 1989 and 1,000% in 1990, dropped to double digits in 1991. In January 1992, a new currency was introduced: the 'peso' equalling 10,000 australes, or one US dollar. The Menem administration also began to eliminate government regulations on private business, to overhaul the country's taxation system and to start an ambitious trade reform, including negotiations for a regional common market, Mercosur. The tremendous success of Argentina's programmes throughout 1992 was a tribute to the imaginative drive and influence of their author, Finance Minister Cavallo.

Bolivia's sweeping plans to open its economy to foreign competition, and Peru's ambitious reforms to restructure its foreign trade and financial systems, both introduced in January 1991, were extended throughout the year and into early 1992. Venezuelan President Carlos Andres Perez (who had implemented populist, nationalist policies as leader of the country in the 1970s) also remained a devoted follower of free-market policies during 1991.

Brazil was the exception to the rule. President Collor began the year under heavy criticism for not propelling the country in any perceptible economic direction after his bold moves to freeze bank accounts and prohibit wage and price hikes had failed. Brazil's economic statistics (growth of only 0.5% and inflation at 460%) pulled down the region's 1991 average, and made it clear that the country has had no significant growth for the twelfth year running. As 1992 began there was some optimism that the new Economics Minister Marcilio Moreira and a new IMF endorsement would put Brazil on a different course, although no significant policy changes were announced.

The Drive to Privatize

Selling government firms to the private sector was a popular ingredient of the region's economic policy packages. In 1991, Mexico sold off 150 state-owned companies, including shares in its telecommunications company and three banks. Chile had already privatized the majority of state-owned enterprises in the 1970s; in 1991, joint ventures with foreign investors became its latest strategy to rid itself of the remaining state-owned copper and public utilities firms. Argentina sold off $2bn worth of railway, airline and telephone companies in 1991, and promised to hand over management of all state and military-owned companies to the private sector by the end of 1992, including its oil and gas companies, power utilities, postal service, steel mills and hydroelectric plants. The Brazilian government sold off six state companies and the shares of several petrochemical plants, while Venezuela, Peru and Bolivia also launched programmes to privatize, or sell partial stakes in, state-owned enterprises.

The privatization drives provoked few protests. Bolivian miners and labour unions led strikes to stop the government from opening up the tin mines and oil industry to private participation. Brazil's attempt was stalled by an opposition movement led by the state oil corporation lobby and supported by the attorney general, who objected to the government's plans on the grounds that foreign banks were converting their debt IOUs into shares of stock of privatized companies (a common financing strategy). In Argentina, fears mounted that a small group of private companies, which was buying stakes in privatized companies, would be able to exert monopoly control over markets. While privatization gave many states an immediate solution to fiscal problems by raising government revenues, these governments also lost a potential source of revenue and political clout, which shifted the foundations of economic and political authority.

Trade, Finance and Foreign Debt

Cooperating with the international community in finance and trade was, once again, an essential item on the new economic agenda, and most Latin American countries returned to the negotiating table to settle their debts and to establish trade linkages. Nevertheless, in terms of volume inflow, foreign investment in Latin America in 1991 remained modest, given the range of investment opportunities in Eastern Europe and the former Soviet Union. The stock and bond markets in Argentina, Mexico and Chile, which were some of the world's most profitable in 1991, provided a strong exception. Lax rules limiting foreign equity investment, the variety of investment instruments (the active secondary market), and the return of flight capital to Latin America helped create a very distinguished performance.

Ten years after Latin America's debt crisis burst open, foreign indebtedness was still a significant burden for the region's policymakers. Although the net transfer of resources to Latin America in 1991 was positive for the first time in a decade, most countries lacked the necessary foreign currency to pay off external liabilities. There were some encouraging developments, however. Argentina and Brazil appear poised to reach debt agreements with the IMF in mid-1992, promising easier negotiations with commercial creditors. Much of Chile's foreign obligations have been serviced, forgiven or traded, while Mexico and Bolivia were also particularly successful in reducing commercial bank debts in 1991. Ecuador and Mexico signed debt-for-nature swaps, following the lead of Costa Rica and Bolivia, but the percentage of overall debt was not greatly affected by these types of deals.

In a step towards increasing the volume of the region's exports, a number of Latin American countries opened negotiations and signed agreements to begin integrating regional trade markets in 1991. The initial euphoria over the Bush administration's June 1990 'Enterprise for the Americas' plan completely evaporated, once the reality of scant US funds and, most important, of restricted access to the US market, was made clear. Negotiations over Mexico's free-trade agreement with the US garnered the most press coverage, but the March 1991 creation of Mercosur, which is preparing a tariff-free common market among the Southern Cone countries of Brazil, Argentina, Uruguay and Paraguay for the end of 1994, reinforced the trend towards subregional economic integration. The Andean Pact, founded almost 25 years ago by Bolivia, Colombia, Ecuador, Peru and Venezuela, was resuscitated and given a neo-liberal cast: in January 1992, free-trade regulations went into effect, albeit with a lengthy list of exemptions. At the same time, a number of bilateral trade agreements were reached: in September 1991, Chile and Mexico signed an agreement to eliminate all duties, while Venezuela negotiated free-trade pacts with both Chile and the Central American countries. This has led to fears that the rising number of bilateral agreements would jeopardize the promise of a Latin American-wide common market.

While the economic orthodoxy of 'getting the state out of the market' has eclipsed other economic models in Latin America, the benefits of growth have not been widely distributed, and the next source of economic conflict will likely be over social policies, such as health, education and public works. In 1991, the increase in GNP in Latin America brought the region up to its 1977 standard of living. The economic contractions that lasted through 1990, and the present economic reforms have worsened poverty in the region, generating greater inequalities of income, unstable employment levels, and have left little leeway for government fiscal policy to improve deteriorated social services. The attempted military coup in Venezuela in February 1992, although a failure, was a reminder of the potential for explosive discontent. Nevertheless, there was relatively little mobilization against the determined austerity measures which, if maintained, carry a promise of improved economic life in the future.

Challenges to Democratic Rule

The emergence of multiparty democracies over the last decade has been the most encouraging development in recent Latin American politics. Consolidation of these gains in 1991, however, was still uneven. Peasant organizations, trade unions, and other private participatory associations are still docile and under-represented. Fragmented political systems, unresponsive and corrupt government bureaucracies and weak judiciaries were the most troubling sources of conflict and instability in most countries. Restive military institutions, many of which retained a high share of residual power and corporate autonomy, increased the risk of military intervention, further challenging governments' ability to rule.

Political Deadlock

Outdated or provisional political arrangements in the majority of Latin American countries created policy deadlock between the executive, the judiciary and the legislative branches. In May 1991, Bolivia's Supreme Court refused to accept President Jaime Paz Zamora's decision to suspend judges on grounds of corruption, creating a tense stand-off. In January 1992, the Peruvian Congress refused to approve the government's budget and instead passed legislation restricting the rights of the executive to enact decrees. The presidents of Uruguay, Venezuela and Ecuador also lacked broad-based support for policy initiatives, and throughout the year they faced major confrontations with both legislatures and judiciaries over executive decrees.

Struggles between the executive and the legislature were most acute in Brazil. In 1991, President Collor de Mello singlehandedly tried to impose price freezes, to lay off thousands of state workers, and to propose sweeping constitutional amendments, initiatives which fizzled out, in part due to lack of Congressional support and the readiness of lower judiciary courts to grant injunctions against executive measures. Collor, who did not rise to power through an established party or movement, remained politically isolated, and few alternative initiatives or leaders emerged from the existing political apparatus.

Argentina's President Carlos Menem also lacked a cohesive political base, after alienating much of his Peronist party apparatus with his liberal economic policies. In 1991 Menem continued to rely on his personal charisma and on executive decrees to push through policies; his mandate, however, was undermined by a series of bribery and corruption scandals. Corruption, more readily uncovered under conditions of a free press and political competition, also shook the credibility of the Venezuelan, Colombian and Bolivian political systems, revealing the dual problems of an underpaid civil service with broad discretionary powers, and a weak judiciary to arbitrate infractions.

More fundamental reforms were under way in Mexico, where the ruling PRI proposed a reform of the country's constitution which would divest the state of ownership of land and would scrap the *ejido* agricultural organization that had been established in the 1920s. Since the collapse of the Soviet Communist Party, Mexico's PRI has become the longest-serving ruling party in the world. In 1991 the PRI made attempts to reform the party, promising to draw up a new electoral roll and to stop hand-picking local party candidates. Although tangible changes that would create greater internal democracy in the one-party political system were slow to appear, the many promised reforms will weaken the traditional pillars of the PRI. The fact that charges of political fraud (ballot stuffing) in the August 1991 by-elections actually led to the resignation of two PRI governors suggested that political change is being taken seriously.

Colombia moved the furthest with its constitutional reforms. In June 1991 President César Gaviria Trujillo dissolved the Congress and, after a month of meetings, submitted a new Colombian political constitution. In October mayors and governors were elected directly, the size of the Congress was reduced, and Colombia's indigenous communities were allotted two special seats in the Congress. Although the two traditional ruling Liberal and Conservative parties polled well, the former M-19 guerrilla group, which had given up arms and formed a new political party earlier in the year, won 10% of the Congressional seats. Talks with the two remaining main guerrilla groups were maintained throughout 1991, but without any significant progress in the effort to entice them into the political mainstream.

The emergence of new leftist parties in Latin America in 1991 demonstrated the capacity for change from within the political system. These parties rejected the now-defunct communist single party platforms and the centrally planned economy and no longer called for violent revolution as a way of gaining power; instead, their agendas opposed neo-liberal economic policies and offered alternative programmes within the democratic system. Colombia's former guerrilla leader, Antonio Navarro, participated in the drafting of the country's new constitution in 1991, founded a new political party, and was poised to run in the 1994 presidential elections. During the 1990 presidential election in Brazil, a candidate from the workers' party (PT) was only narrowly defeated, while the city of São Paulo elected a PT member as its mayor. Even with this success, however, it still was not clear that the 11-year-old PT could sustain its popularity among the proliferation and fragmentation of Brazilian parties. Uruguay's left-wing political party, the *Frente Amplio*, was on the rise in 1991, and the leader of Chile's socialist party was already identified as a candidate with a plausible chance in the 1993 presidential elections.

In Mexico Cuauhtemoc Cardenas' progressive *Partido de la Revolución Democrática* party, which had polled surprisingly well in the last presidential election, made relatively few gains in the August midterm elections, but continued to function, a significant feat in a state where the PRI has been consistently successful in coopting or marginalizing any challenge from its left. After a peace accord with the government of El Salvador was signed in January 1992, the guerrilla organization FMLN began to set up a legal political party. Nicaragua's former Marxist *Sandinista* ruling party continued to play a progressive role within the democratic political system. For most Latin American leftist movements, the collapse of the Soviet-led communist political model will likely remove a major source of divisiveness in the parties, creating opportunities to build broader coalitions among potential supportive constituencies.

Chile faces another challenge to constitutional political reform. Just before the military gave up its rule in 1990 it appointed one quarter of the Senate, almost all Chile's 300 mayors, and many judges and Central Bank functionaries. Electoral regulations were skewed to favour conservative districts, and, after stepping down as head of state, Augusto Pinochet retained his post of commander-in-chief of the army. In March 1991, the President requested that the armed forces acknowledge responsibility for the human rights abuses committed under the military regime, which were itemized and published in a government commission report. The military refused to extend such an apology.

The Armed Forces and the State

A decade after the transition in many Latin American countries from military to civilian rule, the armed forces still retain a significant, but unspecified, share of political power. Civilian governments showed no sign of formulating their own defence or security policies, and idle militaries were left to define their role in a civilian polity now largely free of guerrilla insurgents. In 1991, civilian governments continued to reduce military salaries and budgets, creating a source of resentment and anxiety among the armed forces over their future.

The Caribbean was the site of the region's only successful military coup. In September 1991 the Haitian military overthrew President Jean-Baptiste Aristide, a progressive priest elected in December 1990. The United States immediately condemned the coup and demanded the reinstatement of Father Aristide. Consequent US behaviour was both unimpressive and ineffective, however. It tried to use economic sanctions as a lever to force the military regime to comply, but these turned out to be counter-productive as they merely caused greater hardship among the people. When the population fled the brutality of the regime and the hopelessness of their economic lot, the US forcibly returned them to their unhappy fate.

In neighbouring Central America, years of outright civil conflict financed by the US and its Cold War concerns left a string of strong military institutions. In 1991, the Honduran Army continued to exert control over the country through the civilian government. In Guatemala, a country which appeared the least affected by the growing calm in the region, confrontations between the military and guerrillas led to thousands of civilian deaths and human rights abuses, although peace talks began between the new administration of President Jorge Serrano Elias and the guerrillas of the *Unidad Revolucionaria Nacional Guatemalteca*. The terms of the peace treaty signed in El Salvador in January 1992, ending a 12-year civil war, were largely concerned with a reduction in the size and role of the El Salvadoran army. The accord could still come unstuck due to military intransigence over handing territory over to the rebels (see below). The successes of these recent US-supported peace negotiations in the region, while laudable, meant that Central America was no longer under global scrutiny and thus potentially subject to the whims of local, mostly military, strongmen.

The attempted coup in Venezuela in February 1992 demonstrated the chronic instability created by the armed forces in Latin American polities. In their manifesto, the Venezuelan rebels expressed their opposition to the government's neo-liberal policies, but they also cited the lack of discipline in the armed forces, excoriating, in particular, the drug-related corruption among high-ranking military officers. The revolt's failure to topple President Perez was more the result of poor planning than a lack of popular support. Although the country recorded the highest GDP growth rate in Latin America (8.5%), Venezuelans remained unhappy over the costs of the economic adjustments that the Perez administration were attempting: against a backdrop of apparently widespread corruption the increase in petrol prices, low wages, and the sharp rise in unemployment particularly rankled.

Brazil's armed forces also expressed (more peaceful) opposition to President Collor's economic policies in 1991, citing the 30% decline in their salaries and the loss of military projects. In June 1991 Argentina's Finance Minister Cavallo vetoed military demands for an increase in salaries and budgets. Ecuador's President Rodrigo Borja, whose party faces a presidential election in 1992, also engaged in a battle over the military budget.

Brazil's military-run arms industry, in the 1970s the world's seventh largest arms exporter, and Argentina's military-industrial complex of steel, shipyard and aircraft industries were whittled down by government refusal to subsidize production and by sales of the industries to the private sector. The November 1990 accord between Argentina and Brazil to renounce the manufacturing of nuclear weapons was followed by a December 1991 treaty to open the two countries' military-run nuclear installations to international inspection. President Menem also compelled the Argentine air force to transfer control of its missile activities, which had included the *Condor* II project with Iraq, to a new, civilian space agency in February 1992.

Regional Threats

Drug production, trafficking and money laundering remained a top priority for a growing number of Latin American countries, as signs emerged in 1991 that Brazil and Argentina were becoming new bases for production. The United States continued to emphasize military operations as the cornerstone of its anti-drug strategy in Latin America: from 1988 to 1991, US military aid to Colombia alone increased sevenfold, and, in its 1992 budget, the US earmarked almost 15% of total aid to Latin America for its anti-drug campaign. US efforts to control drug production and trade centred on military training of local troops and surprise attacks on installations in Bolivia, Peru, Venezuela and Colombia. The results were inconclusive, and at the annual February 1992 drug summit attended by President Bush and five Latin American presidents, President Alberto Fujimori of Peru praised the continued regional cooperation but urged a shift away from repressive measures in combatting the drug cartels.

A number of dramatic regional policy initiatives to combat the drug problem were launched. In June 1991 President Trujillo of Colombia, who had assumed office in 1990, offered inducements to members of the drug mafia who would participate in an amnesty plan, and several of its leaders surrendered to authorities on the condition that they were not extradited to the United States. Bolivia's President Zamora offered a similar programme to his country's drug traffickers in July 1991. As a result, the nature of the confrontation between the state and the drug organizations changed: all-out war was replaced by low intensity conflicts, with both sides putting out peace feelers. By 1992, however, drug-related violence had picked up, and new drug cartels, some in the more profitable heroin market, were established. Human rights abuses by the military also increased. In Colombia, a potentially more destructive alliance between politicians of the far right, military officers and narcotic traffickers appeared. In both Colombia and Peru, the violence and corruption from drug cartels began to permeate the guerrilla organizations, the death squads and the para-military organizations, who often worked with the military. These self-defence groups, or popular militia, were on the rise in 1991, and they guaranteed that there would be a continuation of the complex, often private, wars in the region.

In 1991, the cholera epidemic continued to spread from Peru to Bolivia, Ecuador, Colombia, Panama, Brazil, Venezuela, Chile and Argentina, underscoring the inadequacy of basic health provisions in many parts of the region. Cholera killed more Peruvians in 1991 (just over 3,000) than did the attacks by the country's guerrilla movement, *Sendero Luminoso* (Shining Path). There was also a heavy economic impact as export revenue was lost, the tourist trade suffered badly, and public spending for other necessary projects had to be diverted to treat the victims of the epidemic.

New Hope in Central America

The peace treaty signed in January 1992 between the government of El Salvador and its rebel opponents, the FMLN, concluded a civil war which had lasted 12 years, cost over 75,000 lives and displaced over half a million Salvadoreans. The accord, engineered by the departing UN Secretary-General Peréz de Cuéllar, established a general cease-fire and the disengagement of army troops and FMLN forces. Over the course of the 18-month talks, the negotiations had centred on political rather than economic issues, in particular, over reducing the size, and reforming the role, of the armed forces. The January agreement set up a commission to oversee the implementation of these reforms, which included creating a new national police force independent of the military, introducing civilian participation in military training centres, and mandating that guerrillas return to civilian life by the end of October 1992. In February 1992, 1,000 UN observers (UNOSAL) arrived in El Salvador to monitor the implementation of the agreement.

The end of the civil war in El Salvador reflected the overall decline in ideological tensions around the world. During the 1980s, the Reagan administration had viewed El Salvador's left-wing rebels as a communist threat to the United States and poured more than $4bn into the country, of which one quarter comprised military aid. In 1991, US policy-makers no longer feared a communist takeover, and the administration under President Bush played a more active role in supporting the UN-appointed negotiators in the talks.

At the same time, El Salvador's guerrillas lost much of their outside supply of weapons. Their Marxist rhetoric also languished, and by 1991 they had began to support economic policies that were similar to those of the government. In turn, the country's traditional ruling oligarchy, once intransigent in the face of guerrilla demands, grudgingly supported the negotiations, out of fear that prolonging the war would disadvantage El Salvador in trade and economic development.

It remains to be seen, now that the war is formally over, whether the US will pay as much attention to building peace as it did to supporting the military effort. President Alfredo Cristiani has voiced concern over 'uncontrolled groups' who may undermine the agreements, citing in particular far-right terrorist groups who view the treaty as a capitulation of the armed forces. In February 1992, the FMLN's principal leaders were forced to leave El Salvador, fearing for their lives. Given that the region is no longer considered a 'front line', total foreign aid is likely to fall, and the country will be forced to rely on its own resources. The inequalities of wealth, the mistrust and hatred between former enemies after more than a decade of civil strife, and the underlying ethnic divisions between Indians and people of Spanish origin, could continue to produce violent confrontations in the country.

In Nicaragua, the *Sandinistas*, now an opposition party since they lost power in the elections in February 1990, have supported many of the economic policies of the ruling *Union Nacional Opositora* party, which successfully brought Nicaragua out of hyperinflation and economic contraction in 1991. In September, the World Bank and the Inter-American Development Bank announced that the country was again eligible for lending, and the IMF approved its first loan to Nicaragua since 1979, praising the administration for carrying out structural measures to reform the economy.

Strains continued, however, between the ruling party and the *Sandinista* opposition, as Nicaragua's National Assembly voted in

August to rescind the former *Sandinista* government's so-called *pinata* decrees, which legalized the distribution of state property to party supporters immediately before the *Sandinistas* handed over rule in April 1990. President Violeta Chamorro, arguing that its language was too provocative and divisive and that its provisions violated the constitution, vetoed the bill in September. A stand-off between the hardline faction of the ruling ONU and the *Sandinista* legislators over this issue will intensify in 1992.

Meanwhile, the re-armed *Contra* rebels, called *Recontras*, and former *Sandinista* soldiers, known as *Recompas*, increased their military operations in the countryside, and sporadic terrorist attempts and a series of demonstrations which turned violent kept the cities under siege. The Nicaraguan army remained under the command of the *Sandinistas*.

A Just Breaking Dawn

No longer caught in the ideological tug-of-war between east and west, the nations of Latin America and the Caribbean gained a measure of peace in 1991. The negotiated settlement in El Salvador and the election of like-minded, centre-right politicians provided the region with an opportunity to rebuild its economic base through integration and restructuring. However, the region also lost a share of international attention in 1991, as it competed with the new democracies in Eastern Europe and other areas for capital. Despite the increasing optimism over controlling inflation and creating modest growth in their economies, few governments were rewarded for their efforts by the international community. Private foreign investment remained relatively stagnant, and foreign creditors remained unwilling to negotiate debt agreements on easier terms.

It is certainly too early to determine if the raw version of capitalism currently popular in Latin America can save the region. Latin America's populace has not yet tasted the fruits of these more successful economic policies: in 1991 five out of ten Latin Americans lacked access to housing, health care and education. It is not clear how long the public will remain acquiescent, given the lack of organizations, both private and public, to channel their demands. Institutions of government continued to depend principally on presidential personalities for effectiveness, and organized civil society (union and peasant and other groups), remains weak. Nonetheless, the rejuvenation of some political parties, which are seeking to work from within the system, and attempts to reform government bureaucracies provide glimmers of hope for the consolidation of internal democratic political rule.

CUBA: TEETERING ON THE BRINK

The 1990s threaten to be a period of extreme danger for the Cuban Revolution. Deepening economic difficulties could further undermine

President Fidel Castro's leadership and the revolutionary regime's legitimacy, and may well bring on social turmoil and a change of power. For the foreseeable future, the government is trying to implement what it euphemistically calls the 'zero option' for 'the special period in peacetime', namely an economic strategy without the fuel and other basic inputs to generate even minimum growth. In fact, the economy is better characterized as one in free fall, marked by drastic declines in trade, production and consumption.

The Communist Party, itself isolated and with few friends abroad, admitted at its Fourth Congress, held in 1991, that 'Cuba finds itself at the most critical moment of its life as a nation. If we are to continue as an independent and sovereign nation, the Revolution and socialism must be saved'. That the ruling group itself believes that the viability of the nation is at stake, ensures a grim prospect indeed for ten million Cubans with depressed living standards that are going to get much worse.

President Fidel Castro, now 66, still controls the government, the party and the military. He is increasingly perceived as an intolerant autocrat unwilling to recognize the pressing need for change. The President shares the gloomy mood affecting the nation, but refuses to initiate anything resembling *perestroika* or *glasnost*. Neither the one-party system nor the centrally planned economy will be dismantled, because these are viewed as the cornerstones of the system's survival. Not surprisingly, Castro has told his people to 'prepare for the more critical situations that will arise', promising neither relief nor an easy road ahead.

The Crisis and Its Consequences

Cuba's economic crisis dates from the mid-1980s; although exacerbated by the recent difficulties, its causes are structural. In particular, the rigid command model, itself heavily dependent on external support, cannot adjust to rapidly changing global economic currents. The government failed to anticipate just how devastating for Cuba the collapse of communism would be, because to do so would have jeopardized the very relationships that needed to be reshaped. It is now paying the price for its errors, which have been compounded by the failure to begin a process of fundamental reforms.

There is overwhelming evidence that in many sectors of the economy activities have been either drastically reduced or completely stopped. The public transportation system for instance, is in a shambles; workers, government bureaucrats and others are often unable to get to their places of work. Whole industries have been shut down because of lack of fuel and spare parts, and the government has closed or cut back 'non-indispensable' plants and services. The sugar industry is the economy's mainstay, but shortages of fuel imperil the harvest itself. Neither production nor export goals are likely to be met, further reducing hard currency earnings.

No new development projects are going forward, and several that had begun now stand half-finished. This is the case of nuclear energy plants being constructed with (formerly) Soviet and Eastern European technology. Productivity losses and worker redundancies result from the slow-down. In order to save fuel, many workers are paid 60% of their salaries and are told to stay home. The Communist Party Congress declared that 'at the moment there do not exist the minimum conditions that would guarantee our social and economic development in the medium term', almost exclusively as a result of the lack of raw materials and other inputs. The Party admits that 'extraordinarily grave circumstances could come...leading to further reductions in living standards'. In short, Cuba is moving rapidly backwards into a subsistence economy.

The growing shortage of fuel is the fundamental factor affecting the economic collapse. Imports of oil from the former Soviet Union have been declining since 1990, when 13 million tons were imported. Ten million tons were delivered in 1991, and only 4–5 million are expected in 1992. Officials in the Russian Ministry of Foreign Economic Relations attribute the decline to 'a general reduction in oil exports' stemming from internal difficulties. It is quite clear that the oil lifeline is rapidly closing up, and there is little prospect for increased deliveries to Cuba. Nearly 80% of Cuba's trade is now with Russia, the Ukraine, Belarus and Kazakhstan, and officials are seeking to salvage what they can. Barter is part of the exchange, which also includes some 3.5 million tonnes of sugar annually.

There is reason to believe that the government is frantically looking for new suppliers. It seems likely that Cuba's opposition to the allied effort in the Gulf War was in part intended to earn Iraq's goodwill in the hope of obtaining its oil, once that country is permitted to resume exports. Other reports indicate that Mexico and Venezuela have been approached, but neither government has yet agreed to Cuba's proposal to barter the use of its oil refineries in exchange for crude oil. In addition, Cuba has expressed some interest in joining the San José Pact, whose terms provide oil for countries in the Caribbean and Central America at preferential rates. Nothing has come of this initiative either.

In an effort to produce a new source of currency, the regime is moving ahead with plans to make Cuba more attractive for foreign tourists. Ironically, tourism was once held in disrepute by the authorities, because it would generate corruption, illegal trafficking in dollars and prostitution. There are also obvious political risks. Out of sheer necessity, however, very generous proposals intended to attract European and Latin American investors have been advanced. Spanish interests invested some $150m in a chain of hotels around Varadero and other beaches, in what are called 'poles of tourism'. Future investments worth a few hundred million dollars are expected. In 1990 340,000 tourists visited Cuba, and some 400,000 in 1991.

Economists have pointed out that the tourist trade is completely dependent on dollars and has created a new type of enclave economy from which Cubans themselves are segregated. A kind of 'tourist apartheid' exists, catering to the needs of foreigners who spend hard currency. Police often guard tourist installations to ensure that ordinary Cubans do not approach foreigners. Cubans working for foreign firms are paid in local currency (pesos) which employers acquire by selling dollars to the government. Even so, revenues generated from tourism meet only a small share of the island's hard currency needs, and the social consequences may exacerbate feelings of separation and resentment in the country.

Mindful of the need to reach new markets and to attract new technology, the government is rethinking the whole issue of foreign investment. It is looking for joint ventures that increase exports, cooperative enterprises, commercial agreements and other arrangements. The Communist Party is ready to offer 'substantial advantages to Latin American capital and enterprises for investments in our territory', indicating that the old shibboleths about the evils of foreign capitalist penetration are gone. There is little evidence that the foreign investment community is reacting positively to these entreaties, largely because the US embargo is still in effect. In any case, there may be more lucrative investment opportunities in nations where the infrastructure is not crumbling and where the workforce is familiar with capitalism.

Castro is also attempting to bolster international sales from Cuba's biomedical industry in an effort to increase the acquisition of hard currency. The Cubans reportedly sold close to $80m worth of meningitis-B vaccine to Brazil in 1990 and are actively seeking markets in other parts of Latin America. Cuba has also encouraged patients from abroad to seek medical treatment on the island. Neither of these efforts seem significant enough to stem the economic crisis, however.

That crisis continues to fuel illegal migration to the US. Several hundred Cubans arrived in 1990, and 2,200 in 1991. Over 200 more escaped to the US naval base at Guantánamo in 1991, and dozens more arrived as of early 1992. Some Cubans travelling abroad do not return home, instead seeking asylum in Europe or Latin America. The sea trip to the US is fraught with perils; the US Coast Guard estimates that four out of every five would-be escapees drown in the treacherous Florida Straits.

The US Interests Section in Havana has over 30,000 requests for exit visas pending and in all likelihood could receive hundreds of thousands of additional inquiries if migration between the US and Cuba were regularized. Both governments have an interest in solving this problem and may in fact do so before too long. Cuba's policy is to bid good riddance to disaffected citizens, and the US grants political asylum to those leaving the communist nation. Since Castro's accession to power in 1959, some 15% of the population has migrated.

The disintegration of the Soviet Union devastated Cuba's foreign commerce and left a vacuum that simply cannot be filled. Russia is pressuring Cuba to amortize its $17-bn debt. Consumption levels have fallen dramatically, including access to medical and support services. The public health system is overloaded; nutrition levels and the per capita calorie intake are at risk due to growing food shortages. Some reports indicate that meat, milk and fish are no longer available.

The government was slow to recognize the economic collapse and still refuses to reform a cumbersome and unproductive command system. President Castro believes that socialism is vital and that capitalism 'is garbage'. And yet it is doubtful that a development strategy built around mobilization for agriculture, international tourism and pharmaceuticals could succeed. Despite compelling evidence of its global failure, the government is committed to orthodox socialism. It firmly believes that primitivism and the return to 'an agrarian mentality' are preferable to a market system that would loosen central control and restore private initiative.

Dissidence and Political Control

The emergence of a dissident movement has created additional problems for the government and is complicating its efforts to improve Cuba's image abroad. While they are not large in terms of total membership, these dissident organizations are managing to survive in a climate of repression and hostility. In general, they advocate respect for human rights, political pluralism, national reconciliation, an end to political imprisonment and repression as well as a 'dialogue' with the government to bring about a peaceful solution to what they maintain is a national calamity. Some 30 dissident organizations make up two broad alliances, the National Democratic Coalition and the Cuban Democratic Concertation; each has links with human rights and political organizations in the US and Europe.

Led in some cases by intellectuals, political activists and former supporters of the regime, dissident groups are gaining recognition and cohesion. Yet they have failed to generate wide visible popular support and are apparently seen by many Cubans as fostering divisions and unnecessary trouble. If there is 'a silent majority' that identifies with these organizations, it is remaining very silent indeed.

Dissidents challenge the government's assertion that 'the people are united behind their leaders', when in fact there is credible evidence of growing discontent. The economic crisis has exacerbated opposition to the government, particularly when there is no relief in sight and the call is for ever greater sacrifice. Information about the collapse of communism challenges the claim that socialism is irreversible, undermines the regime's domestic legitimacy, and strengthens the moral resolve of dissidents. Quite probably, internal dissidence is expanding and is likely to include bureaucrats, technocrats, members of the armed forces and of the Communist Party itself.

The government's strategy is to tolerate dissent as long as it is politically safe, and to crack down if it becomes open. Repression and intimidation, including the use of street mobs (*turbas*) controlled by the police, are increasingly favoured techniques of political control. A crackdown against the regime's internal opponents is under way, but that in itself is still another sign of deepening political troubles.

Growing dissent is evidence of an increasing polarization among the masses as well as within the elite. It is also a clear sign of discontent and outright disaffection with the system. Vocal criticism is widespread, and there is reason to believe that the Catholic Church, in particular, is breaking its silence. Something approaching a critical mass is building up, which can only be suppressed at considerable political cost. From such confrontations regimes often collapse.

The Regional Situation

In order to reduce its isolation and make up for the loss of trading partners in the former communist world, Cuba is attempting to expand its commercial and political ties with Latin America. Alone, vulnerable and nearly destitute, Cuba must find new friends. It therefore now advocates 'integration and collaboration with Latin America and the Caribbean' and continues to call for regional unity. As noted above, it is appealing to Latin American investors and providing generous terms. In addition, it has renounced its 'export of revolution' on the grounds that circumstances have changed and radical revolutions are no longer feasible.

On the other hand, some Latin American governments are now asking for internal reforms in Cuba before full normalization of relations proceeds. Specifically, there have been explicit declarations from regional summits in Mexico and Colombia for political and economic reforms in Cuba, including free elections. Many governments have protested at Cuba's repression of dissidents, and Argentine President Carlos Menem has publicly called for 'freedom and democracy' for Cuba.

It is also evident that while Latin America would like Cuba and the US to work out their differences over the embargo and other matters, the region is not vigorously calling on the US to change its policy. There is no reason to believe – as Cuba would like – that Latin America is actively pressing for a major change in the US policy on Cuba. This may be a relic of the Cold War but it is not aggravating US–Latin American relations.

Latin America is not united in its approach to Cuba. Mexico and Venezuela prefer quiet pressures, believing that these might be more effective than public demands. These governments are more mindful of the 'non-intervention norm' than others. Argentina, Costa Rica (and the US) are not reluctant to criticize publicly Cuban violations of human rights and they see no reason to pressure Castro quietly, because there is no evidence that he listens. While there is a growing, but as yet not definitive, consensus in Latin America regarding the best means of bringing about internal change in Cuba, there is near unanimity on the need to work out a peaceful and democratic solution. Cuba, however, has continued to reject these calls as interventionist and to reaffirm the 'unmovable position of the Communist party in defence of absolute independence and sovereignty'.

The Cuban community in exile in the United States, some one million strong and concentrated in south Florida (sometimes dubbed 'Northern Cuba'), is also divided on its views of how best to meet the new situation. All perceive the Castro regime as increasingly vulnerable and ultimately doomed, but they do not agree on the best way to spur the inevitable. A new militancy is animating part of the anti-Castro organizations, some of which conduct small-scale paramilitary exercises and carry out extensive propaganda activities. In late January 1992 a small group of infiltrators was captured by the Cuban militia; some were sentenced to death while others received long prison sentences. Despite such failures, some continue to be critical of the Bush administration's Cuba policy, which they view as passive and uninspiring. To them, a more confrontational approach is needed if only to send a signal that the US is concerned with the deplorable conditions on the island.

As the Cuban community in exile has changed, groups that advocate negotiations with the Castro regime have also developed. Their strategy is to send a democratic message to a slowly disintegrating society anxious for 'new thinking'. Like the others, they advocate an end to communism, the establishing of free elections and national reconciliation, but they refuse to legitimize the use of force in order to change the situation. Some of these more moderate organizations have cultivated both international recognition and active contacts with influential European and Latin American governments.

Cuba's efforts to improve its standing in the region have yet to pay off politically or economically. The maintenance of a repressive police state and the unwillingness to enact fundamental reforms discourage those who might give Cuba the benefit of the doubt. The Cuban issue remains important, but it is no longer very high on either the agendas of the US or Latin America. President Castro's intransigence is no longer necessary to stave off an imagined 'US threat' against Cuba; instead it has become more counterproductive and ruinous for the nation than ever before and is now itself the threat.

The Middle East

Against the odds, Saddam Hussein survived in power after the fearsome drubbing his Iraqi forces took in the war that drove them out of Kuwait. Despite uprisings by Shi'is in southern Iraq and Kurds in the north, a lack of unity and a reluctance by the Western coalition to support these forces gave him the breathing space he needed. He had carefully shielded his most trustworthy troops from the allied bombardment, and their brutality and firepower was more than a match for the dissident forces.

Although Saddam has retained enough power to do evil in his own unhappy country, his ability to affect the region is constrained by a continued UN presence and careful watch. This positive outcome to the Gulf War was joined in 1991 by the opening of Arab–Israeli peace talks. Adroit diplomacy on the part of US Secretary of State James Baker, which combined pressure and cajolery, brought unprecedented face-to-face meetings between Israel, the Palestinians, Jordan, Lebanon and even Syria. There has not yet been any real substantive progress, but the fact that none of the parties are willing to torpedo the talks provides hope that in the long run they may prove fruitful. They are certain to be a key issue in the Israeli elections due in July 1992; if the result of these elections is a victory for the Labour Party, the possibility of further advances in the talks will be enhanced.

While Iran has not played a direct role in the dialogue with Israel, its increasingly moderate government did help to remove the irritant of the hostage question from the complex Middle East equation. With Iraq weakened by its failed adventure, Iran is adjusting its policies in the area so as to play a more influential role. It is rearming at an alarming rate, while at the same time reducing the weight of fundamentalist doctrine at home. As it moderates its Islamist practices, however, the threat that they may spread to other areas of the Middle East was sharply pointed up by the success of the FIS party of Islamic fundamentalists in the Algerian election. All the Maghreb countries applauded the undemocratic action of the Algerian government (as did the West more discretely) when it cancelled the second round of elections which would have brought the fundamentalists to power. There is no guarantee that Algiers will be able to make its ban of the party fully effective, however; instead the flame of militant Islam may only be further fanned.

PROSPECTS FOR ARAB–ISRAELI PEACE

That the beginnings of an Arab–Israeli peace process emerged from the Gulf War cannot be disputed. The war provided the necessary impetus for the peace talks to get under way; yet the lion's share of the credit for this encouraging development belongs to the determination of President Bush and the persistent and yet careful diplomacy of US

Secretary of State James Baker. Even so, it is not yet clear if the drift of events in the Middle East and the positions of the key local players have altered sufficiently to enable the process, now set in place by US diplomacy, to move on to a successful conclusion.

The most obvious outcome of the war as it affected the possibility of Arab–Israeli peace talks was the temporary reduction of the likelihood of a new Arab–Israeli war. This second Gulf War, like the first (the 1980–88 Iran–Iraq War), largely neutralized the Arabs' capacity to form an effective eastern front, which historically comprised Jordan, Syria and Iraq, or at least two of these actors, against Israel. Iraq was essentially disarmed; Jordan was weakened and compromised by its stance; and Syria became a member of the same alliance in which Israel was a silent participant. Egypt's role as a catalyst for Arab–Israeli contact was enhanced by its stance in the Gulf conflict. This meant that all sides could at least temporarily consider possibilities of a peace process that involved taking acceptable risks.

Moving To Talks

The US success in prosecuting the campaign against Iraq, and particularly in galvanizing a broad Middle East coalition, gave it new regional credibility, dedication of purpose and, above all, increased influence that it applied to the peace process. As part of the enticement for Arab participation in the coalition against Iraq, it had promised that, following victory over Iraq, it would devote new energies to solving the Arab–Israeli conflict. Alongside this new resolve, Secretary of State Baker and his team astutely embraced a tactic – that of adopting Israeli procedural demands for direct, unconditional negotiations, while backing the substantive demand of moderate Arabs for a territories-for-peace exchange – which effectively neutralized attempts by both sides at obstruction until the process was well under way. Most importantly, the US demonstrated for the first time since Eisenhower that it could say 'no' to Israel on a matter of vital importance to that country, namely, that of the $10-bn loan guarantee for settling Soviet Jews in Israel. About 200,000 Soviet Jews arrived in Israel in 1990; this dropped to 145,000 in 1991. Just over 4,000, the lowest monthly total in two years, arrived in February 1992.

An additional possible contribution to the building of confidence in the process, one far harder to pin down, may have been the unprecedented phenomenon of Israel, Syria and Saudi Arabia siding against an Arab aggressor. The restraint that Israel exercised by not joining the war despite Iraqi missile attacks may also have had a positive impact. Certainly, the commitment of Egypt and the Gulf Arabs to the Palestinians in general, and the PLO in particular, was reduced by the widespread impression that the Palestinians had betrayed them by supporting Saddam Hussein. This in turn suggested the emergence of additional negotiating possibilities dealing with Israel's relationship with the Arab states, and with regional issues, both of which placed the more traditional Israeli–Palestinian route in new perspective. Undoubtedly, the external PLO's impotence and the Palestinians' post-war plight was an important ingredient in moderating their preconditions for joining the process.

Withal, it was an awesome global development, one that interacted but minimally with the Gulf War, that appears to have contributed the most towards catalyzing the new Middle East peace process. The disintegration of the Soviet Union enabled the US to act forcefully and unhindered – for the first time after decades of superpower competition in the Middle East – against Iraq and then in the Arab–Israeli sphere. It also undercut the political and military support of two major actors on the Arab–Israeli scene: Syria and the PLO. President Assad and Yasser Arafat were aware, even before the Gulf crisis, of Moscow's decline as a superpower patron. The dramatic defeat of Soviet arms and military doctrine by those of the West, however, and the emergence of the US, with its special strategic relationship with Israel, as the region's dominant superpower, dealt a devastating blow to any lingering hopes they entertained of wielding a military option against Israel. Clearly, for the time being at least, they were best advised to join the political process and play by American rules, in the hope of gaining at least a modicum of their strategic goals and, in Assad's case, of obtaining badly needed economic assistance from the Saudis and perhaps eventually from the West. Remarkably, Syria was able to convert the potentially disastrous changes of the international scene into new assets, as was demonstrated when Damascus exploited Washington's indulgence at the height of the Gulf crisis in October 1990 to effect a quick takeover of Lebanon.

By persuading Syrian and Palestinian leaders to drop their traditional demand for a prior Israeli commitment to make territorial concessions, Secretary of State Baker essentially offered an American commitment to the same effect. Operating in the euphoric aftermath of the defeat of Saddam Hussein, Baker was able to emphasize that the Arab leaders had a unique opportunity to do business with an American administration that was itself pledged to the territories-for-peace principle, and one that at the time looked as if it was certain to continue in office until 1997, long enough to impose on Israel its views regarding the return of territories. Meanwhile, one immediate way of telegraphing American determination on the territorial issue was for Bush and Baker to insist, more vigorously than previous administrations, that Israel stop its settlement activity in the West Bank and Gaza.

Washington's position on the territorial issue generated among the Arabs a clear expectation that, at some later stage in the process (the sooner the better, from their standpoint), they would be supported by an American demand for Israel's withdrawal from most of the Golan, as well as the West Bank and Gaza, thereby bringing about the diplomatic isolation of Israel. Thus they signed on to the process months before Bush's electoral chances began to sour due to the deteriorating American economic situation.

Positions of the Regional Participants

The negotiating process was to be launched by an international conference that had special significance for the American policy planners. President Bush, in particular, viewed the convening of an expanded conference with the participation of Israel, Palestinians and the Arab states as an achievement that in itself could 'break the taboos' between the parties and, in later stages, that would facilitate fruitful negotiations.

To the extent that it implied early territorial compromises by Israel, this concept was rejected by Prime Minister Shamir. At the end of the Gulf War he tended to see the peace process as a sort of follow-on war for Israel:

> Some will try to use political means to deprive Israel of what they did not succeed in taking from us by force . . . we will not flinch, we will not run away, we'll have to summon all our wisdom and guile . . . we must overcome the Iraqi monster, and overcome the political negotiations confronting us.

Such Shamir statements were accompanied by his declared determination not to yield any territory: Israel would demand 'peace for peace' from the Syrians and Palestinians, and would continue to settle Jews in the disputed territories as an implicit indication of its unyielding position regarding the territories (although Shamir granted that Arab territorial demands could be presented for negotiation).

This emphasis on its traditional opposition to territorial compromise points up the only genuine innovation in the Likud's approach to the peace process: *vis-à-vis* Jordan. In the aftermath of the Gulf War the Israeli government displayed a particular willingness to involve King Hussein in the process. Israel's position grew out of its recognition that the King had been successful in providing a more or less neutral buffer between Israel and Iraq before and during the war, and that Hashemite Jordan appeared increasingly to constitute a convenient partner for Palestinian autonomy talks. Jordan had forsaken any claim of its own to the West Bank in July 1988, and assuming that it shared Israel's fears of militant Palestinian nationalism, it could conceivably collaborate with Israel in constraining the extent of Palestinian autonomy. Hence Israel's early insistence on a joint Jordanian–Palestinian delegation to peace talks, and its later insistence, in the State Department corridor gatherings in winter 1991–2, on a Jordanian role of some sort in the autonomy talks.

Like the Palestinians, however, the Hashemite Kingdom had been weakened by its war experience and it did not feel that it could attempt to impose its will on the Palestinians. There was even a pro-Hashemite faction in Amman, known there tongue-in-cheek as the 'East Bank

Likud', that advocated a separate Jordanian–Israeli peace, regardless of the fate of the West Bank.

Finally, Shamir's government faced a possible deterioration in the American–Israeli relationship due to his position on territories and settlements. In the months after the war, tensions between Shamir and Bush over this issue focused on the American attitude toward Israel's request for US government guarantees for the $10bn in bank loans. The US administration, alarmed by a sharp increase in settlement construction in the West Bank and Gaza after Labour had left the Israeli government in March 1990, linked the loan guarantees to a cessation of the building programme, lest the Likud succeed in 'creating facts' that precluded any reasonable territorial compromise. While Shamir sought to isolate the settlements/loan guarantees disagreement and avoid substantive damage to the relationship (Israel's wartime restraint in the face of Iraqi attacks was a prime example of Shamir's calculations), a decade-long slow decline in American support for Israel had clearly crossed a major psychological threshold. Israel could only note that the US Congress was no longer willing to thwart the administration's decision. Nor did subsequent US allegations about the transfer of sensitive technology by Israel to China improve matters.

Given the overt expressions of determination in Cairo, Riyadh and Washington during and following the Gulf War to replace the traditional PLO leadership with more moderate figures, it is remarkable that Yasser Arafat and his colleagues once again survived a major Middle East upheaval, and were able to play a major role in determining Palestinian policy towards the peace process. Nevertheless, the war had produced changes in Palestinian attitudes. Arafat's near total identification with Saddam Hussein, and his inability to provide alternative means of support for hundreds of thousands of newly displaced Palestinians and for PLO factions that no longer received Saudi and Kuwaiti funding, left the local 'insider' West Bank and Gazan leadership in a position of relatively greater independence with regard to the Tunis-based 'outsiders'. This, coupled with American assurances, ultimately produced agreement by Faisal al-Husseini and his colleagues – with the blessings of Tunis – to enter peace talks without direct representation of the PLO, the Palestinian diaspora or East Jerusalem, and without insisting on an advance Israeli commitment as to the final outcome, beyond interim self-rule.

The war also produced a newfound readiness among moderate Palestinians in the Territories to criticize the excesses and failures of the *intifada* – especially the wholesale internecine violence against 'collaborators' and the failure of the economic boycott – without first seeking the sanction of Tunis. This was not a risk-free stance, however. In the aftermath of the Gulf War, grassroots Palestinian attitudes reflected both disillusionment with the peace process and hostility towards America, Israel and the moderate Arab states. The Palestinian 'street' in Nablus and Gaza at times offered little support for the moderate intellectuals centred in East Jerusalem who had sought to play down support for Saddam Hussein during the war, and who now undertook to negotiate with Baker.

The Saudi Arabian position remained ambiguous. Riyadh's anger at the PLO over its support for Iraq was joined by a postwar desire to enter the circle of contacts with Israel to an extent sufficient to ensure American understanding for Saudi postwar security needs. This dictated a forthcoming attitude towards the peace process, even if only rhetorically. On the other hand, in the early stages of the process, the Saudi leadership refused to sanction any direct contact with Israel or to push Syria too hard towards moderation. Here it may have been both reacting to the resurgence of traditional conservative circles inside the country, and reflecting a preoccupation with the lack of resolution of the Iraqi challenge to regional stability, and the hesitancy of American and regional efforts to delineate a new Gulf security regime.

If, however, the Saudis appeared in some ways to be reverting to a traditional stance of fence-sitting in the Arab–Israeli conflict, they nevertheless contributed to the momentum of the process with surprising initiatives: an offer to suspend the secondary economic boycott of Israel in return for a freeze on settlements; Prince Bandar's presence and influence at the Madrid conference; participation, along with the other Gulf emirates, at the Moscow multilateral conference; and the opening of contacts with the American Jewish community.

The Process Unfolds

Prior to the convening of the historic peace conference in Madrid on 30 October 1991, the United States outlined its position, and summarized the undertakings made during the long pre-negotiation process, in 'letters of assurances' to the various actors. These were an exercise in creative diplomacy – at times, in constructive ambiguity – that defined, in writing, the parameters within which Washington intended to channel the process.

Thus, while the Palestinians were told that 'the United States is determined to achieve a comprehensive settlement of the Arab–Israeli conflict', Israel, in reply to its demand that the goal of the process be peace agreements, was granted that 'the United States wants to establish peace in the Middle East'. While Israel was informed that 'the US will not support the creation of an independent Palestinian state', the Palestinians were told that the US 'will accept any outcome agreed by the parties . . . confederation is not excluded' (confederation with Jordan presupposes the prior and continued existence of an independent state of Palestine). And while the Palestinians were offered 'an end to the Israeli occupation . . . Palestinians should gain control over political, economic and other decisions that affect their lives', the administration acknowledged that Israel held 'its own interpretation of Security Council Resolution 242', according to which it need not give up more territory.

Several of the assurances are not balanced symmetrically. Jordan and the Palestinians are given an undertaking that Jerusalem, though not represented in their delegation, may be discussed in the talks; that the US does not recognize Israel's annexation of East Jerusalem; and that Jerusalem Arabs should be allowed to participate in autonomy elections. Jerusalem is not mentioned in American assurances to Israel, however, presumably because the two sides could not agree. Moreover, the Palestinians are guaranteed an opportunity to put their case individually, despite being part of a joint delegation with Jordan.

For its part, Israel is assured unilaterally of US intentions to end the Arab economic boycott of Israel and to support a repeal of the 1975 UN 'Zionism-is-Racism' resolution (which the UN did by a large majority, in December 1991; the very Arabs with whom Israel was negotiating, however, refused to support a repeal). The US accepts that Israel is 'entitled to secure and defensible borders'; reconfirms 'the importance of the Golan Heights to Israel's security' and offers to 'give its own guarantees to any border agreed upon between Israel and Syria'; and reaffirms its commitment 'to Israel's security and to the maintenance of Israel's qualitative edge'. Syria (which alone did not publish its assurances) was presumably told that Washington would support an extensive territories-for-peace settlement on the Golan, as well as Israeli withdrawal from southern Lebanon.

All the parties to the conference were assured by the United States that a Palestinian autonomy agreement was sought within one year of the start of negotiations; that it would last five years; and that in the third year, negotiations would be renewed regarding the final status of the territories.

The Madrid Conference itself featured a series of addresses and replies by the heads of delegations, followed by the opening of direct bilateral talks between Israel and its Arab neighbours. The speeches were remarkable for their dedication to a rational peace process; Syrian Foreign Minister Farouq al-Shar'a was the lone exception, setting a tone that Damascus then maintained by an abortive last-minute attempt to sabotage the talks. Certainly, little happened at Madrid to substantiate American hopes that this face-to-face confrontation would effect a dramatic breakthrough in the regional actors' attitudes towards one another, a conclusion reflected in James Baker's powerful summing-up of the proceedings on the last day.

Negotiating on the Surface

Following these bumpy beginnings in Madrid, talks continued throughout the winter in a series of bilateral meetings held in Washington in December, January and February–March. Little progress was made, as the substantive gaps between Israel and each Arab partner were laid out, and the United States – pressed in particular by Israel to give the parties a chance to sort out their differences on their own, and mindful of Israeli internal political considerations – dismissed Arab pressures to intervene actively.

In particular, the case of Israel and Syria appeared to confirm the common belief that, for the most part, the Arabs and Israelis were going through the motions only to please the Americans: Syria insisted that Israel commit itself to returning all of the Golan, and withdrawing on all other fronts as well, before substantive talks could begin; Israel demanded a prior detailed Syrian commitment to a genuine peace agreement as the goal of negotiations, before agreeing to hear Syria's territorial claims. Israeli–Lebanese talks were more relaxed, reflecting the two sides' history of contacts through the years. But they were equally unproductive, as the Lebanese delegates clearly could not proceed without a green light from Damascus.

Against the backdrop of impending Israeli elections and heightened tension in southern Lebanon in February 1992 following Israel's assassination of *Hizbollah* leader Sheikh Abbas Musawi, two aspects of the Israeli–Syrian–Lebanese talks are of interest. First, Syrian and Lebanese readiness to attend the late February talks in Washington despite Israel's increased military involvement in southern Lebanon appeared to reflect a sober assessment in Damascus that Israel's actions were tolerable, indeed perhaps desirable (*Hizbollah*, with its Iranian backers, enjoyed at best ambiguous support from Damascus). Second, given the difficulties of bridging the substantive gulf between Jerusalem and Damascus in the short term, the only chance for progress appeared to be an American-orchestrated effort to bring about a minimalist interim agreement – one that probably would focus on an Israeli withdrawal from southern Lebanon, or perhaps would deliver a symbolic slice of Golan territory to Syria, in return for a series of Syrian confidence-building and non-belligerency gestures. Yet this required that both Syria and Israel solicit American intervention and see some benefit in an agreement, however minimal.

A second 'triangle' of talks in Washington – Israel, Jordan and the Palestinians – progressed along different lines during the winter meetings. Here the initial centre of controversy was the procedural issue of the nature of the Jordanian–Palestinian negotiating 'partnership'. The Israeli government, with its more positive orientation towards the Hashemites, insisted that the principle of a joint Palestinian–Jordanian delegation be maintained even when autonomy issues were discussed. The Palestinians, never happy with the partnership with Jordan that had been forced upon them, wished to detach themselves to the greatest extent possible. Jordan, weakened economically and politically, and fearful of antagonizing its many enemies on the inter-Arab scene, remained neutral.

As a result, in December and January the three delegation heads met in a State Department corridor – unable to agree even on a format that would allow the delegations to meet in conference rooms. Once this obstacle was finessed (with a symbolic Jordanian presence at the autonomy talks), Jordanian–Israeli talks took on a friendly but largely procedural tone, as Amman insisted on prior progress towards Palestinian autonomy before discussing its few minor territorial and other disagreements with Israel.

It was the autonomy talks that were the most eventful. The moment the very notion of autonomy surfaced on the agenda, the Likud's extreme right-wing coalition partners left the Israeli government. This precipitated a political crisis that culminated in an agreement between Likud (now leading a minority government) and Labour to advance the Knesset elections, originally scheduled for November 1992, to June.

This probably ensured that little progress would take place in Israeli–Arab peace negotiations prior to the autumn of 1992, and perhaps later if US elections became a factor. It also guaranteed, however, that the peace process and its satellite issues – the fate of the Territories, the wisdom of building Israeli settlements there, the effect of Israeli policies regarding these areas on the alliance with the United States, and the consequent plight of the Israeli economy and ramifications for the immigration of Russian Jewry – would dominate Israel's elections.

As for the autonomy talks themselves, once Israel and the Palestinians did sit down together, they each presented their concepts of the interim period arrangements. The initial gaping discrepancy in the two positions that this showed quite clearly represented each side's internal political considerations rather than negotiating tactics. Thus Israel offered a bare version of autonomy, focusing on aspects of self-government that did not involve any Palestinian control over the land or security, and that left the Israeli government as the source of authority. This was a significant retreat from some provisions of the 1978 Camp David Autonomy Framework that Shamir had once reluctantly embraced. For example, those provisions postulated the withdrawal of Israeli armed forces to 'designated locations' in the Territories and the delineation of limited responsibility for security to an enhanced Palestinian police force, buttressed by Jordan. It was also a retreat from the readiness to discuss an alternative source of authority that Israel had displayed in the earlier autonomy talks that ended a decade before. While Shamir's present position obviously reflected his own ideological predilections, it also reflected changed realities (there were now perhaps ten times as many Israelis in the West Bank as in 1979). In addition, it exposed his fear of alienating right-wing voters yet further; even the minimum Israeli autonomy offer was embodied in a draft document that bore no official letterhead, and was called 'Ideas for peaceful coexistence in the territories during the interim period'. It also bespoke Israel's claim that the spread and extent of its settlements in the West Bank now made it impossible to consider giving security authority to the Palestinians, as specified at Camp David.

The Palestinians, for their part, presented a 'model of the Palestinian Interim Self-Government Authority (PISGA)' that described a sovereign state in everything but name, and rendered largely meaningless the concept of an interim, confidence-building period. They too appeared to fear the reaction of constituents who doubted the entire process. Moreover, the Palestinian delegation displayed a natural tendency towards escalation, as competition was intense among diverse circles of negotiators and advisers: West Bankers and Gazans in the actual negotiating team, East Jerusalem intellectuals in a primary advisory capacity, pro-PLO exiled academics from Europe and the US in a secondary advisory capacity, and a high-level PLO official, usually Nabil Shaat, calling the shots from a nearby hotel room.

Multilateral Talks

In late January Moscow hosted the opening of the multilateral conference. It was designed to deal with a broad spectrum of issues that concern most Middle Eastern countries, regardless of the specifics of the Arab–Israeli conflict. Like Madrid, the Moscow conference was little more than a procedural beginning, and it attracted relatively little media attention from a world by now accustomed to the sight of Arabs and Israelis sitting together. Yet the Moscow conference was notable for the presence for the first time of all the Gulf states and some of those from North Africa (Morocco, Tunisia and Mauritania) at the same table with Israel. From the Israeli standpoint, it also served as the ultimate incentive for Moscow, Beijing and even New Delhi to establish full diplomatic relations so that they could qualify either to host or attend the conference.

From a substantive standpoint, however, the absence from Moscow of two key delegations signalled the implicit limitations of the multilateral process. Syria refused to attend because, it argued, no bilateral progress had yet been made with Israel; this spelled difficulty for the arms-control 'basket' of the Moscow process. The Palestinians were not allowed to be seated because they insisted on including 'outsider' diaspora representatives, in violation of the guidelines they had accepted before the Madrid summit; this meant that refugee rehabilitation discussions could not effectively begin. Nonetheless, spring dates and host country venues were fixed for these and the other three baskets for the beginning of their substantive discussions: 'Regional Security and Arms Control' in Washington, 'Refugees' in Canada, 'Regional Economic Co-operation' in Brussels, 'Water' in Turkey or Austria, and 'Ecology' in Japan.

New Factors in the Equation

Whatever the short-term fate of this peace process, it was clear by early 1992 that much had changed in the fundamentals of the Arab–Israeli conflict. Syria had recognized the principle of direct, unconditional negotiations with Israel. The Palestinians appeared to accept the utility of progress through limited interim measures. Jordan's appetite was growing for a proper peace agreement with Israel, to replace years of tacit cooperation. Saudi Arabia had placed its prestige, and potentially its wealth too, behind the process. Alongside the natural conservatism of experienced Middle East leaders like President Assad of Syria and King Fahd of Saudi Arabia, the Arabs, with few exceptions, seemed to have become reconciled to the notion that they could not solve the problem of Israel's existence by war. The Camp David process and even the substance of the Camp David autonomy provisions, were now fully in the Middle East mainstream.

As for Israel, its government was talking directly with Palestinians associated with the PLO, and the Likud had accepted that it would confront Arab territorial demands at the conference table. Moreover, the entire process had accelerated political change in Israel. Faced with early elections, Labour chose Yitzhak Rabin as its leader in place of Shimon Peres; this improved Labour's electoral chances, and enhanced the possibility that Israel's next government would again be one of national unity, in which the moderate left-wing element would ensure a modicum of progress through territorial compromise, while the moderate right would guarantee sufficient popular support to fend off extreme-right wing opposition to any move towards peace.

Perhaps most significantly, the Arab–Israeli peace process was now a multi-track, multi-state operation – perhaps the most complex peace effort since Versailles. And the US was resolutely at the helm; the talks owed their beginning and continuation entirely to American determination.

Yet beyond the Washington and Moscow conference rooms where Arabs and Israelis, however hesitantly, were working on the foundations for progress towards peace, strong and dangerous currents of change were eddying in and around the Middle East, with long-term ramifications for the peace process that were impossible to assess. The arms race, and particularly the prospect of further nuclearization of the region and the post-Gulf War race to acquire ballistic missiles; massive Iranian rearmament; the resurgence of Islamic fundamentalism in Algeria, Jordan, Iran and southern Lebanon; and the uneasy vicissitudes of the former Soviet Muslim republics of Central Asia, with their potential for enhancing either the best or the worst in the Middle East – all spelled danger for this admirable attempt to normalize Arab–Israeli relations.

IRAQ AND THE GULF STATES

The most remarkable feature of Iraqi politics in the year following the war for Kuwait was the survival of Saddam Hussein as President. Iraq's infrastructure had been crippled by the allied bombing campaign of January–February 1991. Its armed forces had been decisively defeated in Kuwait, suffering enormous losses in manpower and matériel. The Kurdish rebels in the north of the country, as well as the Shi'i rebels in the south, sought to exploit this defeat by rising up against the central authorities and seemed at one point on the verge of taking over most of the country. The Iraqi economy was in a shambles, with billions of dollars in claims for reparations now added to its spectacular pre-war indebtedness. In addition, the continued United Nations sanctions regime prevented the export of Iraqi oil and severely restricted the nature of whatever imports Iraq could afford. Nevertheless, Saddam Hussein and those around him in Baghdad kept their nerve, dealt piecemeal and in a characteristically ruthless manner with their domestic foes, gradually reasserted their control and gained in confidence. The result was that by the first anniversary of the war, in January 1992, Saddam Hussein could portray the endurance of his regime as a kind of victory.

How Did He Do It?

In March 1991, following the defeat of the Iraqi armed forces in and around Kuwait, uprisings broke out in the southern, predominantly Shi'i cities of Basra, Nasiriyah, Najaf and Karbala. What began as spontaneous revolts against a hated regime which appeared about to collapse, were soon being organized by members of the underground Islamic *Da'wa* party (the 'Voice of Islam'). The rebels succeeded in seizing a number of cities in the south, but, despite the defection of some army units, they clearly lacked the heavy military equipment needed to march on Baghdad. At the same time, the forces of the Kurdish Front (grouping together the main Kurdish parties as well as a number of smaller ones) took advantage of the disarray and distraction of the Iraqi armed forces to seize control of all the major towns in Kurdistan. However, they too were prevented from taking their fight further into the heartland of central Iraq by their relative weakness beyond the mountains and territory of Kurdistan itself.

Despite initial reports of panic and indecision in Baghdad, it soon became clear that Saddam Hussein was well equipped to deal with rebellions of this kind. In late March and early April his forces struck back. Units of the Republican Guard, particularly the divisions recruited from Saddam Hussein's own provincial and tribal territory which had been kept prudently in reserve during the previous six months, were thrown into the fray. In the north, they recaptured Kirkuk and a number of other major towns in Kurdistan, brutally suppressing the rebellion. This caused roughly 1.5 million Kurdish civilians to flee into the mountains, seeking sanctuary across the Turkish and Iranian borders. In the south, a campaign of equal brutality soon isolated the rebels and then closed in on the towns they held, recapturing these and reasserting Baghdad's control. Roughly 40,000 refugees fled to the relative safety of the zone occupied by the coalition forces in the south. Thousands more crossed the border into Iran or simply fled to the southern marshes in an attempt to escape the relentless pursuit of the Republican Guard.

Saddam Hussein had demonstrated his own relative strength, as well as the difficulties facing the opposition forces in Iraq. In the first place, he had ensured that, however bad the defeat on the battlefield, he still had at his command, in the shape of the key divisions of the Republican Guard, coercive power greater than anything which the opposition forces could mobilize. Furthermore, faced with such an internal threat, he could rely on the cohesion not only of the inner circle of his clansmen, but also on all those whose obedience allowed the regime to function. These people may have had little cause to love, or even admire, Saddam Hussein, but the spectre of communal conflict and civil war raised by the outbreak of revolts in the Kurdish and Shi'i areas evidently terrified them more.

Nevertheless, whilst Saddam dealt with the most pressing danger of open rebellion by force, he clearly felt it prudent to hold out some promise of a more open political system in the aftermath of the defeat. Consequently, in March he appointed as Prime Minister, Saadoun Hammadi, a member of the Revolutionary Command Council, but a Shi'i, who was portrayed as more 'liberal' and as the harbinger of 'fundamental change'. In April, the leaders of the Kurdish Front, recognizing their own weakness, but also perhaps believing that serious political concessions might be wrung out of a weakened regime in Baghdad, began negotiations with Saddam on the question of Kurdish autonomy. In May, the Revolutionary Court, used since 1968 to try 'enemies of the revolution and the state', was abolished and some rather vague promises of future press freedoms were made. In July, this was followed up by moves in the People's Assembly to allow the formation of opposition parties, while Saddam Hussein, in the first speech to the nation since the defeat in Kuwait, promised the institution of a pluralist political system. In September, the RCC finally approved the formation of opposition parties, while making clear the limitations under which they would have to operate.

All the talk of pluralism, liberalism and the promises of change were simply intended to buy time. They were aimed at those who had not joined in the revolts, in an effort to persuade them that the existing regime held out the best prospects of substantial but orderly change. They were also aimed at the leaders of the Kurdish Front, to persuade them that it was still worthwhile to keep talking to Baghdad. This both separated them from their allies among the Shi'is, and forestalled further intervention on their behalf by the Western powers. It may also have been intended to persuade the UN that Iraq was somehow a changed and better place, with the hope that this would lead to a dilution or even elimination of the economic sanctions.

Having recuperated sufficiently, and having presumably decided that the promises of liberalization had served their purpose, Saddam

Hussein reasserted himself in the old style in September. The *Ba'th* Party congress during that month indicted Saadoun Hammadi and paved the way for his dismissal as Prime Minister and ejection from the RCC. Saddam explicitly ruled out any 'Western-style democracy' for Iraq, making it clear that those who advocated it would be regarded as enemies of the state. The talks with the Kurdish leaders continued, although to little purpose, whilst the Iraqi armed forces began to put in place the blockade which was intended to put a stranglehold on Kurdistan.

There was little doubt that the prospect of Saddam Hussein resurgent horrified many Iraqis who saw him as primarily responsible for the disasters which had befallen the country in the preceding year, and for the continuing suffering of large sections of the population. This discontent, logically in such a regime, appeared to have found its focus in groups of conspirators within the Iraqi armed forces. Reports of failed coup attempts are always difficult to substantiate in Iraq, but there appear to have been three such attempts between February and June 1991. The last seems to have been serious enough to have led to the dismissal of the Chief of the General Staff, Hussein Rashid al-Takriti, one of Saddam Hussein's clansmen.

Similarly, the reported uncovering of another serious conspiracy in the armed forces in October may have been the reason for the sudden shake-up in Saddam's inner circle in November. He dismissed his son-in-law, the Minister of Defence, Hussein Kamil al-Majid al-Takriti, replacing him with another clansman, Ali Hassan al-Majid al-Takriti. The latter had hitherto been the Minister of Interior and this post was now filled by Saddam Hussein's half-brother, Wathban Ibrahim al-Takriti, while another half-brother, Sibbawi Ibrahim al-Takriti continued as head of the Intelligence Services. These reshuffles and the associated rumours of intra-elite jealousies and rivalries, do not contradict the principle on which Saddam Hussein has generally relied in his rule of Iraq: a secure power base can only be founded on blood relationships. If anything, the setbacks of the past year, the discontent apparent in the armed forces and elsewhere in the country, as well as the continuing economic crisis have reinforced for him the wisdom of relying on such methods.

In such circumstances, it was scarcely surprising that, by January 1992, the familiar pattern of close surveillance and control had been re-established in Iraq. The talks with the Kurdish Front had reached an impasse, and the blockade of those areas of Kurdistan which the Front controlled had been tightened. Wariness of the possible response of the Western powers, should the Kurdish areas come under open Iraqi army attack, as well as the difficult nature of the terrain, had prevented any outright assault on the areas of *de facto* Kurdish autonomy. No such inhibitions attended the reassertion of central government control in the south. Periodic campaigns against those who had fled to the marshes, combined with an intensifying campaign to root out the Shi'i-based resistance organizations in the cities of the south, marked the re-establishment of Saddam Hussein's power.

Iraq and the UN

So confident was Saddam of this power, both among his inner circle and in the country at large, that in February 1992 Iraq withdrew from the negotiations with the UN over the sale of Iraqi oil. Despite the suffering of the Iraqis caused by the continued inability of the government to raise money for imports through oil sales, the conditions which the UN laid down for permitting such sales were rejected by Iraq as an infringement of its sovereignty. The proposed UN control over the funds ($1.6bn) which would thereby be realized, was evidently too great a public humiliation. However, Saddam Hussein was unable to avoid other intrusions into Iraq during 1991–2, whether by the forces of the allied coalition or by the UN, backed implicitly by the threat of these same forces.

In April 1991, under the terms laid down by the UN Security Council, Iraq provided details of some of its missile sites and of some of its chemical weapons production facilities. At the same time, under explicit threat from the Western partners in the allied coalition, the government in Baghdad agreed to withdraw its forces from areas in Kurdistan to allow the creation of a 'safe haven' to which the thousands of Kurdish refugees could return. In May, the first UN inspection teams arrived in Iraq to verify the extent of Iraq's non-conventional arsenal and to supervise its destruction. These inspections were to continue throughout the following twelve months and became progressively more revealing, uncovering the surprising extent of Iraq's biological and nuclear weapons programmes.

The intrusiveness of these inspections, as well as their inexorable thoroughness, clearly rankled the Iraqi authorities. Equally, in such an obsessively secretive regime, the obligation to give up information of such a sensitive nature went against all precedent. The result was that, periodically, the Iraqi authorities would try to obstruct the work of the inspection teams, either by harassing individual members, by seeking to prevent them from entering certain sites, or by denying them the facilities which would allow them to make thorough and independent investigations. These delays, obstructions and obfuscations were to no avail, however, since the UN inspectors were backed by the implicit threat of the use of military force. Occasionally, this threat became explicit, as in the summer of 1991, when President Bush warned that with the UN's approval, force could be used in the event of Iraqi non-compliance.

Iraq was thus forced into making available more and more detailed information on its non-conventional arms programmes. In July, the Iraqi authorities admitted the construction of the much publicized 'supergun' and opened the site for inspection and destruction. In the same month, Iraq admitted the existence of a programme for uranium enrichment, confirming the intention of acquiring a nuclear weapons capability. In August, further revelations forced the Iraqi government to admit to the manufacture of biological weapons. Finally, the discovery in October 1991 of the vast nuclear research site at Al-Atheer wrung the admission out of the Iraqi government in January 1992 that there had indeed been a nuclear weapons programme. By that stage, the admission was largely superfluous, since the UN inspectors had uncovered the details and infrastructure of a programme of startling scope and sophistication.

Iraq made further efforts to evade the UN mandate when it sent a letter to the Secretary-General on 28 February challenging the authority of the UN to destroy Iraqi equipment used in the improvement of *Scud* missiles. If it had hoped to split the Security Council so that it could avoid further UN action, it was bitterly disappointed. The members of the Council insisted on the validity of their mandate, demanded Iraq's continued adherence to its measures, and threatened military action if it did not concur. On 11 March, Iraq sent the Deputy Prime Minister Tariq Aziz to New York to plead its case. When the Security Council stood firm, Aziz agreed that destruction of the equipment could begin at the end of the month. Despite this climb-down, suspicious Western nations readied military forces in the Gulf and stepped up their warnings of military action in the event that Saddam again attempts to block UN action.

Faced with the threat of military force, the Iraqi government had no alternative but to comply. Nevertheless, in public, Saddam Hussein tried to make a virtue of these otherwise humiliating developments. In a defiant speech in January 1992, for example, he claimed that Iraq might have lost a battle, but had in effect won a triumph in the war against the '30-state aggression'.

The theme of the victimization of Iraq by malign forces was used repeatedly in government propaganda throughout the year. Continued UN sanctions, as well as the UN-supervised destruction of much of Iraq's military potential, were portrayed as evidence of this victimization. It was, of course, harder to maintain that Iraq had triumphed: thousands had died in the war and in the rebellions following the war; economic hardship and disease were taking their toll a full year after the end of the fighting; the country's economy was crippled, even if parts of the infrastructure had been patched up; much of Iraq's conventional military arsenal had been destroyed; equally, the non-conventional weapons, on which the government had lavished such resources, were being systematically destroyed. For Saddam Hussein and his clan, however, a kind of victory had been won: they were still in power one year after the ending of the war, despite the economic and military prostration of Iraq itself. It was this disturbing fact of life which troubled most of Iraq's neighbours.

The Security of the Gulf States

The lesson learnt by the Arab states of the Gulf about the organization of their own security in the aftermath of the Gulf War seemed to be one which stressed the value of increased reliance on the Western powers. This irked Iran and annoyed Egypt and Syria, but as far the members of the Gulf Cooperation Council were concerned, it appeared to hold out the best prospect of secure defence. Western technologies had been impressively deployed in the war against Iraq. The Western states, specifically the US, seemed better able than any others to provide the kind of guarantees of protection that would defer future aggression in the uncertain future of the Gulf. Furthermore, despite the relative political sensitivity of close alliance with Western powers in the region, this was evidently thought to be less heavy a price to pay than to allow regional powers, with their own agendas and affinities, too great a say in guaranteeing the security of these kingdoms.

This process gradually played itself out in the year following the 'Damascus Declaration' of March 1991. A meeting in Damascus that month had brought together the six states of the GCC (Saudi Arabia, Kuwait, Bahrain, Qatar, the UAE and Oman), as well as Egypt and Syria. They had publicly declared their joint commitment to guaranteeing the future security of the Gulf and seemed to suggest that Egypt and Syria would provide, in some systematic way, the military manpower which would act as an effective Arab deterrent force against future aggression in the region. Follow-up committees were established to examine the modalities of these new forms of cooperation, and it was intended that a new framework for Gulf security, rooted squarely in the region, would be established. In reality, nothing very much happened. The follow-up committees never met and differences emerged at head-of-state level which effectively prevented any further progress in this direction.

Impatient with these delays, conscious of the extraordinary resilience of Saddam Hussein's regime in Iraq, and fearful that in the absence of any concrete agreement, the Gulf states would be as vulnerable as ever, the leaders of the GCC held an emergency meeting in May. It appears that they agreed then to look to the Western powers for their immediate defence needs. This development, as well as the simultaneous visit of US Defense Secretary Cheney to the Gulf, seems to have precipitated the Egyptian announcement on 8 May that it would begin to withdraw its 38,000 troops from the Gulf. It appears that the Egyptian government had differed with the rulers of the Gulf states on a number of issues, including the apparent *rapprochement* between these states and Iran, the role which they still envisaged for Western powers in ensuring their defence, as well as the crucial question of the payment which Egypt expected for its participation in such a security arrangement. In June, Syria followed suit and began the withdrawal of the bulk of its forces from the Gulf.

The attempt in July by the foreign ministers of the GCC states to resolve their differences with Egypt and Syria failed. In fact, the divergence of views between the Gulf states and the other two Arab states became more pronounced. Instead of reaching an agreement for joint defence, the meeting merely produced a declaration stating that each country was entitled to seek military help from its allies whenever necessary. The rather *ad hoc* impression given by this statement was echoed by the fact that 4,000 Egyptian troops and 1,000 Syrians had been sent back to Kuwait on a bilateral, contract basis outside the terms of reference of the Damascus Declaration.

By August 1991, the shape of the GCC states' ideas of how best to ensure their security was becoming apparent. On the one hand, there were moves to set up ambitious arms procurement programmes, concentrating on some of the new technologies which had been deployed to such effect during the war with Iraq. On the other, there was a determined effort to reach bilateral defence agreements with a number of the Western states which had participated in the US-led coalition. As might have been expected, given its experiences and the continued uncertainty of developments in Iraq, Kuwait was the first to sign such an agreement. Originally, the Kuwaiti government had attempted to persuade the US and the UK to base troops in Kuwait itself. This offer had been declined, but bilateral defence cooperation agreements were drawn up. In September, the US signed a ten-year security accord with Kuwait, allowing the prepositioning of US military equipment, providing for joint military exercises and giving the US access to Kuwaiti airfields. US bilateral agreement with Bahrain followed in October and negotiations to update older agreements, or to establish new ones, continued with other GCC states well into 1992. In October, the UK signed a similar agreement with Kuwait, and France began discussions with the Kuwaiti authorities along similar lines.

The most important deal may be the US–Saudi accord which hinged on agreement of Saudi defence needs. The government had announced in 1991 ambitious military procurement plans, envisaging arms purchases from the US of at least $10bn in the context of a wide-ranging security accord with the US. Its complexity, its size and the implications for Saudi force restructuring and for the regional balance of power, meant that though a large proportion of the arms sales had been agreed to in principle by the US administration in 1991, the negotiations on it could drag on for months into 1992.

This bilateralism dominated the thinking of the Arab Gulf states when they considered how best to ensure their own security. Whatever their rhetorical commitment to the principle of 'regional defence' or 'Arab defence', it was evident that they saw in Western technology, military assistance and security guarantees a more effective and, ironically, less intrusive form of security arrangement than anything offered by their Arab allies. Whatever the longer-term plans, in the short term such guarantees appeared to them to offer a more reliable form of security against the regional threats which still faced them. Meetings of the GCC chiefs of staff to discuss the establishment of a GCC deterrent force – much urged on them by the Western powers – stumbled on disagreements over command and control, finance, national troop contributions, and where to station such forces. The most that can be expected may be the 'earmarking' of national forces for a collective structure on paper only.

Across the Gulf, Iran under Rafsanjani had been cultivating its own principally economic ties with the West, and this helped to encourage the *rapprochement* with the Gulf states. Nevertheless, they were aware of the uncertainties of Iranian politics and unsure, therefore, of the reliability of the apparent 'pragmatic' trend of Iranian policy towards its fellow Gulf states.

At the time they considered Iran to be relatively weak militarily and unable to act as a deterrent to further aggression by Iraq. Consequently, they were unwilling to listen either to the blandishments or to the threats of Iran concerning its own capacity to guarantee the security of the Gulf. Whilst seeking to open up diplomatic and economic links with Iran, the states of the GCC have clearly been reluctant to grant it any security role, preferring instead the reassurance which bilateral Western agreements provided.

Even more extreme uncertainty characterizes their views of Iraq. As long as Saddam Hussein remains in power, Iraq will be seen as the major military threat to the security of Kuwait and possibly of Saudi Arabia. Recognition of this fact has led these two states to set up whatever security arrangements would appear to protect them best against future Iraqi aggression. In the case of Saudi Arabia, it has also led to thoughts about how to engineer the removal of Saddam Hussein himself. Insofar as one can tell, however, these efforts have been as unsuccessful as all previous attempts by outside powers to foment serious revolt against the Iraqi leader. In the absence of any certainty about the political future of Iraq, and thus of the policies which it will pursue in the region, the more ambitious ideas of wide security frameworks for the Gulf have been suspended. In their absence, the rulers of the Gulf states have clearly decided that it is wiser to secure what they have by the trusted methods of massive arms purchases and the protection of stronger outside, and distant powers.

IRAN SHEDS ITS RADICAL IMAGE

The government of President Hashemi Rafsanjani has been trying for some years to repair the damage done to its international standing by the radical positions that were adopted while the Ayatollah Khomeini insisted on theocratic rule. During 1991 Iran adopted two significant foreign-policy initiatives which helped considerably in recovering some of its earlier position. The first was its neutrality in the Gulf War in 1991; the second was to press the pro-Iranian *Hizbollah* party hard enough to secure the release of all the American and British hostages held in Lebanon. By adopting policies that fall more in line with state interests than with untempered ideological objectives, both these initiatives helped the government to enhance Iran's image as a rational player on the international stage.

Iran, Iraq and the Gulf

Despite reports and fears that Iran was secretly aiding the Iraqis during the US-led war against Iraq, it became clear that President Rafsanjani understood very well the political and strategic opportunities that would accrue by sticking to neutrality. The US and others in the coalition had supported Iraq during the eight-year Iran–Iraq War and, as a result, Iran had only narrowly escaped defeat. It made no sense at this juncture for Rafsanjani to support Iran's old, and now desperate, enemy. Despite pressure from his radical opponents at home to join a Muslim brother in fighting America, he defended Iran's position of neutrality. 'We will not become involved in fighting to shed our blood so that either the US attains victory or to shed blood so that the Iraqis may remain in Kuwait,' he said in January.

Yet Iran could ill afford to do nothing; instead it tried to project a statesman-like image by offering to mediate between the two sides and by sending food and medicines to Iraq, which did not contravene the spirit of the UN trade embargo. Iraq continued trying to court Iran throughout the war with visits by the then Deputy Prime Minister, Saadoun Hammadi, and Foreign Minister Tariq Aziz, although relations deteriorated in the spring and summer when Iraq accused Iran of aiding uprisings by the Shi'i in the south of Iraq. That the West recognized the careful position Iran had adopted was reflected in the fact that at no point in the year did the West recommend to the UN that Iran be requested to return the more than 100 Iraqi combat aircraft which had crossed the border in February. This was as much a *quid pro quo* for Iranian neutrality as it was a lack of desire to see the aircraft back in Iraqi hands.

The defeat of Iraq and the restoration of Kuwaiti territorial sovereignty altered the balance of power in the Gulf region and has led to alternative interpretations of a new security structure. Iran's position was made clear by Mahmoud Vaezi, a Deputy Foreign Minister. 'As the most powerful country in the region it is natural that we should be concerned about the security and the stability of the region', he said in March. 'Our proposal for the seven regional countries – as well as Iraq as the eighth country if the right conditions are present there – [is] to create the nucleus of a system by which they can, on their own, without the interference of others, restore security and stability in the region'.

For this reason, Iran opposed the abortive Damascus plan, which would have included Syria and Egypt in a Gulf security scheme, even though this stance subsequently led to tensions with Cairo. To promote its policy of cooperation and 'neighbourliness' and to win trust, Tehran was diplomatically active, exchanging visits with the GCC states and restoring diplomatic relations with Saudi Arabia and, further afield, with Morocco. Particular care was taken over Kuwait, with which, except for Saudi Arabia, Iran had had the worst relations of all countries during its own war against Iraq. Tehran sent firefighters to help put out the oil-well fires in Kuwait, while Kuwait paid $10m in compensation for losses incurred by former Iranian workers in Kuwait as a result of the Iraqi invasion in 1990.

The GCC states responded diplomatically by seeking to argue that the Damascus proposal was a partial, not comprehensive, security plan. The Qatari Foreign Minister, Mubarak Ali al-Khater said after the GCC ministerial council session in May that, 'Iran is a friendly and neighbouring state and since past times we have had historic relations with it. It must have a role in the proposed arrangements'. Nevertheless, Iran's worst fears were realized later in the year when it became clear that the US was to be involved in the region through bilateral pacts with all GCC states. It is a measure of the increased pragmatism of the Tehran government that even this news did not provoke the kind of outburst that would have been expected during the Khomeini era.

The Kuwaiti ambassador in Tehran was summoned and asked for an explanation of Kuwaiti agreements with the US, and though some members of the Iranian government were outspoken about the alliance, in general, the Iranian response was restrained. A commentary on Tehran radio in October stuck to a line of persuasion and logic rather than threats: 'Defence pacts with other countries – such as Britain and France – rather than increasing defence capability, are designed for the creation of balance among those countries who pursue their own varied interests in the region. As has been said many times before, security is a reality that is achievable when, primarily, there is understanding in the region, and when a basis exists in the cultural, economic and social fields.' Iran managed to maintain cordial relations with Kuwait, promising to return six Kuwaiti passenger aircraft that had been flown to Iran by Iraqi pilots, and in November Iran Air resumed flights to Kuwait for the first time since the fall of the Shah.

The importance of Iran for the region was still being acknowledged at the end of the year, even though no concrete security plan had emerged. At the end of November, Abdullah Bishara, Secretary-General of the GCC said that, 'Iran is an essential partner of the GCC in ensuring the security of the Gulf waterway. The security of this waterway cannot be ensured in the absence of agreement with Iran.' Later he was to admit that it would be some time, however, before a full security partnership can evolve between the GCC and Iran, arguing, for example, that 'joint patrols' could not yet be considered.

Freeing the Hostages

Serious moves to obtain the release of the Western hostages had begun back in 1990, when President Rafsanjani acknowledged, somewhat disingenuously, the adverse image Iran suffered as a result of being associated with the hostage-takers: 'The Americans and others are always using the issue as a lever to portray the Lebanese as terrorists and portray us as their supporters'. Two Americans and an Irishman, Brian Keenan, were released that year, but the release of other hostages had become bogged down in tricky diplomacy, involving *Hizbollah* and the Syrian-backed *Amal*, while enduring the occasional kick from Israel by its attacks on *Hizbollah*-held territory in Lebanon.

By the summer of 1991, however, the good offices of the UN Secretary-General, Javier Pérez de Cuéllar, and the fact that Syria had been given a free hand in Lebanon as a result of its participation in the Arab forces arrayed against Saddam Hussein, brought about a breakthrough. Another important factor was the US insistence to Iran that there would be no normalization of relations, including the release of Iran's frozen assets and the removal of its trade sanctions, while Americans were being held captive. The decision to link the issue of Western hostages with those Lebanese being held at Israel's Khiam prison and seven missing Israeli servicemen also helped. All Western hostages, apart from two Germans, were released by the end of the year, even though Iran's attempts to secure information about four of its own nationals abducted in 1982 were ineffective, and despite the fact that efforts to achieve the release of Sheikh Abdel Karim Obeid, the Lebanese cleric kidnapped by the Israelis, also failed.

Wider Foreign Relations

These two initiatives led to an overall improvement in Iran's relations with the West, including the US, despite Iranian misgivings about the exact import of President Bush's vision of a new world order. The US became Iran's sixth-largest supplier of goods over the year, with a relaxation of the ban on Iranian oil imports and a payment of $278m to Iran as compensation for Iranian-owned military equipment which was undelivered after the 1979 revolution. The US studiously avoided blaming Iran or Syria for any involvement in the destruction of the Pan Am flight over Lockerbie, though Iran said it would condemn any US military action taken against Libya as a result of the US holding Libya solely responsible for action.

The improvement in foreign policy is tied in with President Rafsanjani's attempts to improve the Iranian economy by boosting productivity through the import of raw materials for industry and attracting foreign investment and technology transfer. Although potential foreign investors remain cautious, a spate of contracts were signed during the year with Germany, Japan, Italy and the UK, with lines of credit arranged by consortia of European banks. The financial dispute with France over the return of a $1-bn loan made by the Shah to Eurodif, the French nuclear company, was finally resolved, but a visit to Tehran by President François Mitterrand was postponed *sine die* after the murder in Paris of Dr Shahpur Bakhtiar, the leader of Iran's liberal opposition group, the National Resistance Movement, and the Shah's last prime minister. The assassination, which led to a warrant for the arrest of an adviser to the Iranian Minister of Post and Tele-communications, reminded the world that the Iranian government will still resort to terrorism to further its own ends. The minimal international condemnation of the murder is testimony of the success of the 'moderate' image that President Rafsanjani has managed to project.

Iran kept a wary eye on developments in the Soviet Union. Although it belatedly recognized the independence of Azerbaijan, fears of the potential for the breakdown of security along its northern borders led to a round of diplomatic activity by Foreign Minister Dr Ali Akbar Velayati. In the early months of 1992 he visited the former Soviet Muslim republics to establish a cordial working relationship and to secure an early foothold in what may develop into a rivalry with Turkey and Saudi Arabia for influence in the area. The Iranians also promoted revitalization and expansion of the Economic Cooperation Organization, adding Tajikistan, Azerbaijan, Uzbekistan, Turkmenistan and Kyrgyzstan to the three original members (Iran, Turkey and Pakistan) and established a Caspian Sea Council, made up of Iran, Russia, Kazakhstan, Azerbaijan and Turkmenistan. The secretariats for both organizations are in Tehran.

Iran found itself both cooperating and competing for influence with Ankara in Transcaucasia and Central Asia. Given Tehran's cautious line towards Azeri assertiveness and its relatively benign role towards its own Armenian community, Iran could attempt to play the role of honest broker in the dispute over Nagorno-Karabakh. It would be something of a paradox if Islamic Iran came to be seen by the international community as displaying more understanding towards Christian Armenia than constitutionally secular Turkey.

In Afghanistan too, Iran worked with the UN in its efforts to arrange a final settlement to the crisis, even though it would not necessarily be one that wholly favoured the fundamentalist cause. Towards the end of 1991, however, charges that Iran was continuing to fuel fundamentalism resurfaced in relation to Algeria. The Iranian relationship with Sudan, however, naturally took on a higher profile. The Sudanese opposition claimed that Iran was providing funds for a $300-m Sudanese purchase of Chinese helicopters to use against the Christian rebels in the south. Iran denied sending military personnel to train Sudanese fighters, but after a series of exchanges between delegations of both countries, Iran found it necessary to admit that military cooperation was being discussed and that there had been a meeting between the Chief of Staff of the Sudan Army, Hassan abd al-Rahman Ali, and the commander of the Iranian Revolutionary Guards, Mohsen Rezai. In December, after a visit by Rafsanjani to Sudan, the two countries signed agreements on economic and military cooperation. In early March, Sudan launched a new offensive against the rebels in the south, reportedly using Iranian-supplied weapons. The ties between these two militant Islamic states are a cause of deep concern to Egypt and Saudi Arabia.

Military Procurement

The increase in the price of oil as a result of the Iraq–Kuwaiti crisis helped foreign exchange earnings in 1990–91. Some of this newly available money was spent on rebuilding the armed forces, which Tehran considers a priority because Saddam Hussein is still in power in Iraq and the collapse of the Soviet Union has destabilized Iran's northern borders.

Military purchases were made from the Soviet Union, China, North Korea, Brazil, Pakistan and Argentina. Arms purchases from the Soviet Union date from the ten-year accord signed in 1989 between President Rafsanjani and then President Mikhail Gorbachev. During 1991 Iran is reported to have purchased or ordered from the USSR and China 72 F-7 fighters, 25 Su-24 bombers, 50 MiG-29s, a number of MiG-31s and Su-27s, and 200 T-72 tanks. In the summer of 1991, Iran's air force commander, Brigadier-General Mansour Sattari, visited Moscow as head of a military team. In February 1992 he said that in addition to the Soviet and Chinese aircraft, many of Iran's US-built planes, grounded during the Iran–Iraq War, have become serviceable. In March 1992, a North Korean vessel, which reportedly was carrying an unknown number of advanced *Scud*-C missiles, docked at the Iranian port of Bandar Abbas. US intelligence suspected that some of the missiles were also intended for Syria, and although there had been rumours that the US would board the ship to check its cargo, it landed without interruption.

Speculation increased during the year that Iran might also be trying to acquire nuclear weapons with the help of China. In June 1990, China signed an agreement to provide a small research reactor at Isfahan. It has confirmed that it had a nuclear cooperation programme with Iran, but insists it is for peaceful purposes only. India has also announced it would be selling Iran a ten-megawatt research reactor, under a transaction guaranteed by the IAEA. There was also speculation that Iran was seeking nuclear expertise and materials from the Central Asian republics of the former USSR. Iran admits having a nuclear energy programme, while arguing that it is intended to make up for the considerable shortage of power which is hampering the country's industry and household domestic needs.

The IAEA has so far shown little concern, although White House spokesman Pat Williams voiced anxiety in November 1991, noting that the remarks made by Iranian officials cast doubts over Iran's commitment to the NPT. The IAEA visited Iran in February 1992 and team leader Jon Jennekens concluded that, 'I and my colleagues have inspected different parts of Iran's nuclear facilities and have found nothing suspicious'. Nevertheless, the IAEA is likely to seek cooperation from the Western intelligence community and to make a request for the inspection of specific sites, should this collaboration raise the level of suspicion.

A Continuing Struggle for Power

The year started badly for President Rafsanjani when in January the radicals in the *Majlis* were able to carry through the impeachment of his Minister of Health, Dr Iradj Fazel – the first time a cabinet minister had been unseated by the parliament since the 1979 revolution. At the same time, a new and critical daily paper, *Salaam*, was launched with Mohammad Musavi Khoeini, the leader of the students who took over the American Embassy in 1979, as its publisher. The hardliners in parliament, however, failed in their attempt in April to unseat another minister, Mohammad Ali Najafi, the Minister for Education. The pro-Rafsanjani daily, *Ressalat*, commented that hardliners had 'drawn up a list of ministers to impeach one after another in order to deliver a telling blow to the government. But will our people sit down silent and watch a group in the Majlis slaughter Rafsanjani, the dignity of the revolution?'

Rafsanjani was to have his revenge on the extremists later in the year, when two MPs were summoned before a Special Clerical Court on conspiracy charges. The two hardliners had met the disgraced Ayatollah Hossein Ali Montazeri, the man once designated to succeed Ayatollah Khomeini, but who was pushed aside after showing liberal tendencies. The meetings may have been connected to the rumours during the early part of 1991 that the spiritual leader, Ayatollah Ali Khamenei, was dying of cancer; although these rumours were not proven it is still suspected that he is suffering from a malignant illness. By the end of the year, Rafsanjani's foreign-policy successes, in particular the release of the hostages in Lebanon, and at home, the release of Roger Cooper, the Briton imprisoned on espionage charges, demonstrated that, although they remain an irritant, the radicals were being successfully marginalized.

Pressure continued on the main opposition groups outside the country. In March 1991, the communist opposition radio station, Radio Iran Toilers, a pro-*Tudeh* station based in the USSR, declared it would be shutting down – a casualty of the reforms that had swept through the Soviet Union. The murder of Dr Shahpur Bakhtiar rid the opposition of one of its more credible figures. In December the government cracked down on pro-Shah activists in Iran itself, killing some of their number.

Economic discontent sparked disturbances in a number of Iranian cities during 1991. Unrest was particularly marked during the summer, when several arson attacks took place in Tehran's bazaar, and a demonstration against the veil in Isfahan turned into a wider protest. Oil income had increased after oil prices rose in the wake of the Iraqi invasion of Kuwait in 1990, but by the middle of 1991 they were falling again. Imports totalling $22bn in 1990 had to be reduced to $17bn in 1991, while domestic productivity remained low and inflation increased once again. Trying to turn the ailing economy around remains one of the greatest challenges for the government.

The government took some measures to improve the situation. The multi-tiered foreign exchange system was simplified as a step towards devaluing the rial. The private sector was encouraged to play a greater role in the economy, and Mohsen Nourbakhsh, the Economic Affairs and Finance Minister, invited a cross-section of Iranian expatriates to return home and participate in the country's reconstruction. Many Iranians have been gradually returning, though few have settled permanently. Once again these policies aroused the opposition of the hardliners, but it is expected that their position in their main power base, the *Majlis*, will be substantially weakened after the parliamentary elections scheduled for April 1992.

Rafsanjani has been slowly improving his position despite the constant efforts of the more radical followers of the Ayatollah to thwart him. With the opening up of foreign relations and some relaxation of social conditions inside the country over the year, what might be described as an intensification of the Rafsanjani line has gradually become clearer. Although human rights abuses continue and the government remains politically unpopular, Rafsanjani was able to turn the sensitive issue of the Gulf War into a political victory for Iran and to outmanoeuvre his hardline opponents on this and on the question of the hostages in Lebanon. The more militant days of the Iranian Revolution seem at last to have ended; conversely, the rise of Islamic Iran as a great regional power may have only begun.

THE MAGHREB: THE RISE OF RADICAL ISLAM

Crisis in Algeria, where one of the most firmly established of Arab regimes crumbled in the face of popular opposition led by Islamist radicals, has forced policy-makers to reassess long-held assumptions about stability in North Africa and the consequences of conflict for the southern flank of the Mediterranean basin. This is made more pertinent because the region is undergoing profound change as the EC adjusts to the single market and new political configurations, and Turkey and the Arab east come to terms with a new Middle Eastern order in the wake of the Gulf War.

In the Arab west, established regimes face the challenge of a new generation of opponents, led by Islamist radicals, who have articulated the demands of largely youthful populations for housing, jobs and what reformists in the former single party in Algeria, the National Liberation Front until recently called 'a better life for all'. The resolution of this conflict is of deep concern throughout the region, with Western European planners making support for the *status quo* in North Africa a central, if fragile, plank of their Mediterranean policy.

This is seen as essential to reduce the threat of what Brussels, Paris, Rome and Madrid fear could be a new generation of radicalized, anti-Western states emerging on their southern flank. Attempts are being made to promote projects which can create sustainable economic growth as a way to support stability in the Maghreb and to staunch the flow of North African populations in search of a better life in Europe. This factor was explicitly written into the EC's Redirected Mediterranean Policy, drawn up in 1989–90. However, the trade concessions and financial commitments necessary to sustain such policies remain insufficient. Recent reports of the arrival of the first Maghrebi 'boat people' in Spain, and the improving political fortunes of the radical right in France and Italy have given impetus to this policy – even when helping existing North African regimes means overlooking human rights violations. This finds expression in efforts by EC governments to provide the maximum possible political and, to a lesser extent, financial support for Algeria, Morocco and Tunisia, and for closer security cooperation – a process in which Arab states to the east, mindful of the possible consequences of Islamist revolution in the Maghreb for their own people, are now also involved.

Algerian Islamists Take on the Establishment

In 1989–91, President Chadli Bendjedid's move to open the way for greater democracy was thought to provide a possible political formula to begin solving Algeria's economic and social problems – for example, by bringing new faces into government as a precondition for breaking down the structures of a heavily centralized economy, and by opening the way to political democracy. Opinion was divided in the states of the Arab Maghreb Union, with the governments in Morocco and Tunisia making little secret of their concern that Chadli's initiatives, which opened the political arena to the Islamist opposition, would have a knock-on effect throughout the region. The Algerian move divided Algiers and Tunis, with Tunisian Interior Minister Abdallah Kallel and other officials publicly proclaiming that Algiers was too soft on exiled Islamist opponents. At the same time, President Zine el-Abidine Ben Ali led an onslaught against the illegal Tunisian Islamist party, *Nahda*, arresting thousands of its militants and sympathisers.

The Moroccan and Tunisian leaders felt that developments in Algeria from December 1991 to February 1992 proved the validity of their fears. Even though its leaders had been jailed for most of the election period, the Islamic Salvation Front won a surprisingly large victory in the first round of the legislative elections on 26 December. Round two of those elections, which would undoubtedly have seen an absolute FIS majority, was cancelled before its scheduled 16 January date, and Chadli Bendjedid resigned. The extent of the Algerian crisis was highlighted by the imposition of a one-year state of emergency on 9 February, and on 4 March the government (the Higher Council of State) put the FIS on the banned list, where it joined other Maghrebi Islamist parties, such as *Nahda* in Tunisia or *Al Adl wal Ihsan* in Morocco. With the army dominating political life, Algeria had moved from reformist model to repression pure and simple, with little prospect of an early restoration of stability. The Algerian crisis has been interpreted as confirmation of widespread fears that radical Islam could prove an unstoppable force for unwelcome change in North Africa and beyond, and that democratization would not necessarily lead to liberalization, but would go in the opposite direction.

Other Arab Maghreb Union governments made no attempt to hide their approval of a military-sponsored takeover which underlined their arguments that Chadli's democratic opening had moved too far too fast, threatening to undermine their own strategies for containing popular discontent and demands for change. Tunisia led the way, giving the new military-backed HCS regime its full support while it continued its own crackdown on *Nahda*. Independent analysts believe that *Nahda* could also win if it were allowed to stand in elections.

Although European governments expressed concern at the human rights situation in Algeria, and the European Parliament suspended a new EC financial protocol until the political situation became clearer, there was tacit support in much of Europe and the West, as well as from most other Arab governments, for the HCS takeover in Algiers as the only way to avert rule by the FIS. Outside the Islamist movement, very few observers believed that stability in the Mediterranean would be advanced if the FIS formed a government. Rather, they argued that thousands of arrests were perhaps acceptable if they crippled the movement and allowed Algeria to avoid the election of Islamic fundamentalists, who were suspected of wanting to abolish democratic rules as soon as they were in power.

However, this view overlooked the fact that the causes for the emergence of FIS are still present. For several months before the elections, the Algerian authorities had put the Islamist movement under intense pressure, including the arrest of FIS leaders Abbasi Madani and Ali Belhadj, and many of their supporters. The FIS was apparently deeply divided over strategy as well. It was widely felt that as a result Islamist militants would not do as well in a general election as they had in the very different conditions of the historic June 1990 local elections, when the FIS took over town halls throughout the country.

The results, however, were quite different. Analysis of the 26
December election reveals a depth of anti-establishment feeling and
gives a rare empirical view of how North Africans are actually thinking. Although the percentage of FIS votes dropped by around 10%
from the two-thirds level reached in the pre-1990 elections, a convincing majority of those who voted opted for the change represented by
the FIS, the only party to offer a credible national alternative to rule by
the FLN establishment. The size of the FIS vote in the first round was
such that even if a higher proportion of voters had been frightened into
voting for the FLN and secular opposition parties in the second round,
the FIS would not only have been called to form a government, but it
would have been able to claim a substantial popular mandate. The
voting also showed, if anyone doubted it, that the FLN was finished as
a popular force. The FIS took 188 of the 231 parliamentary seats
decided in the first round, which put it only 28 seats short of an absolute majority in the 430-member *Assemblée Populaire Nationale*. Of
the remaining seats allocated in the first round, the FLN, with 15 seats,
was beaten into third place by the FFS, with 25 seats (largely concentrated in the Berber-speaking part of the country).

It has been argued that a voting system originally introduced to
give the FLN an advantage actually worked in favour of the FIS. Certainly, the distribution of seats did not reflect the actual voting pattern: the FIS won 3.25 million votes, against 1.61 million for the
FLN, and 510,000 for the FFS. More than 900,000 ballot papers were
disqualified as many electors failed to understand the system of voting.
Only 59% of eligible voters – 7.82m out of a 13.26m electorate – took
part in the first round, and the results confirmed a widespread fear that
a low turnout would undermine plans to bring political stability
through the ballot box by favouring the FIS, whose supporters were
more mobilized to vote.

Nevertheless, the size of the FIS vote was sufficient to say that
Algerians – and potentially other North Africans, even if cross-border
conditions are different – would vote first and foremost for change. In
the early 1990s change is represented not by the leftist, liberal and eth-
nocentric parties which had also stood in the Algerian elections (and
were largely obliterated), but by radical Islamists. Part of radical
Islam's appeal is that it advocates a new political system to replace the
present 'corrupt' governments, one based on the higher moral values
of Islam, a value system known to all the voters. This has particular
resonance when structural adjustment throughout the region has
meant rising prices, less job security and new fears for the future
among a population largely unable to comprehend the wider
macroeconomic goals of reform.

Prior to the elections, the FLN establishment and the reformist
middle class believed that the threat of a massive FIS vote leading to
an Iranian-style Islamic republic would frighten the majority away
from voting FIS. In the event, while many Algerians have deep reser-

vations about rule by Islamist radicals, anti-establishment feeling was so strong that faced with a choice between more FLN rule (and structural adjustment), or a genuine change of government and (perhaps illusory) hope for the future promised by the country's largest opposition party, the majority of those who voted opted for the FIS.

The HCS regime now has a short period to respond to the popular demands for a better life which propelled the FIS into the centre of North African politics. The initial signs are that it will offer only limited changes, of either personnel or economic policy. An indication of the shape of HCS policy was given by a limited government reshuffle announced on 23 February, which confirmed that Sid-Ahmed Ghozali would remain head of a government which includes reform-minded technocrats and senior members of the security establishment, notably Major-General Khaled Nezzar as Defence Minister and Major-General Larbi Belkheir as Interior Minister. In a bow to Islamist sentiment, the reshuffle also included the appointment of a disaffected FIS founder member, Said Guechi, as Vocational Training and Employment Minister and the allocation of the sensitive Religious Affairs Ministry to an Algiers *imam* with opposition connections. These appointments were too limited to convince FIS members to drop their opposition.

Perceptions of political risk are now so bad that international confidence in Algeria's ability to manage its finances has also collapsed, even though the successful signing of a $1.46bn commercial debt refinancing in March 1992 signalled the way for a partial rehabilitation. Unless the HCS regime can take a firm hand, Algeria is threatened by even worse civil disorder and economic chaos. Despite the massive security crackdown, restoration of stability will not be easy, especially as the regime seems very fragile. Maintenance of cohesion and unity of purpose within the military will prove a critical factor in the months ahead. If the army were to divide on ideological or generational grounds, Algeria would be threatened with civil war. This point has been acknowledged by the 72-year old HCS chairman, Mohamed Boudiaf.

If the HCS regime is overwhelmed – which, given its military backing is far from certain – the FIS could yet be best placed to form a government. Indeed, whether Boudiaf's regime survives its first year will be determined by its success in quelling opposition on the street. Experience from 1988–91 suggests that the military can control the situation in the short term, but in the longer term the Islamist opposition will bounce back. The authorities will look for allies, such as the FFS or even Islamists who renounce the FIS. It remains a fact of Algerian political life, however, that only the FIS has consistently proved itself a popular and nationally-based opposition party. In prospect is a further period of chronic instability as the authorities and FIS supporters continue to clash.

UMA Takes Root

The Arab Maghreb Union, known by its evocative French acronym, UMA, the Arabic word for community, was founded in Marrakesh in February 1989 by Algeria, Morocco, Tunisia, Libya and Mauritania. It represents a long-held aim to bring North African states, often divided by political rivalries, closer together, both economically and socially. One consequence of the HCS takeover is that political relations between UMA states have improved after a tense period in 1991.

The UMA itself is an increasingly significant factor in the complex nexus of relations binding the northern and southern flanks of the Mediterranean. Through the even newer 'Five Plus Five' grouping, which brings the UMA states together with four EC members (France, Italy, Spain and Portugal) and Malta, there is the potential to build a regional dialogue. This could even include the maverick Libya, whose reintegration into the wider international community was speeded by its UMA membership, at least until its alleged implication in the Lockerbie air crash and the bombing in September 1989 of a French UTA jet flying over Africa.

The question of Libyan membership is one of several problems to be resolved if UMA relations with the West are to be placed on a stable, institutionalized footing. Maghrebi regional integration initiatives have foundered in the past, leading to widespread scepticism that the UMA could survive as a viable entity. Despite a strong historical, economic and social impetus towards integration in a relatively homogeneous region, decades of unity initiatives have brought few results. To a certain extent, however, the time is now ripe for UMA. Its member governments are increasingly condemned to work together by external pressures, not least the advent of the EC's single market, and internal problems. The UMA has already begun to act as a channel for dialogue with the EC.

Although bilateral differences can still sink the organization in its present form, the UMA is likely to remain a fact of North African life, despite a slower than desired pace of integration. This process was given some impetus at the fourth ordinary UMA summit, held in Casablanca on 15–16 October 1991, when it was finally agreed to establish permanent structures, including a secretariat, development bank and other institutions. Previously Tunis (which would like to be the 'Brussels of North Africa') had argued for a permanent headquarters, but it was outvoted by its larger neighbours who preferred a more flexible formula, with UMA institutions regularly moving from capital to capital. The decision to establish permanent bodies pointed to a recognition that, given the UMA's ambitions for a customs union and eventual economic integration, a lack of institutional structures would become an increasing problem.

Under the new system, each UMA state houses part of the union's machinery. Morocco won the headquarters, Tunisia got the post of UMA Secretary-General, who is charged with implementing policies and providing a secretariat for the Presidential Council, the Council of Ministers, the *Comité de suivi* and other specialized commissions. Tunis is also to house a regional investment bank, *Banque Maghrebine d'Investissement et de Commerce Exterieur*, to be established with $500m capital. Algeria is to host the Consultative Assembly (*Majlis Es Shoura*), the 100-member UMA Parliament; Mauritania gets the judiciary, including an UMA supreme court; and Libya is to house the Maghreb university and Academy of Sciences. This is an apparently attractive prospect for the Libyan leader, Muammar Gaddafi, who will hope to influence a new generation of North African students at a time when the current generation of Libyan students are showing signs of tiring of his regime.

The Casablanca summit also agreed that henceforth decisions would be made on a majority basis, rather than by consensus. Majority voting promises to create a more flexible organization, better able to react quickly to crises and to implement policy. However, it could also threaten problems when states are outvoted; consensus is thus still required in exceptional circumstances.

If UMA is to keep to its timetable of achieving customs union by 1995, it is now essential that it make these structures work efficiently. Efforts to increase trade and show that UMA initiatives are economically viable are also critical. This will require that the five members work out a payments system that is acceptable to all, and that they carry through with microeconomic projects which will demonstrate that North African states can profit from working together, rather than only looking north for the bulk of their business. UMA's longer-term economic prospects depend to a large extent on Algeria's abandonment of state-owned industry and central planning.

Morocco Looks for New Political Formulas

Despite the UN initiative to resolve the protracted conflict for sovereignty over the Western Sahara, the war between Morocco and the Polisario Front liberation movement retains the potential to undermine regional unity. King Hassan has not been able to mobilize support within UMA for his energetic efforts to ensure recognition of his possession of Western Sahara, even though this received a boost when Mohamed Boudiaf, an exile in Morocco for nearly three decades, returned to head the HCS in Algeria.

In the second half of 1991, the UN slowly deployed a peacekeeping force, MINURSO, to oversee an eventual referendum in the disputed territory. However, by early 1992 it was clear that the referendum proposed by the outgoing UN Secretary-General Javier Pérez de Cuéllar would not go ahead as planned. Morocco will certainly not give up the territory, whose integration into the kingdom remains a focal point for Moroccan nationalism; indeed, it is one of the few areas of consensus for all Moroccan political factions. Instead, Hassan will try to force a 'Maghreb' solution, persuading his neighbours that Polisario should be ignored in order that the Sahara will remain part of Morocco. For the King there are clear advantages in maintaining the *status quo*, having effective possession of Western Sahara while keeping the legal issue open. Once the issue is closed in legal terms, be they favourable or not, the Moroccan opposition will have no reason to hold its political fire.

In a parallel move, it was announced that a major political initiative would be launched in August 1992, involving a referendum on a new draft constitution to be followed by general elections. A cautious opening to limited democracy was expected as Moroccans started to ask questions about the evolution of their society once the Saharan dispute was resolved. In his annual *Fête du Trône* speech on 3 March, Hassan promised 'to establish a better balance' between the legislature and executive. The implication is that a parliament which includes opposition parties will have a greater say over policy. General elections should have been held in September 1989, but following a referendum were delayed for two years in order to give more time to resolve the Sahara question.

This represented the last act of the so-called Saharan consensus, by which all but fringe groups in Moroccan society agreed to moderate their political and economic demands while the territory was 'reintegrated' into the kingdom. Hassan's promise that elections would be held before 9 October 'in total transparency and far from ambiguity' seems to acknowledge this fact. A royal commitment to insuring free and fair elections, after persistent irregularities in past polls, may signal a recognition that some degree of change must follow. However, it remains to be seen whether such a move will be undercut by a growing movement for more sweeping change – best represented by the local Islamists. Under intense police pressure, Moroccan Islamists have largely remained underground. Hassan will continue to wield the stick of police power, while offering the carrot of rewards to the secular opposition, in order to insure that this remains the case. He hopes thereby to avoid repeating Chadli Bendjedid's move out of power and into the history books.

East Asia

There is a certain smugness in the way some East Asians have reacted to the demise of the Soviet Union and the end of the Cold War. Looking at other inhabitants of Eurasia, whether in South Asia or Europe, it is easy to see there the risks of new conflicts. To some extent, East Asians have good cause for *Schadenfreude*. They have the world's fastest growing economies and they see a relatively simple succession from the Soviet Union to a Russia that knows it must withdraw much of its military punch from the region.

And yet, part of the reason East Asia appears more calm may only reflect a cultural preference not to face unpleasant realities, at least in public. The disintegration of the Soviet Union has led the United States to withdraw elements of its military forces in the Pacific, thereby raising the prospect that East Asians will be left to come to terms with their own long-standing rivalries that were often suppressed under the blanket of the Cold War.

While some old conflicts are winding down, as in Cambodia, others, for example in Korea, may well be shifting into a dangerous phase where the risks of nuclear proliferation lead to a major crisis in the short run and to a wrenching reappraisal of existing security choices in the longer run. Disputes over islands in the South China Sea are far from resolved, and even the Russo–Japanese territorial dispute seems to defy a swift solution. The end of the Cold War also puts trade disputes across the Pacific in a harsher light. Perhaps most important, at least two of the major powers in the region, China and Japan, are facing choices about how to reform at home and adjust their foreign policy to the new world. As Europeans cope with the new realities through their multilateral institutions, and the East Asians flounder with at best a patchwork of bilateral relationships, some of the smugness may begin to fade.

CHINA ON THE MOVE

At the end of 1991 it looked as if China had embarked on a new tack. Most of the year was taken up with the continuing struggle between reforming members of the leadership and their hardline opponents. Since the end of the year, however, the reformers have launched a new offensive on both the political and economic fronts. It is too early to tell if the uneasy balance of power that has existed at the top for the past three years has shifted decisively in favour of the reformers, but there is no question that there is jostling for a commanding position from which to fight the inevitable succession battle.

On the international scene there were also changes of emphasis. China has moved beyond the reactive diplomacy into which it had retreated after the international uproar at the government's repressive actions at Tiananmen Square and has begun to take some initiatives in its approaches to the world community. While the collapse of the Soviet empire has weakened China's bargaining position towards the US, it has significantly improved its security environment and increased its leverage in dealing with both India and Vietnam. In effect, China has almost fully recovered from the damage caused to its international standing by the Tiananmen massacre in June 1989, and by adjusting to a new post-Cold War world it is poised to improve that standing even further.

Politics and the Succession

China is governed by a gerontocracy: a group of senior leaders, now in their late eighties, with no formal positions of legal importance who exercise power via their proxies who do hold these positions. These relics have long held quite contradictory notions of the right directions in which China should move, and they continue to balance each other as they scrabble for the power of making the final decisions. They refuse to transfer any real authority to the younger leaders, perhaps because these lack popularity, global vision and sufficient strength of personality to lead the country out of its current uncertainties.

Since the summer of 1991, the 87-year-old Deng Xiaoping has been using Shanghai as a power base from which to challenge the conservative elders in Beijing. A number of editorials appeared in Shanghai's local newspapers sharply criticizing the political policies of the hardliners and calling for further reform and openness. The entrenched conservatives, led by 68-year-old Chen Yun, struck back by continuing a campaign against 'peaceful evolution', their codeword for bourgeois liberalism and capitalist encroachment. That the equilibrium of power was maintained through most of the year, however, was demonstrated by the Eighth Plenum of the Communist Party's Central Committee which, although postponed for two months until November 1991, was unable to make any advance on major economic or political issues. It is clear, however, that the leaders believe that some decisions, particularly on personnel, will have to be made soon if they are to take advantage of the Fourteenth Party Congress which is due at the end of 1992.

Chen Yun and his cohort were clearly disappointed by the failure of the August coup in Moscow. They had held high hopes for the success of the reactionary forces; after the coup they issued a number of internal documents censuring both Gorbachev and Yeltsin for 'undermining the socialist system' in the former Soviet Union. The Chinese government tightened its control over public affairs, imposing new restrictions on ideology and cultural affairs. It reorganized military and security forces and began to implement new personnel policies, especially at key government, party and military institutions.

The tensions within the governing bodies eroded their ability to maintain complete control. Central government was no longer capable of organizing effective mass political campaigns. The increased power struggle and its attendant political instability enabled bureaucrats at lower levels to avoid promoting the more conservative policies with which they might disagree. Nor can the government rely on corrupted party organizations or discredited official theology; neither command respect any longer. Even the security and military forces have become shaky; the conservatives cannot be relaxed if they must rely on them as their sole instruments for retaining power.

Despite the restructuring of the military leadership which has been carried out, efforts by the hardliners to strengthen their political control over the army has had no real success. Particularly since the end of the Gulf War, there has been increasingly stronger demand within the army for further defence modernization and military professionalism. All of the 103 military academies were still operating according to the principles defined before the July 1989 crackdown. More than 400 internally circulated military publications still focus on military technology, strategies and new development in foreign armies rather than on Party ideology. Promotions have been made on the basis of an officer's professional performance rather than his loyalty to ideology. It is doubtful that the military would support the highly unpopular and ineffective hardline leaders if they were called on to do so in a succession crisis. They are more likely to back future reformers, particularly if these have succeeded in mobilizing popular support.

Another indication of the decline in the authority of central government was the strengthening of power on the part of local government, especially at the provincial level. Central government controls only about 40% of the total state budget. It is dependent for the remainder on the willingness of the provinces to forward funds collected there, and in the past few years the provinces have increasingly refused to agree to such a transfer. Given the wide regional gap in development, progress in reforming the economy and access to international markets, this trend will further weaken the centre's ability to project its power, especially in the rapidly expanding South China coastal areas and in other advanced economic development areas in inner China.

The political tensions and economic difficulties have heightened the antagonism that has developed between the state and the people, particularly among urban residents. The progress of economic reform from 1987 to 1989 created new interest groups, which pursue their own increasingly independent political and economic goals. In both rural and urban areas, there are protests against corruption, inflation and low wages.

The government also faced new, and fairly determined, defiance from ethnic minorities encouraged by the political developments in the former Soviet Union. There is still ethnic hostility in Tibet, where small-scale demonstrations continue to be mounted. In Xinjiang an ethnic resistance movement, under the leadership of an Islamic fundamentalist religious leader based in Turkey who is partially financed by some Muslim states of the Middle East, has reportedly expanded its organizational network and has begun to smuggle in weapons. The independence of the Turkic-speaking republics of the former USSR is bound to have an effect on the kindred populations of Xinjiang. In Inner Mongolia, activists of an independence movement, encouraged by the democratic transition under way in the Republic of Mongolia, have increased their demands for greater autonomy.

Deng Xiaoping seems to have recognized the urgency of a resumption of his reform programme to encourage greater participation by a disillusioned populace. Accompanied by a few top leaders, he spent January and February 1992 in Guangdong and Shanghai, key areas in the drive for modernization. During this trip he repeatedly called for further economic reform and openness, going so far as to encourage 'the use of capitalism' to support what he calls 'socialism with Chinese characteristics'. He pointedly criticized Gao Di, director of the Party newspaper *People's Daily*. His offensive finally was effective: on 24 February *People's Daily* published an editorial based on his speeches on reform and the need for an open-door policy.

An even more important indicator of the direction in which Chinese politics is moving came on 12 March, when the major newspapers reported the results of a Politburo meeting which had been held over the previous three days; all the key points covered were those championed by Deng and the reformers. While the internal political struggle is far from ended, it appears that Deng has managed once again to force the pace on economic reforms. If he can maintain the momentum he has built up (and if he survives until then), there will probably be personnel changes at the autumn Party Congress that will help assure that the succession will be moulded by the hands of the reformers.

Economic Growth and Reform

On the surface, and according to official figures, the economy performed well in 1991. GNP grew by 7%, industrial output increased by 13.6%, inflation was kept below 3.5% and the trade surplus totalled $8.2bn. Most of the growth, however, came from the non-state sector, light industry and export-oriented enterprises. The growth of the state sector was only 1.3%; although the government pumped in huge subsidies, capital investment, soft loans and foreign exchange, 70% of state-owned enterprises posted losses. For the first time since 1949 the state sector's total 'losses' exceeded its total 'profits'. Moreover, the drag on consumer spending and the disjunction between what pro-ducers produced and what consumers wanted created a 15% increase in inventory, which was a major cause of high company debts and low tax revenue. Central government continued to rely heavily on macro-economic instruments to control the economy without undertaking a well-coordinated overall reform programme. As a result, the pressure of inflation and fiscal deficit and debt remained high.

This was the basic reason why the central government decided to significantly revise, if not abandon, its newly created Eighth Five Year Plan, which had maintained a strong emphasis on macro-economic policies rather than institutional reform. In January 1992, Premier Li Peng pointed out that the central government's priority for the year was to reform the state sector. In February, both Shanghai and Guangdong announced their plans to expand local financial markets, develop a shareholder system in the state sector, and provide more favourable conditions for foreign investors.

While competition for capital, market shares and raw materials between the state sector (which in 1991 made up only about 40% of total industrial output) and the non-state sector sharpened, the tensions between a free market and a government-controlled market continued to rise. Although it has tried, the centre failed to recentralize decision-making and fiscal power. Holding 60% of the total government budget, local authorities became increasingly independent, pursuing their own reform programme, development strategy and open-door policy, regardless of the desires of central government. This development, while protecting the local economy from the centre's frequent attempts at intervention, strengthened the ability of the outlying regions (particularly those on the coast) to expand their business abroad. At the same time, however, it also increased China's internal trade barriers and monopolistic competition between the various provinces.

China's foreign economic relations continued to expand; in 1991 foreign trade rose 17.5% from the previous year. The imposition of new import controls and the rise in import taxes substantially reduced imports from OECD nations. Having sharply devalued its currency in 1990, the government employed a 'flexible floating' foreign exchange regime to depreciate the currency gradually. Central government, as well as local authorities, encouraged Hong Kong, Taiwanese and South Korean companies to relocate their labour-intensive manufacturing operations, which are mainly export-oriented, to the Chinese coast. The average labour cost in China was only one-eighth that of Taiwan, and one-sixth that of Hong Kong. As a result, Hong Kong remained China's top trade partner and investor, while Taiwanese investment increased sharply, notably in Fujian.

Since the G-7 Houston summit in June 1990, when Japan decided to end its sanctions against China, foreign investment has recovered its momentum. A number of European countries have followed the Japanese lead, resuming their economic aid and loans to Beijing. Both the World Bank and the Asian Development Bank have increased their lending to China, and private banks have also expanded their business there, particularly along the coast. China's foreign debt reached $54bn by the end of 1991; its total foreign exchange reserves, however, rose to $40bn.

China's trade relations with a number of OECD nations have become strained, however. Post-1992 Europe is likely to increase trade barriers, and Tokyo is now complaining of China's reduced import of Japanese goods. After a long and difficult negotiation, in which Washington took an unusually firm stand, the two sides reached an agreement in the middle of January 1992 over the protection of intellectual property. Further difficulties are in store, however. The Bush administration managed again to extend its MFN status to China, but opposition from Congress put pressure on Beijing to make more compromises in a new round of Sino-American trade talks which opened on 14 February 1992. Together with strengthened competition from South-east Asian nations, these trends may jeopardize China's position in the international market for labour intensive goods.

Adjusting to a New World

The collapse of the Soviet empire changed the international scene irrevocably and strongly affected China's foreign and security policies. On the one hand, the removal of the Soviet threat and the progress that has been made in East–West arms control and disarmament reduced China's strategic importance to the OECD nations. On the other hand, the West grew concerned about Beijing's arm sales and the transfer of nuclear technology to the Near East. In some senses, the death of the Soviet Union has meant that China has assumed new importance in international security; for example, with regard to the positions it is willing to take in the Security Council to support a revived UN.

The US and China were in sharp disagreement over many policy issues, including human rights, trade and weapons proliferation. On its foreign-policy agenda Beijing has given priority to bridge-building with Washington. Under US pressure, it released some political prisoners (while at the same time sentencing others for their part in the Tiananmen riots) and allowed some of their relatives to go to the US for family reunions. It signed the NPT, and promised to encourage North Korea to join the UN together with Seoul and to agree to accept IAEA inspection of its nuclear facilities.

In November, US Secretary of State Baker met Premier Li Peng in Beijing, where talks focused on trade, human rights and China's sale of weapons to the Middle East. In January 1992, at the special meeting of the UN Security Council, Li Peng met President Bush; immediately thereafter China announced its intention of adhering to the Missile Technology Control Regime. In turn, President Bush decided, despite strong Democratic Congressional opposition, to support China's MFN status and to lift sanctions on the sale of sensitive technology to

China. US–Chinese relations were moving to a new plane, but because of its weakened bargaining position, Beijing had to pay for this advance with actions it might not have endorsed happily, and to maintain good relations it will have to continue to do so.

Although the collapse of the USSR diminished Moscow's direct military threat to China's security, and the progress made in Russian–US arms control improved the military balance between China and Russia, it created a new set of foreign-policy and security problems. Beijing quickly approached Russia and the new Central Asian states to ensure the effectiveness of previous Beijing–Moscow agreements on their border disputes and the reduction of troops along the border. It also immediately established diplomatic relations with all the new states of the former Soviet Union in order to counter Taiwan's 'flexible diplomacy'. When Latvia established consulate-general relations with Taipei, Beijing decided not to open its own embassy in Riga, but it did not cut off diplomatic ties; and it was willing to accept the reality that many of the new states have established official commercial relations with Taiwan. Beijing was also deeply concerned about the influence of Central Asian states on China's ethnic groups, and as a result it has increased its military forces in Xinjiang and Inner Mongolia.

The changing nature of international politics provided the backdrop for a shift in Beijing's foreign-policy priorities from its concentration on, and support for, the Third World to its Asian neighbours and OECD nations. The loss of their Soviet patron had significantly improved China's leverage in dealing with Vietnam (see pp. 145–6) and India (see p. 165), and China followed up by consolidating its ties with Iran and Pakistan, including further developing its military cooperation with them. China re-established diplomatic relations with Israel, thus allowing it an opportunity to participate in the Middle East peace process.

It also became increasingly active and flexible in many international organizations; at the UN it supported the US-led actions to press Iraq to destroy all of its non-conventional weapons systems. Although its application to join GATT was delayed, Beijing managed to lobby OECD to delay Taipei's application as well. In September, it agreed that the three Chinas (China, Hong Kong and Taipei, under the title of 'China, Taipei') could take up full membership in APEC.

China remained a major player in the political and security affairs of the Asian–Pacific region. It pursued with some vigour its key objectives on the Korean peninsula: to maintain stability, to reduce tensions and hostility between the North and the South, and to preserve its relations with Pyongyang while expanding its ties with Seoul. It remains to be seen whether China will be able to reconcile these objectives as North Korea moves closer to a nuclear capability. It continued to place emphasis on its special ties with Tokyo. There was a flurry of top-level official visits between the two countries; during a trip to Tokyo in July, Foreign Minister Qian Qichen even extended an invitation to the Emperor to visit China. Beijing continued to play down the sensitive and troublesome issues that have long divided the two countries: there was little mention of Tokyo's treatment of the history of the Sino-Japanese war, of the pace of Tokyo's rearmament, or of Japan's role in Asian security.

Beijing was very active in wooing ASEAN states. During the year, PRC President Yang Shangkun, Li Peng and Qian Qichen visited almost all the ASEAN states, and China's economic relations with them expanded rapidly. Nonetheless, disputes between China, the ASEAN states and Vietnam over the sovereignty of islands in the South China Sea were still very much in evidence. Vietnam and some ASEAN states, pointedly excluding China, have signed agreements for the joint exploitation of off-shore resources in the South China Sea, while Beijing, proposing that the sovereignty issue be set aside, suggested 'joint exploration of natural resources' with these countries. At the same time, however, it has strengthened its Air Force and Navy in the region and has expanded its own cooperation with multinational oil corporations in ventures there. China has also put emphasis on the development of air-refuelling technology, and announced that it is considering the construction of a medium-sized aircraft carrier. In February 1992, China formally reaffirmed its claim to both the Spratlys in the South China Sea, and the Senkakku islands to the south-west of Okinawa.

In essence, China has managed to recover from the short period of international isolation that followed the Tiananmen Square massacre. It has stabilized its ties with most of its neighbours, while expanding its relations with OECD nations. As the Central Military Commission concluded in its annual review of China's security environment, for the first time since 1949 China does not face a major direct threat to its national security. The international scene is fast shifting, however, and Beijing will have to remain flexible and deft to assure stable foreign relations while tending to its internal difficulties. As the political succession at home draws nearer, the leadership power struggle is certain to intensify. To ensure further expansion of economic ties with market economies abroad, China will need a well-coordinated economic reform programme, which would do best if it focused on a growth in private ownership, a new price structure and a solid financial system. The country may no longer be in immediate crisis, but the underlying causes of the previous one remain to be overcome. Domestic and international challenges still loom larger than easy opportunities.

JAPAN: STILL SEARCHING

Japan entered 1992 in the same mood of agonizing self-appraisal in which it had started the previous year. All that seemed certain was that the Japanese were still uncertain about whether they should be playing an enhanced international role, and if so, what that role should be. The debate had moved forward, particularly with the commitment of Japanese mine-sweepers to duty in the Gulf after the war there had ended, but domestic political complications, the subsequent inconclusive debate over peace-keeping forces, and mixed international reactions stalled further significant legislation.

Despite a public opinion rating which made him one of the most popular of post-war Japanese prime ministers, Toshiki Kaifu was forced by intra-party manoeuvring to retire. The intellectual internationalist, Kiichi Miyazawa, who was chosen as his successor, found his own political honeymoon short-lived. Indeed, a number of apparently self-inflicted setbacks in his early months in power cast considerable doubt on the notion that he would prove a more dynamic and effective prime minister than his predecessor. Even the economy, a sustaining force during all the political turmoil of 1989–90, began to falter, and a succession of new scandals tarnished Japan's image. The Japanese found their self-confidence dented.

Back to 'Normal' Politics

In early October 1991, Toshiki Kaifu, whose term of office was due to expire later in the month, gave up any chance of remaining prime minister by announcing that he would not stand for re-election as president of the Liberal Democratic Party. Although he had just failed to push his proposals for electoral reform through the *Diet*, Kaifu's political demise was not the result of a loss of popular or even parliamentary influence. Rather, he lost the support of key LDP faction leaders, who then haggled behind the scenes to install either themselves or one of their protégés as leader. This reversion to the traditional pattern of leadership reshuffling confirmed that, after more than two years of turmoil, Japanese politics were back to 'normality'.

Initially chosen for, and subsequently sustained by, his image as 'Mr Clean', Kaifu proved unable to alter the fundamentals of the Japanese political system. Plucked from obscurity in 1989, at a time when the LDP was reeling under a succession of political and financial scandals, Kaifu had made a brave try, but he never had the political power base necessary to push through his ideas. His main programme, a package of political reforms which would have introduced single-member constituencies and made political fund-raising more transparent, was criticized by the opposition parties and, more seriously, was sabotaged by some members of his own LDP, who feared losing their lucrative seats. He was also vulnerable because of his reputation for indecision in responding to major international emergencies such as the Gulf crisis and the August 1991 Soviet coup attempt. As a member of the smallest of the LDP factions, Kaifu had always been forced to rely on the support of bigger and more powerful ones; his fate was sealed when his main backer, the faction committed to former prime minister Noboru Takeshita, decided to drop him.

The election to succeed Kaifu was fought out between three older politicians, excluded from consideration in 1989 because of their own involvement in the Recruit scandals. Kiichi Miyazawa, a good English speaker with lengthy ministerial experience at senior level, was the oldest, and he clearly saw this election as his last chance to become prime minister. His main rival was Michio Watanabe, a more colourful and outspoken character, who has an even more solid record in party positions. A third faction leader, Hiroshi Mitsuzuka, was a relative newcomer to this top league and faced strong opposition within his own faction when he moved to assume the mantle of his predecessor, Shintaro Abe, who had died in May; a small group did, indeed, later break away to form a new faction. The largest LDP faction, under the joint, though often rival, tutelage of Takeshita and Shin Kanemaru, vacillated, but finally tipped the balance by deciding to support Miyazawa. The two rising stars of the Takeshita faction had excluded themselves: Ichiro Ozawa, because of his mismanagement of the LDP's candidature in the Tokyo gubernatorial election in April and his subsequent ill-health, and Ryutaro Hashimoto, because of the succession of financial scandals for which, as Finance Minister, he had had to take responsibility. In the future, as Shin Kanemaru, the most powerful, but elderly, member of the faction, weakens both physically and politically, the rivalry between Ozawa and Hashimoto could well split the Takeshita faction.

Miyazawa won by a comfortable margin. Watanabe, however, made a better showing in second place than had been expected (partly because some Takeshita faction members voted for him in order to deflate Miyazawa), and against Miyazawa's wishes he was rewarded with the post of Deputy Prime Minister and Foreign Minister. Nonetheless, the Takeshita faction was the main winner, taking six important posts in the new cabinet. Miyazawa's cabinet and party appointments also marked the political comeback of several other politicians involved in past political and financial scandals. Miyazawa himself has not only come under increasing pressure to disclose fully the details of his own involvement in the Recruit scandal, but was embarrassed by the arrest in mid-January 1992 of one of his close factional aides, Fumio Abe, on bribery charges. A more serious scandal, revolving around the payment of billions of yen to hundreds of parliamentarians by the Sagata Corporation (a haulage company also involved with Japan's gangster gangs), is brewing. The first result has been the loss of a safe seat by the LDP in a February by-election.

Beyond the scandals, Miyazawa has been a disappointment to those who anticipated greater leadership than Kaifu was able to display. In particular, he has proved inexperienced in the behind-the-scenes manoeuvring and deal-making which are the essence of the Japanese political system. The LDP, handicapped by its first loss of an overall majority in the Upper House as a result of the 1989 election, had carefully constructed a working relationship with two of the smaller opposition parties, the *Komeito* and the Democratic Socialist Party, to assure passage of its legislation in the Upper House. This marriage of convenience, however, broke up in December 1991 as the tactics used by Miyazawa and the LDP to support yet another bill for participation in UN peace-keeping operations (an earlier one was aborted during the Gulf crisis) managed to upset both parties. The idea of a new 'international contribution tax', hurriedly concocted as a substitute and just as quickly dropped, was yet another example of the Miyazawa administration's ineptitude.

Ironically, Miyazawa's failure to hold together the relationship with the *Komeito* and the DSP has completed the reversion to another feature of pre-1989 Japanese politics, a disparate and divided opposition. The Gulf crisis and war proved traumatic for the opposition. Its largest member, the Social Democratic Party of Japan (formerly the Japan Socialist Party, which chose a new English name in January 1991 but kept the same Japanese one), abruptly and dramatically lost the popularity it had gained in 1989. The SDPJ's dithering on the deployment of the Self-Defense Forces overseas (it was critical of such action but could not offer a realistic alternative) exasperated even those Japanese who doubted the desirability of breaking long-standing constraints on the use of the SDF. The incompetence of the leadership helped to ensure a humiliating performance in the Tokyo gubernatorial and local elections, and in June 1991, Takako Doi, the heroine of 1989, was forced to resign as party leader. The run-up to the Upper House elections due to be held in mid-1992 will see the usual inter- and intra-party manoeuvring to form temporary coalitions, but a major political regrouping remains more a speculative than an immediate prospect.

Seeking a Role

The Kaifu government had responded to the outbreak of the Gulf War with a substantially increased financial contribution, but its efforts to contribute personnel in a number of different forms had been stymied by parliamentary opposition (see *Strategic Survey 1990–1991*, pp. 192–4). At the end of the Gulf War the Japanese government was left frustrated by its failure to participate in any way other than financially. Public opinion polls, in contrast to those in the early days of the Gulf crisis, had begun to indicate majority support for the use of the SDF overseas. In April 1991, emboldened by this shift and by the expression of support for a peacetime SDF role overseas from the leader of the influential business organization, the *Keidanren*, the government decided to send Maritime SDF mine-sweepers to the Gulf.

This was the first deployment of the SDF overseas since its establishment in 1954. During the Iran–Iraq tanker war in 1987 then prime minister Yasuhiro Nakasone had seriously considered similar action, but had abandoned the idea because of strong opposition. The dispatch of forces in 1991, therefore, was a radical departure. The government justified the action under Article 99 of the Self-Defense Forces Law, which assigns the task of clearing mines from the sea to the Maritime SDF. In addition, it argued, the mine-sweepers would be operating for the 'peaceful and humanitarian purpose' of securing the safe passage of ships. The opposition parties, with the exception of the DSP, opposed this action, but public opinion, while divided over its constitutionality, nevertheless broadly supported this modest and belated attempt to contribute to the international effort in the Middle East. Views amongst Japan's Asian neighbours were mixed. The Koreans and Chinese expressed reservations, but many ASEAN nations, appreciating Kaifu's explanations during his visit to the region in late April and early May, were cautiously positive. The mine-sweepers in fact docked in three ASEAN ports on their way to and from the Gulf, where they spent three months on duty.

The deployment was only possible because the SDF missions did not include any combat-related activities in which the 'threat or use of force', banned under the Japanese constitution, might arise. The sensitivities about the possible use of force were exposed in the summer and autumn of 1991 during the renewed debates about SDF participation in UN peace-keeping operations. The progress that had been made in the Cambodian settlement raised the prospect of the establishment of a UN peace-keeping force in which Japan might be expected to participate.

Accordingly, in mid-September, the Kaifu administration proposed a bill which would allow up to 2,000 SDF members at any one time to participate in UN peace-keeping efforts. They would be allowed to carry small firearms for self-protection only, but would be forbidden to use them against those forcefully resisting UN peace-keeping operations. Any breakdown in the cease-fire would lead to a withdrawal of the SDF from the UN mission in the area. The 1991 bill differed from its 1990 predecessor in two respects: participation was limited to UN peace-keeping operations (so that the SDF could not join forces such as that put together by the anti-Iraqi coalition in the Gulf War); and the scope of the SDF's activities were widened from merely surveillance of cease-fires to all UN non-military peace-keeping activities. A parallel bill allowed for the dispatch of SDF members to assist in disaster relief operations overseas.

In drafting the new legislation the LDP had worked closely with the *Komeito*, but not as closely with the DSP, which has traditionally been the party most enthusiastic about an enhanced SDF role. Feeling slighted, the DSP argued for a provision in the legislation which would require *Diet* approval of each SDF deployment, something which the *Komeito* considered superfluous. LDP prevarication and eventual desperate railroading of the bill through the Lower House in December

1991 alienated both parties and precluded an early submission of the bill to the Upper House. Indeed, it might well have to wait until the *Diet's* deliberations on the budget, which often stretch into April, have finished. Such a delay would be tantamount to killing the legislation yet again.

Although the *Diet* discussions on the UN peace-keeping cooperation bill were couched in legal and technical terms, the debate was really about a more fundamental issue: whether the Japanese could be trusted, or, indeed, trusted themselves, to participate in overseas military operations without becoming a militaristic power again. Apart from the fate of the peace-keeping legislation, regional neighbours and outside observers saw two other elements as crucial to answering this question. First was Japan's attitude to its past wartime actions, which was of particular political significance in the year that ended with the fiftieth anniversary of the attack on Pearl Harbor. Second was the manner in which Japan adjusted its defence programme and philosophy to the post-Cold War world.

In its efforts to cope with Japan's past, the government managed to take a step backward almost every time it moved one step forward. First, Prime Minister Kaifu, during his tour of South-east Asian countries in the spring, and then Emperor Akihito, in a visit to the same region in October (which was not only his first trip overseas since becoming emperor, but also the first by a Japanese emperor to that region), expressed their 'remorse' for Japanese actions there during the war. These gestures were appreciated by the ASEAN countries.

The goodwill this engendered soon dissipated. Feelings became heated in the run-up to the anniversary of Pearl Harbor. A deputy cabinet official argued that it was too early to decide who had been responsible for the war, and a senior LDP politician, notorious for his anti-American writings, argued for reviving the wartime Greater East Asia Co-prosperity Sphere. The *Diet*, after intense wrangling, balked at issuing a formal apology for the attack on Pearl Harbor, so it was left to Foreign Minister Watanabe to condemn the Japanese military's 'reckless attack' and to express 'deep remorse' for the sufferings caused by the Pacific War. Yet, the net result showed at least some symmetry, for President Bush, in his speech at Pearl Harbor (the Japanese were not invited to the anniversary commemoration) apologized for the internment of Japanese-Americans during World War II. He made no reference, however, to the dropping of the atomic bombs at the end of the war, a gesture the Japanese felt would have been appropriate. The Japanese took another conciliatory step on the eve of Miyazawa's visit to South Korea in January 1992 by apologizing for the Japanese Army's enforced prostitution of Korean women during World War II, though the idea of financial compensation demanded by some of the victims, and endorsed by the South Korean government, was rejected.

The rapid changes in the international security scene also presented the Japanese government with a difficult dilemma. The new

1991–5 Mid Term Defense Program had been built on the continued qualitative extension of Soviet military capabilities in the Far East (a point stressed in the 1991 Defense White Paper). Just as the Program had begun, the Soviet Union disintegrated. Caught between demands from the United States for greater burden-sharing, both financially and operationally, and efforts by the Finance Ministry, who were anticipating a large revenue shortfall, to slash the defence budget (an endeavour supported by the SDPJ, which called for zero growth), the Defense Agency and the Foreign Ministry were forced onto the defensive. They therefore supported their arguments for a continued defence build-up by citing the dangers of regional instabilities. On taking office, however, Miyazawa made it clear that he preferred to emphasize social welfare expenditure rather than a sustained military build-up.

The draft 1992–3 budget allotted only ¥ 4.5 trillion ($36.4bn) to the Defense Agency; although high by comparison with the budget-slashing in Europe and North America, this was a 3.8% increase, the lowest for 32 years, and accounted for only 0.94% of the estimated GNP, the lowest ratio in nine years. Faced with the popular desire for a greater 'peace dividend', the Defense Agency will have to work hard at mending political fences to avoid deeper cuts in future years. Miyazawa has already instructed the relevant ministries and agencies to begin a review of the five-year defence procurement programme, well ahead of its intended 1993 date. Although few senior government officials wished to accept it, any such review would further stimulate reconsideration of the rationale of the crucial US–Japanese security relationship.

Global partner . . .

In fact, both pillars of the US–Japan relationship – economic interdependence and security cooperation – came under strain during the year. President Bush's brief collapse at a state banquet during his January 1992 visit to Tokyo was more symbolic of the state of a relationship suffering from a mild, though not yet lethal, sickness, than was the rhetoric accompanying the 'Tokyo Declaration' made during that same visit. Many Americans felt that the Bush administration's two-tier approach, based on the Structural Impediments Initiative talks and the 'global partnership' concept, was faltering. Amongst the Japanese, the litany of US complaints over rice, cars and trade in general, provoked more condescension and less concession than had been the case earlier.

Japan's prevarication during the Gulf crisis heightened Washington's demands that Japan should shoulder greater responsibilities for maintaining international peace and stability. This, in turn, provoked disappointment and anger amongst the Japanese, who felt that their considerable financial support for the US had not been appreciated. Wrangling over America's requests for the Japanese to make up the exchange-rate losses on their financial contributions to the US effort in the Gulf, and over increasing the Japanese financial share of the costs of US forces in Japan to 70% by 1995 typified the more suspicious approach on both sides. (Japan eventually agreed to both demands.) What was needed was not fine tuning, but a fundamental adjustment of the US–Japanese security framework. The Americans were more willing to admit this than the Japanese; it was US Defense Secretary Dick Cheney who took the initiative in April 1991 to open discussions on changing the scope of the existing arrangements so as to enhance their cooperative ability to guarantee stability in the entire Asia–Pacific region.

President Bush did not follow this through effectively. He not only postponed his planned visit to Japan because of domestic criticism of his economic policy, but he also changed the focus, from pursuing partnership in non-economic areas to a thinly disguised trade mission. Although two follow-up meetings during the year dealt with the implementation of the 1990 SII agreements, the slowing down of the Japanese economy and the failure of the US economy to emerge from recession only exacerbated commercial frictions. Japan recorded its worst growth rate in five years (3%); a succession of banking and securities scandals dented, but did not destroy, the financial system; and import and overseas investment growth peaked and exports rose again. The trade surplus with the US went up for the first time for five years, to $41bn. Despite the fanfare that his trip to Japan would result in 'jobs, jobs, jobs', President Bush went home with an economic 'action plan' which was naïve in its expectations and unlikely to produce a quick turnaround in the economic relationship. In addition, the US–Japanese relationship was badly shaken by the new Japanese contempt engendered as a result of the visit.

. . . Or Regional Friend?

The Japanese government continued to argue that a sound US–Japanese security alliance was an important prerequisite for its dialogue with the Soviet Union. A significant opportunity to warm up that chilly dialogue came in April 1991 with the first ever visit to Japan by a Soviet head of state. President Mikhail Gorbachev came, saw, but certainly did not conquer. A much vaunted 'land for yen' deal did not materialize. Gorbachev failed both to elicit substantial economic assistance from the Japanese government, or to convince the Japanese business community that, despite the increasingly chaotic state of the Soviet economy, there were real commercial opportunities to be had in the USSR. For his part, Kaifu failed to persuade the Soviet leader to revert back even to the 1956 Soviet–Japanese Declaration on the disputed four 'Northern Territories', and had to settle for an admission that 'territorial demarcation' was one of the problems to be settled in the peace treaty negotiations.

Disappointing though the summit may have been, both sides were beginning to show greater flexibility. The Japanese government gradually developed a new approach of 'expanded equilibrium', which would allow an improvement in some aspects of the relationship, provided that there were positive changes inside the Soviet Union/ Russia. The Japanese announcement in October 1991 of a $2.5-bn loan/export credit package to the USSR was a sign of this loosening up. The Russian Republic, under President Boris Yeltsin, appeared more positive too, and, after the abortive coup in August 1991, Russian officials called for 'accelerated' negotiations with Japan over the disputed territories. Yet the very decentralization of Soviet/Russian power complicated the issue, for the local Sakhalin administration, in turn, made clear its opposition to a territorial reversion.

For the Japanese, the territorial question remains the key issue in their relationship with Russia. Just as a year before, when expectations had been built up prior to the Gorbachev visit, so too in 1992 the Japanese are looking for a political decision from Yeltsin on his planned visit. Once again, domestic determinants will decide whether Yeltsin can, or for economic reasons needs to, offer more than his predecessor.

While Japan stayed one step behind its G-7 partners on relations with the Soviet Union (it displayed the same caution during the attempted Soviet coup), it continued to be more forward in its relations with China. In August 1991 Kaifu became the first prime minister from the industrialized countries to visit China since the Tiananmen Square massacre. Although successive Japanese visitors pushed harder than before on issues of human rights and arms exports, including, most bluntly, Foreign Minister Watanabe in January 1992, the Japanese found it difficult in the Chinese case to put into effect the new policy, announced in April 1991, of adding political criteria to overseas aid allocation. In sum, however, the Japanese considered that the bilateral relationship was back on a normal footing.

Japan was still attempting to begin a normal relationship with North Korea. Five rounds of negotiations were held during 1991, in which North Korea's claims for compensation and its reluctance to open its nuclear facilities to international inspection were the main sticking points (see pp. 138–40). The Japanese had succeeded in slowing the negotiations down to their own pace, and have been rewarded with increasing signs of North Korean flexibility. If a solution to the nuclear conundrum can be found, it is likely that formal diplomatic relations will be established in 1992. Conversely, a nuclear-armed Korea would pose a major new security challenge for Japan.

All these dialogues were in tune with Japan's step-by-step approach to security in the Asia–Pacific region. This approach gives priority to bilateral forms of political cooperation which would lead on to sub-regional forms, and the Japanese government did gradually show greater interest in broader regional dialogues. In July 1991, Foreign Minister Taro Nakayama proposed using the annual ASEAN

Post Ministerial Conference (which from 1991 had featured six dialogue partners of ASEAN) as a means of enhancing political and security dialogue. Reactions were cautious, but, at the least, Japan had advanced a proposal which would have been unthinkable even a year earlier.

From the Japanese viewpoint, whether in the embryonic political or the more advanced economic dialogues, the inclusion of the United States was crucial. In the economic field this accounted for Japan's endorsement of the APEC process, but also for its negative attitude to a Malaysian initiative which, even in its watered-down form of the East Asian Economic Caucus, specifically excluded the US. The Malaysian idea had actually been posited on Japan taking a leadership role in the region. Japan is not yet ready to seize that poisoned chalice.

Despite its success in building into the July 1991 Japan–EC Declaration and the January 1992 Japan–US Declaration elements of political cooperation over their partners' preference for economic commitments, Japan still looks unready to play a major role globally. With few signs of significant political reform in the offing, the continuing immobilism leaves little room for generating leadership. Indeed, Japan's search for a 'respectable place' in the world community has only just begun.

THE TWO KOREAS: COOPERATION OR CRISIS?

The Korean Peninsula has often seemed stuck in a time-warp. During 1991, however, there were significant moves towards untying what South Korean President Roh Tae-woo called the 'last knot of the Cold War'. Despite the tensions that rose as the threat of North Korea's nuclear-weapons development programme loomed large, a series of dramatic agreements between the North and South were reached which, for the first time, opened up the prospect of a top-level summit and real exchanges developing across the border.

Domestic developments on the other hand, were not as encouraging. South Korea suffered from the effects of politicians' manoeuvring to secure the succession to President Roh, and from a faltering economy, epitomized by a trade balance which was badly in the red. Once again, however, Roh was able to find compensation in diplomatic successes: visits by both the Soviet and US presidents, entry into the UN (simultaneously with the North), and, most significantly of all, the apparent breakthrough in relations with the North.

The North, too, had cause for concern, with the parlous state of its economy and its own succession process. Aging President Kim Il-sung began the formal process of handover to his son, but he showed no interest in loosening his grip on real power. The concessions he made to external powers were ones which he felt would not undermine the stability of his dynasty; indeed, they were intended to enhance its survivability. Economically strapped and politically isolated, Kim needed assistance from outside, but found himself threatened by the South Koreans, the Americans and the Russians, coaxed by the Chinese and alternatively tempted and pressured by the Japanese. He tried to sell the nuclear card dearly – and did achieve a withdrawal of US nuclear weapons from South Korean soil – but was forced to realize that the price of diplomatic relations with the Western countries best placed to aid him economically would have to be the opening up of his nuclear facilities to intrusive international inspection. It is as yet uncertain whether this will be effectively conceded or whether North Korea has been playing for time.

South Korean Politics: More of the Same

The learning process of democracy continued to prove a difficult one. Politicians both within the ruling Democratic Liberal Party (DLP) and amongst the opposition spent most of the year positioning themselves for the crucial National Assembly elections in March 1992 and the presidential elections due at the end of that year. At times, the DLP came close to splitting apart, while the opposition, after achieving a measure of unity, found its ground contested by new parties.

A succession of corruption scandals, the pervasive factional feuding within the DLP, and the inability of the opposition to cooperate disillusioned the public. The first local elections for three decades, for small and medium-sized cities, were held in March 1991 and were marked by the lowest voter turn-out (only 55%) in South Korea's history. Although the parties were not legally able to endorse candidates, affiliations were quite clear and the DLP drew some satisfaction from winning around 50% of the seats. However, this was a vote for stability rather than for the party itself, which continued to hover around the 20% level in public opinion polls.

Radical students and workers were frustrated by the apathy which prevented popular complaints against government corruption and economic mismanagement from translating into systemic change. In an effort to awaken the conscience of the country, a number of students resorted to self-immolation during the spring, but neither these horrific acts, nor the beating to death of a student demonstrator by the police, were sufficient to evoke the middle-class support which had been so crucial in 1987. Indeed, after Chung Won-shik, who replaced Roh Jai-bong as prime minister at the end of May 1991, was pelted with eggs during a visit to Hankuk University, public sympathy actually began to swing away from the students. As a result, in late June, in the second round of local elections for the larger cities the DLP took 65% of the seats and the opposition parties did badly.

All the parties recognized that there were grave problems in the election system, and leading DLP and opposition politicians held well-advertised discussions about ways to clean up politics, reduce regionalist influences and restore public faith in politicians. There were no actions to match the impassioned rhetoric, however. Party politics remained stuck in the familiar mire. With the older politicians insisting on yet another try for the top position, there was not even hope of a generational change to enliven the stale agenda.

Kim Young-sam, the executive chairman of the DLP, tried without success to push Roh into endorsing him early as the DLP's presidential candidate. Strong counter-pressure from other factions within the DLP, especially from that led by Kim Jong-pil and the group tied to former president Chun Doo-hwan (who had returned from exile), and Roh's own desire not to turn himself into a lame duck, led to continual hedging on this issue. A disappointed Kim was finally forced to agree that the candidate should be chosen at a party convention in May 1992. However, Roh and Kim Young-sam did come to an arrangement whereby Roh would handle economic and inter-Korean affairs, while Kim would take charge of party matters in the run-up to the National Assembly elections. Kim's political future, therefore, may well be tied closely to the results of those parliamentary elections. So too is the DLP's future, for Kim has threatened to leave the party if he fails to gain the nomination.

Kim Young-sam's old rival, Kim Dae-jung, also showed his determination to take another shot at the presidency. Initially, he changed the name of his party to the New Democratic Party, but after humiliation in the June local elections he agreed to merge with the smaller Democratic Party and adopt its name. The old DP's leader, Lee Ki-taek, was named joint leader with Kim Dae-jung, but Kim's insistence on taking the higher profile has not helped this particular marriage of convenience.

Towards the end of 1991 two new parties emerged and threatened once again to divide the opposition. Kim Dong-gil, a university professor, inaugurated the new, 'clean', Saehan Party. More significantly, Chung Ju-yung, the powerful founder of the Hyundai conglomerate, fell out with the Roh administration, which presented him with a massive tax bill for illegal stock deals, and began recruiting former politicians to his newly-established Unification National Party. Chung poured millions of won into the UNP, and it merged with the Saehan Party in early February 1992. In the 24 March 1992 National Assembly elections, the people sent a clear message of frustration with the old crop of politicians. The DLP lost its majority in parliament, the opposition Democratic Party did well, and the new UNP won a surprising 31 seats. Although the immediate victim is likely to be Kim Young-sam, in the longer run the election's importance may be the evidence it provided that a more pluralist democracy is emerging in South Korea.

Roh had earlier postponed a further round of local elections (for mayors and provincial governors), due in 1992, ostensibly because of the financial costs involved. Even so, with the presidential election scheduled for 1992, plenty of money will be flowing into electioneering rather than into more productive areas. This will not help the economy recover from its comparative slump. While GNP growth continued at an enviable level (7%, compared with 9% in 1990), this masked a number of serious problems, which successive reshuffles of ministers with economic portfolios did little to alleviate. Because of the declining competitiveness of its export industries, Seoul's trade and current account balances deteriorated quite severely. Inflation rose to 10%, and the government, by pushing for wage rises at around half that of the spring 1992 wage round, is set on a collision course with workers. The economy, like South Korean society, is in a difficult transition, and on both counts the country's traditional resilience will be tested to the full.

Northern Dilemmas

The economic problems of the South pale into insignificance by comparison with those faced by the North. North Korea's economy has been plagued by shortages and production inefficiencies for some time, but during 1991 the situation deteriorated considerably. Official statistical data is, as always, fragmentary and unreliable, but outside experts calculate that in 1990, for the first time since the end of the Korean War, North Korean GNP actually declined (by 3.7%), and that there was negative growth again in 1991. A senior South Korean businessman who visited the North in January 1992 estimated that the operational rate of industrial facilities has dropped to around 50% because of shortages of energy and materials. A succession of grain production targets have not been met, and in 1991 the North was particularly keen to import rice from the South – although the South stopped these imports after the initial test shipment when the North failed to provide proper payment. Foreign trade has stagnated; imports are handicapped by the lack of hard currency and exports are rarely of sufficient quality to sell well in international markets.

North Korea has suffered from adjustments to its economic relationships with its two main backers, the former Soviet Union and China. As the Soviet Union/Russia insisted on hard-currency dealings from January 1991, imports from the former USSR in that year virtually disappeared to around 2% of the previous year's total; exports held up slightly better, but still fell to around one-third of the 1990 level. Kim Il-sung, therefore, had to rely more on the Chinese. Partly because of its own economic problems, however, and partly for political reasons, China reduced its subsidized exports to the North. For example, it stopped using 'friendship prices' for oil (one of the North's major imports) and began charging close to world prices.

Kim Il-sung made a lengthy visit to China in October 1991 to ask for more substantial economic assistance, but, apart from some food supplies, he went home disappointed. Instead, the Chinese leadership spent much time trying to explain to Kim that only by introducing certain controlled elements of capitalism, such as special economic zones (he was taken to Shenzhen), could he expect to revive his economy. The North did become involved in discussions sponsored by the UN Development Programme about developing an ambitious economic zone straddling the borders of North Korea, China and the Soviet Union, but there are significant infrastructural, labour and capital problems to be solved.

Although Kim was forced to begin to toy with elements of capitalist economics, the pace at which he moved was inhibited by his determination to exclude any 'contaminating' political influences. The North Koreans had found their hosting of the annual Inter-Parliamentary Union conference in May 1991 a mixed blessing, for they came under strong criticism from some of the European delegates for human rights abuses. This must have reinforced Kim's reluctance to open up his society, even though, despite rumours of unhappiness, there was no overt evidence of domestic unrest against his regime.

In December 1991, Kim Il-sung appointed his son Kim Jong-il as Supreme Commander of the Armed Forces, thus moving to consolidate his plans for the succession. This was the first time that the younger Kim had taken a military post, suggesting that Kim was attempting to overcome opposition to his son's succession which many believe exists in the senior ranks of the military. The possibility that the father might transfer power to his son during the spring of 1992, when Kim Il-sung celebrates his eightieth birthday and Kim Jong-il his fiftieth, has been strengthened by changes in propaganda adulation of the two: Kim the younger is now referred to as the nation's 'Great Leader' and 'father', and Kim the elder as 'grandfather'. Even if the transition is made formal, however, Kim Il-sung, as long as he remains robust in body and mind, will be the power in the land.

When Vice-Prime Minister Kim Yong-nam publicly argued in September 1991 that Marxism could not be 'applied to present day realities', he said nothing to imply that Kim Il-sung's own variant of Marxism-Leninism – the *Juche* philosophy – was unsuitable. Yet even Kim Il-sung has had to countenance some modifications to his much vaunted self-reliance. Economic imperatives have forced North Korea to look away from its traditional socialist allies towards new sources of economic assistance. Since the Americans have remained hostile and the Europeans preoccupied, he turned to Japan. Kim has dangled the carrot of political relations before Japan, but his attempts to extract 'compensation' – economic assistance – speedily and on a large scale, were frustrated. The Japanese set the agenda and the pace.

By the autumn of 1991, the North Koreans had begun to realize that Tokyo could not be hurried into establishing relations and giving aid and investment, and they switched their attention to South Korea and even to the US. There were a number of obstacles in the Japan–

North Korean negotiations, but the sticking point rapidly became the question of international inspection of North Korea's nuclear facilities. Although Japan, through its direct negotiations with the North, took a central position on this issue, it was not the only country concerned by the North Korean threat to nuclear non-proliferation.

The North Korean Bomb

Under Soviet pressure, North Korea had joined the NPT in 1985, but had failed to sign the linked nuclear safeguards agreement with the IAEA within the 18 months required under the NPT. By 1989 suspicions about the nuclear facilities that were being constructed at Yongbyon, 100km north of Pyongyang, began to surface. In addition to a small and old Soviet-built research reactor (regularly inspected by the IAEA), overhead intelligence has subsequently revealed: two Korean-built reactors; an older Soviet-built research facility (regularly inspected by the IAEA): a 30-MW reactor capable of producing irradiated fuel, which began operating in 1987, and a much larger reactor nearing completion. The latter reactor can produce enough weapons-grade plutonium for an estimated two to five bombs a year. A large reprocessing plant necessary for this task is also nearly finished. Since neither Yongbyon facility has any electric power-generating and transmission capacity, they cannot be for domestic energy supply purposes.

Although the advanced stage of development of the North Korean nuclear programme suggests that the decision to go this route was taken in the early 1980s at the latest, the relatively cheap alternative of nuclear weapons has probably become increasingly compelling. North Korean concerns about the rising costs of trying to match the more advanced South Korean conventional weapons capabilities, about cutbacks in Soviet arms supplies, and the failure of the Chinese to offer any real substitutes, can only have been reinforced by the disturbing parallels that could be drawn from the ease with which the technologically superior US-led forces defeated the Soviet-armed Iraqis in the Gulf War. The North Koreans have consistently denied that they have either the capability or the intention to produce nuclear weapons, but these denials have become more and more unbelievable. During the course of 1991, the international argument shifted from whether, to when, North Korea would produce its first bomb. As evidence from satellite intelligence and from a senior North Korean foreign ministry defector altered the time-span considerably from 1995 to 1993 or 1992, the question became how North Korea could be forced into abandoning this programme.

As the IAEA experience in Iraq shows, it is difficult for international inspections to detect secret nuclear weapon facilities – at present the Agency can only inspect those sites designated by the host country. The military option, such as an Israeli-style pre-emptive strike against the Yongbyon reactor, suggested by the South Korean

Defence Minister Lee Jong-koo in April 1991, was considered extremely risky because of the damage that would be sustained by South Korea in the inevitable retaliation. Instead, the South Korean and US governments decided to put together an informal international coalition to put pressure on the North. Japan, the US and other Western countries made it clear that no diplomatic relations – and attendant aid – would be possible unless Pyongyang submitted to IAEA inspections. The Russians suspended all technical assistance to North Korea, and even the Chinese, while warning the West against putting excessive pressure on the North, quietly encouraged Pyongyang to be more realistic about inspection.

In July 1991 the North initialled an inspection agreement with the IAEA, but refused to take the next step, planned for September, of signing it. It reverted to its former precondition, which had been dropped in July, of a removal of US nuclear forces from South Korean soil. Realizing the difficulty of securing direct negotiations with the United States to achieve such an objective, it called for the two Koreas to make the peninsula a nuclear-free zone, which would be guaranteed by external nuclear powers.

The US and South Korea then shifted to a more complex carrot-and-stick approach. President Bush's declaration in September about reducing the number of US tactical weapons around the world had clear implications for America's nuclear presence in South Korea. Even though US government officials persisted in their 'neither confirm nor deny' approach, the removal of the ground- and air-launched nuclear warheads (approximately 150) stored at Kunsan was quietly begun. On 8 November 1991, President Roh announced that South Korea would not 'manufacture, possess, store, deploy or use nuclear weapons'. On 18 December Roh was able to declare that there were no nuclear weapons on South Korean territory, and he suggested the simultaneous inspection of all facilities in the two Koreas, including American military bases in South Korea. At the same time, both South Korean and US officials made it clear that this would not mean the removal of the US nuclear umbrella from South Korea, nor a lessening of the US commitment to defend the South. Indeed, Secretary of Defense Cheney agreed with Defence Minister Lee in late November to postpone the second phase of US troop withdrawals, scheduled to begin in early 1993, until North Korea complied with international inspection requirements. A decision over whether to scale down the annual US–South Korean *Team Spirit* exercises was said to depend on North Korean actions (after the December North–South denuclearization agreement the 1992 exercises were cancelled), and the US agreed to supply the South with *Patriot* missiles, designed to cope with the North Korean *Scud* threat.

Although there was close consultation between the two allies, the South Korean government seems to have been nudging Washington along, and some US officials, including President Bush on his visit to

Seoul in January 1992, cautioned the South Koreans about pressuring the North. This new approach by South Korea – and the United States – aimed to undermine North Korea's arguments against opening up its facilities, leaving it no reason for not complying. In the process, of course, they actually helped North Korea to achieve one of its long-standing aims, the removal of US nuclear weapons from South Korea. Kim, therefore, had succeeded in using his only bargaining tool – the nuclear threat – with some effect, but he had failed to achieve diplomatic relations with Japan or the US. Once the US nuclear weapons were removed, he lost much of his leverage. As international diplomatic pressure mounted, and it became increasingly clear that the only way out of his diplomatic isolation was compliance with inspection demands, Kim turned to the South.

Following on from the prime-ministerial level agreement on general relations in mid-December 1991, the North and South on 31 December issued a joint Declaration on a Non-nuclear Korean Peninsula, in which both sides pledged the peaceful use of nuclear energy, no nuclear weapons and no nuclear reprocessing and uranium enrichment facilities. Subsequently, on 30 January 1992, North Korea signed the full-scope nuclear safeguards agreement with the IAEA and in March announced that it would be implemented in June. However, the past record of North Korean stubbornness and foot-dragging, and the inadequacy of existing IAEA inspection procedures, still leave doubts as to the timing and effectiveness of the implementation of both the North–South denuclearization accord and the IAEA nuclear safeguards agreement. Whether by these methods North Korea can be stopped from developing a nuclear weapon remains an open question whose answer may put US–South Korean relations to a severe test. If North Korea were to become a nuclear power, the repercussions would be grave for North-east Asian security and for the global non-proliferation regime.

North–South Reconciliation

As a result of its own economic difficulties, South Korea has begun to ask itself whether it wants to add the North's problems to its own. Ironically, since the initial euphoria engendered by the collapse of the Berlin Wall and the hope that this would lead to a similar dismantling of Korean barriers, the Koreans have seen the economic and social difficulties that the Germans have been suffering and this has induced new, more sober feelings about reunification.

After the North postponed a planned prime-ministerial meeting in February 1992 because of the *Team Spirit* exercises, the South concentrated on furthering its contacts with the Soviet Union and China. To the humiliation of the North, Mikhail Gorbachev became the first Soviet president to visit either Korea when he dropped into Cheju-do in April 1991. Gorbachev's main concern was to ensure that South

Korean economic assistance to the USSR was on track; this was later suspended as the Soviet Union disintegrated, but it is likely to be resumed with the successor Russian state.

South Korea's trade contacts with China developed strongly, but of more importance was the Chinese decision not to veto a South Korean application to join the UN. This triggered a change in North Korean policy in May 1991, after Chinese premier Li Peng's explanatory visit to Pyongyang. Determined not to allow the South to enter alone, the North agreed to simultaneous entry; the two states took their seats in September. The Chinese remained cautious about full relations with the South, but when the foreign ministers of the two countries did meet for the first time ever, a trade agreement was signed and the quasi-diplomatic status of their trade offices was enhanced.

Although lengthy North–South negotiations had produced a joint table-tennis team (which actually won the world championships in Tokyo in June), the intra-Korean dialogue moved painstakingly slowly until the North agreed in the autumn to restart the prime-ministerial meetings. Then discussions moved much faster than expected. The October meeting in Pyongyang produced a draft, which was fleshed out into an Agreement on Reconciliation and Non-aggression, signed on 13 December in Seoul. In this most significant breakthrough in North–South relations since the July 1972 North–South Declaration, the two Koreas guaranteed non-interference and non-aggression, proposed military confidence-building measures, and agreed to stimulate economic exchanges (trade, investment and transport links) and to facilitate the flow of mail and people.

Both sides had made concessions, but both could draw satisfaction from the terms. The South had accepted the North's non-aggression concept, but in the medium term could open up the North's society to the kinds of influences which would slowly undermine the power of the Kim dynasty. The North was, of course, wary about these broader humanitarian contacts (and balked at the South's suggestion of unrestricted exchanges of newspapers and television), but it had gained a way out of its international isolation and a more immediate infusion of economic inputs than was likely to come from either Japan or the US and the West. While the Japan–North Korean negotiating session in January 1992 was rancorous, and the US continued to link an upgrading of US–Korean relations to the implementation of nuclear inspection, the visit to the North by Kim Woo-choong, the president of the Daewoo conglomerate, was marked by a spate of proposals for promoting joint ventures and direct intra-Korean trade.

Implicitly, both sides found themselves in accord on two objectives. First, Kim Il-sung clearly wants to bolster the Kim dynasty by relieving the worst of the North's evident economic hardship. The South, for its part, wants to do enough to keep the North Korean economy alive, but not thriving, in order to ensure a controlled, steady

winding down of the North which is far preferable to a traumatic disintegration. Second, should an unprecedented summit meeting follow,
it would have domestic benefits for both presidents. Kim could use it
as a means of gaining the South's acquiescence in his succession plans.
The various signs of Northern flexibility during the year – entry to the
UN, North–South reconciliation and the nuclear inspection agreement – can only be seen as concessions made by Kim if they do not
fundamentally affect his position or that of his son. Roh, on the other
hand, could draw support for his party in the forthcoming National
Assembly and presidential elections and prolong his own influence
during the final year of his presidency by acting as the statesman who
stretched out his hand to the North. Almost all of this, however,
depends on clear and acceptable assurances that the North has given
up its ambitions to become a nuclear power. This still hangs in the
balance.

INDOCHINA: A FRAGILE PEACE

After almost 12 years of fighting and two years of what seemed to be
inconclusive talking, an agreement on a comprehensive political settlement of the Cambodian conflict was reached in Paris on 23 October
1991. The terms of the agreement were based on a framework document produced in August 1990 by the five permanent members (the
so-called Perm-5) of the United Nations Security Council. The UN plan
had been designed to overcome the seemingly intractable problem of
power-sharing among the warring Cambodian factions in the transitional period between the first stage of a political settlement and general elections to determine the future government of the country.

The essential central element of the peace plan was the establishment of a United Nations Transitional Authority in Cambodia which
would assume powers of administration in the transitional period,
including responsibility for verifying the withdrawal of foreign forces
and organizing free and fair elections in a neutral political environment. Those powers would be delegated to UNTAC by a Supreme
National Council, a body made up of representatives of all of
Cambodia's factions. As if to illustrate the difficulties in store, the
members of the Council, which was formed in September 1990, took
over a year of acrimonious wrangling before they could agree on its
procedures and role, as well as on the UN plan itself.

The first steps of political settlement, a formal cease-fire and the
return to Phnom Penh of expatriate members of the SNC, including its
chairman, Prince Norodom Sihanouk, were completed by the end of
1991, although not without disruptive incident. The United Nations
Advance Mission in Cambodia, with Australian and French military
contingents among others, was also deployed to the country.
Difficulties in organization and lack of money, however, prevented the

appearance of the full complement of UNTAC in Cambodia during the first quarter of 1992 and this delayed the proposed monitoring of demobilization of the warring factions. Under the terms of the Paris accord, the transitional period would end when an elected constituent assembly approved a constitution, transformed itself into a legislative assembly and then established a new government.

The Cambodian conflict had been detached from both Sino-Soviet and Soviet–American relations by the middle of 1989; the Paris accord probably marked its end as a problem of international politics. That it had continued beyond 1989 was due to antagonism among the Cambodian parties, sustained by a corresponding enmity between their principal Chinese and Vietnamese patrons, whose historical differences have long existed separate from major power relations. The deep engagement of competing Sino-Vietnamese interests retarded the process of settlement until the end of June 1991. The progress to peace was accelerated and brought to a successful conclusion only four months after a weakened and vulnerable Vietnam signalled its willingness to come to terms with China. The end of the Cambodian conflict followed the well-established pattern for conflict resolution in Indochina: the end of fighting is due more to a loss of political will than to outright military victory.

Breakthrough at Pattaya

The SNC had been set up in Jakarta in September 1990, but its members remained deadlocked over the detailed terms of the UN peace plan. A symptomatic contentious issue revolved around the basis of representation on the SNC. Agreement had originally been reached on an equal representation of six members each from the State of Cambodia on the one hand, and from the tripartite coalition National Government of Cambodia on the other. Although it was recognized that this agreement made the participation of the *Khmer Rouge* in the political settlement a legitimate one, it was accepted as the only way to prevent a continuing civil war. The agreement quickly broke down, however, because the sponsoring Perm-5 had recommended that Prince Sihanouk become a thirteenth member, and chairman, of the Council. The Phnom Penh government then made its acceptance of that recommendation conditional on the appointment of its Prime Minister, Hun Sen, as vice-chairman of an enlarged 14-member Council in order to sustain numerical parity and equal status between the two competing sides.

Meetings of the SNC in Paris in December 1990 and in Jakarta at the beginning of June 1991 failed to resolve the issue of representation; the strongest resistance to its revised composition came from the *Khmer Rouge*, which was insisting on a larger equalizing membership for itself. Substantive opposition to the UN plan itself was also raised in Paris. Hun Sen objected to any change in both the political and military *status quo* in Cambodia before general elections, thus refusing to dismantle the Phnom Penh administration and to demobilize its forces. Since March 1991 he had also insisted that the UN plan be amended to incorporate concrete measures to prevent the *Khmer Rouge* from returning to power.

Here he was pitted against Prince Sihanouk who would not accept any accord with the Phnom Penh government at the expense of the *Khmer Rouge*, which enjoyed China's patronage. Sihanouk's position reflected a recognition that a political settlement would not be possible without China's endorsement. He valued China's support in particular because, unlike Vietnam and Thailand, it had a natural interest in upholding Cambodia's territorial integrity.

An unexpected breakthrough occurred in late June when the members of the SNC reconvened in the Thai resort of Pattaya at Sihanouk's initiative. Given the sensitivity on the part of the military regime which had assumed power in Bangkok in February to shifting priorities in Beijing, the chosen location suggested Chinese approval of the meeting. Procedural differences were resolved when Hun Sen withdrew his demand to serve as vice-chairman. Prince Sihanouk then joined the Council as an ordinary member in place of one of his faction and was accorded the task of convening future sessions. Other major achievements were: an agreement making permanent an informal cease-fire concluded at the end of April; and an undertaking by all factions to stop receiving external military assistance. In addition, they decided to establish the headquarters of the SNC in Phnom Penh by the end of 1991.

The pace of *rapprochement* was sustained with another surprising development. In mid-July an informal meeting of the SNC, including representation from Phnom Penh, was held in Beijing with the conspicuous political blessing of the Chinese government. Indeed, a Chinese official attended the meeting as an observer. The four factions reaffirmed their acceptance of the UN framework agreement and announced that a single delegation, headed by Prince Sihanouk, would be sent to the annual session of the world body. This was followed by a meeting between the SNC, representatives of the Perm-5 and the French and Indonesian co-Chairmen of the Paris International Conference which reconfirmed the commitment of the participants to free and fair elections under UN auspices.

The Sino-Vietnamese Dimension

The delayed Seventh National Congress of Vietnam's Communist Party met in Hanoi at the same time as the SNC meeting in Pattaya. Although the documents endorsed by that Congress did not suggest any formal change in Vietnam's insistence on treating Cambodia as a client state, a position which China had never been willing to accept, changes in the composition of the Vietnamese Politburo were interpreted as a concession to China. This was especially true of the removal of Foreign Minister Nguyen Co Thach, who was regarded as an implacable Sinophobe, from his government and party posts.

Sino-Vietnamese dialogue was renewed in July when Defence Minister and second-ranking Politburo member, General Le Duc Anh, the commander of the forces which had invaded Cambodia, visited Beijing unannounced for private talks. In August Vietnam's Vice Foreign Minister returned to China for a fresh round of talks with his counterpart. Their meeting prepared the ground for another in Beijing between Vietnam's new Foreign Minister, Nguyen Manh Cam, and Qian Qichen of China; (it was the first such encounter since the Sino-Vietnamese border war in 1979). Normalization of relations was sealed in November, after the Paris accord, with a four-day visit to Beijing by Vietnam's new party leader, Do Muoi, and new Prime Minister, Vo Van Kiet, who were received by their Chinese counterparts, Jiang Zemin and Li Peng.

The key to the restoration of Sino-Vietnamese relations was primarily Vietnam's willingness to acknowledge that its invasion of Cambodia had turned into a grievous mistake. Isolated and increasingly vulnerable, Vietnam could no longer reconcile the imperative of economic reform with trying to preserve a special relationship with Cambodia in the face of American as well as Chinese objections. The US had made it clear in April 1991 that any normalization of relations with Vietnam depended on a Cambodian settlement and backed this up with a renewal of its trade and investment embargo against Vietnam in September. In the face of these actions, the restoration of the China connection gained even greater importance. Moreover, China and Vietnam were drawn together from a common pragmatic interest in upholding the socialist model of politics, especially after the abortive coup in the Soviet Union in August. The restoration of relations was a purely business-like undertaking with none of the effusive warmth of an earlier era. It reflected a grudging deference to China's priorities by Vietnam. This could be seen in Vietnam's suspension of direct flights to Taiwan only three days after their restoration in August.

The Road to Paris

The changing terms of Sino-Vietnamese relations were reflected in successive concessions by the Phnom Penh government which reinforced progress towards a Cambodian peace agreement. A further session of the SNC was held in Pattaya in late August, following additional talks between the Vice Foreign Ministers of China and Vietnam in Bangkok. All factions agreed to reduce their forces by 70% and to regroup the remainder, with their equipment, under UNTAC supervision. In addition, the Phnom Penh government withdrew its insistence that specific provision be made to prevent the *Khmer Rouge* from resuming power and that reference be made to *Khmer Rouge* 'genocide' when it was previously in power, in return for general undertakings on human rights. It also accepted the central decision-making role of Prince Sihanouk within the SNC.

Negotiations among the Cambodian parties were resumed in New York in late September when an SNC delegation attended the annual session of the UN General Assembly. All outstanding issues appeared to be resolved. Agreements were approved on demobilization of forces, elections through proportional representation on a provincial basis and acceptance of the ultimate authority of the representative of the UN Secretary-General in the transitional period whenever the SNC could not find a consensus. The nominal constitutional position of the Phnom Penh government remained unchallenged, but the SNC, under the chairmanship of Prince Sihanouk, had assumed the semblance of an interim government, notwithstanding remaining ambiguity over the precise relationship between the incumbent Phnom Penh administration, the SNC and UNTAC.

The series of agreements among the Cambodian parties between the end of June and the final settlement in October indicated the change that had taken place in the structure of the conflict. It had been signalled by the way in which Prince Sihanouk had been able to reach agreement with the Phnom Penh government with evident approval from China and grudging acquiescence from the *Khmer Rouge*. China no longer appeared to view an accord which did not provide directly for dismantling the Phnom Penh government in the transitional period as working against its interests.

China's concern about the role of Vietnam as a proxy of the Soviet Union had long vanished. A corresponding concern about Cambodia as a proxy of Vietnam had evidently also diminished as its government made concessions in the negotiations leading to the Paris accord. Indeed, less than a week before the conference convened, the Kampuchean People's Revolutionary Party, which had been established under Vietnamese aegis, held an extraordinary congress; its first since 1985 and significantly in the absence of delegates from any foreign communist parties, including Vietnam. It dropped its ideological identity by abandoning both its name and its Marxist-Leninist principles. The emergence of a renamed Cambodian People's Party which endorsed multiparty democracy could not have been congenial to China on ideological grounds. It was certainly acceptable in balance of power terms, however, because it was a deliberate attempt by Phnom Penh to distance itself from a Hanoi which no longer had the capability or will to act as a patron.

From Paris to Phnom Penh

The Paris accord was a notable diplomatic achievement which only became practical at the end of 1991. The conflict had involved sponsorship of contending domestic clients who between them represented the range of tensions that had existed in Cambodian politics since the end of the Pacific War. Although the UN plan was intended to bypass the power-sharing obstacle, its implementation required cooperation among factional rivals in observing rules which could be politically disastrous to some of them in the event of free and fair elections. The key to that cooperation was the translation of the SNC to Phnom Penh as a working institution.

Prince Sihanouk returned to Phnom Penh in mid-November, significantly on a direct flight from Beijing. He was greeted with popular acclaim, and Prime Minister Hun Sen declared that he would be regarded as head of state until elections in 1993. On 19 November Prince Sihanouk signed a treaty of cooperation with Hun Sen's government and then announced that his faction, led by his son Prince Ranariddh, would form a coalition with the Phnom Penh administration and that a bipartite government would be established before the end of the month. This initiative suggested that an attempt was being made to sidestep the SNC and the UN plan.

Soon after Sihanouk's return, one of the two *Khmer Rouge* representatives on the SNC and the movement's military commander, Son Sen, returned to Phnom Penh from Thailand to a hostile but restrained reception. Son Sann, leader of the non-communist Khmer People's National Liberation Front, followed, and the first meeting in Cambodia of the SNC was expected to be convened shortly thereafter. However, when the second *Khmer Rouge* representative and nominal leader, Khieu Samphan, returned to Phnom Penh on 27 November, he was met by a stage-managed demonstration which reportedly got out of hand and became violent. The demonstration was apparently intended to underpin the political *fait accompli* which Prince Sihanouk and Hun Sen had contrived at the expense of the other parties to the SNC. The *Khmer Rouge* residence was attacked while local police looked on, and its representatives were manhandled. Khieu Samphan came close to being lynched. Eventually, security forces restored order, rescuing the *Khmer Rouge* leaders and, after only eight hours in the Cambodian capital, Khieu Samphan and Son Sen were put on a flight to Bangkok.

The violence in Phnom Penh exposed the fragility of the Paris accord. There was an immediate attempt at political damage-limitation, especially by Sihanouk, who now expressly disavowed a coalition government outside the terms of the UN plan. He was almost certainly disturbed by the vehemence of the official Chinese response which insisted that the Phnom Penh government was responsible for the incident. It was stressed that the Cambodian issue could not possibly be settled, nor could peace and stability be maintained 'so long as one side of Cambodia is excluded in the settlement'. With the peace process in danger of breaking down, the SNC convened an emergency one-day meeting in Pattaya on 3 December, at which terms were agreed for protecting the *Khmer Rouge* representatives on their return to Phnom Penh. They were to reside and work in the headquarters of the SNC, which would also house offices for the UN mission. Senior *Khmer Rouge* officials returned to Phnom Penh a week later to take part in establishing an SNC secretariat.

The return of the *Khmer Rouge* representatives was planned to take place in time for the visit to Phnom Penh of China's Foreign Minister, Qian Qichen on 27 December. Several days before, a second outbreak of violence occurred, this time directed against the Phnom Penh administration, whose members had acquired a notorious reputation for corruption. Faced with the prospect of a loss of power and perquisites, ministers and their senior assistants had been plundering government assets wholesale. The rumour that Ros Chhun, the Minister of Communications, had evicted a number of families from a government-owned house in order to sell it for private profit infuriated students and slum-dwellers who then mounted five days of demonstrations. These culminated in riots on 21 December which were quelled only after at least eight people had been shot dead by police and a night curfew imposed.

The government's attempt to blame *Khmer Rouge* involvement for the violence fell flat. It was widely acknowledged that it was corruption that generated spontaneous public fury. Indeed, the focus of popular anger had begun to shift from the *Khmer Rouge* to the Phnom Penh government, recalling the situation in Cambodia in early 1975 when the *Khmer Rouge* had first taken power. The violence led to a second postponement of a meeting of the SNC and prevented a visit by China's Foreign Minister and also one by his Vietnamese counterpart. The SNC convened eventually on 30 December under the chairmanship of Prince Sihanouk, shortly after the return once more to Phnom Penh of Khieu Samphan, under heavy military escort and this time without incident. Although the major significance of the meeting was that it could take place at all, given the background of violence and acrimony, agreement was reached on a common appeal for the urgent deployment of UN forces to assume UNTAC's military role. Khieu Samphan returned to Bangkok the following day and then flew back to Phnom Penh for a second meeting of the SNC in early January. The lack of progress by the SNC in moving forward the process of political settlement led Prince Sihanouk to threaten to resign as chairman. Although Sihanouk uses this threat frequently, it remains a potent one since he is the essential link in the whole process.

Building Peace

By the end of 1991, the UN had deployed a small advance military mission (UNAMIC), led by a French general, to evaluate the conditions for the planned peace-keeping operations and to provide a liaison network among the four Cambodian factions, which had themselves formed a Mixed Military Working Group in the last days of 1990. Early in 1992, Yasushi Akashi, an Under Secretary-General for Disarmament, was appointed as the UN Secretary-General's Special Representative to Cambodia. He arrived in Phnom Penh on 22 January 1992 on an initial fact-finding mission with the disappointing news that the UN had not yet approved the budget for the peace-keeping operation and that there was little likelihood of forces under its auspices being deployed to Cambodia before April. If they do arrive by then it will be wholly due to the determination of the Secretary-General himself. In mid-February Boutros Boutros Ghali was reported to have overruled his senior advisers by insisting that the 26,000 peace-keeping soldiers and administrators must be in place by spring 1992.

The Secretary-General's determination is a reflection of his concern that any delay will mean a breakdown in the cease-fire and a loss of the gains that have been made over the last year. Boutros Ghali's timetable includes the disarming of the Cambodian fighters by summer 1992 and elections in the spring of 1993. Few feel that the Secretary-General is over-dramatizing the need to move quickly; the problem lies in the cost of the operation, which has been estimated as high as US$2bn. It is difficult to see where the debt-ridden UN will find the necessary funds, since, at the same time, it is to spend at least $600m for the estimated 14,000 soldiers and civilians to keep the peace in Croatia. In the meantime, the Security Council has approved the despatch of more than 1,000 military and civilian personnel to Cambodia for mine-clearing operations.

By January 1992, the cease-fire among the combatants appeared to be holding, but at the end of the month heavy fighting erupted in the central province of Kompong Thom between Phnom Penh and *Khmer Rouge* forces. In addition, a significant rise in banditry was reported in the countryside, together with claims of intimidation by the *Khmer Rouge*. The SNC convened again in late January, all four factions pledged themselves once again to uphold the fragile cease-fire, and the *Khmer Rouge* withdrew a demand that the SNC should be extended to the provincial level.

Despite these expressions of goodwill, Yasushi Akashi was soon publicly claiming that the *Khmer Rouge* had breached the Paris accord by restricting the freedom of movement of UN military liaison officers. There has been undoubted progress towards a peaceful settlement in Cambodia, but a serious question remains as to whether the UN presence, even when fully deployed, will be able to fill the evident political vacuum in the country and permit effective implementation of the Paris accord. The inveterate enmity and suspicion among Cambodian parties, which have never developed a culture of compromise, remain a fundamental obstacle to a viable settlement.

Central and South Asia

Just as the retreat of the Soviet empire from Eastern Europe necessitated a radical reassessment of the geostrategic borders of Europe, so the emergence of the newly independent states of the Soviet Muslim periphery requires a complete re-evaluation of the frontiers of Central Asia. The Iron Curtain which divided the Soviet Central Asian republics from their ethnic and religious brothers in Turkey, Iran and Afghanistan to the South, and in China to the East, was just as rigid and impenetrable as the division between East and West Europe. With that curtain now lifted, the traditional map of Central Asia, which viewed all of Iran, Afghanistan, the new Central Asian states and Western China as a geopolitical whole, is re-emerging. The formation of a new regional identity for Central Asia is still in its early stages but there is a general consensus that the weakening of Russian influence has created a potential vacuum for other regional powers to extend their political, economic and cultural influence.

In South Asia, the strategic metamorphosis that has transformed the globe has been accompanied by regional transmutations as well. The two major actors of South Asia, India and Pakistan, while trying to adjust their policies to the new global realities which followed the end of the Cold War, the aftermath of the Gulf War, and the disintegration of the Soviet Union, are grappling with a variety of internal political and security problems that pose the dual threats of political destabilization and territorial disintegration. The smaller powers of the region – Bangladesh, Sri Lanka, Nepal and Bhutan – are having to deal with similar problems resulting from global change and the Indo-Pakistani military confrontation. They have also been coping with their own domestic political pressures arising from opposition efforts to topple existing governments, and, in some cases, they face armed separatist insurgencies that threaten to destroy the state in its existing territorial form. Perennial domestic economic pressures in South Asia – external debt crises, shortages of foreign exchange and essential commodities, and inflation – further complicate this unhappy picture.

These problems are now being addressed in what is essentially a new regional political and economic environment, characterized by the establishment of democracies in almost all the states of South Asia, and by efforts on the part of their governments to establish more liberal free-market economies to replace the old state-dominated 'mixed' economies. At least in the short run, the maintenance of Western-type democracies in South Asia will face increasing political pressures from violent ethnic nationalism and widespread economic dissatisfaction. In addition, the promotion of private sector competitive capitalism may run into resistance from the entrenched public sector bureaucracies and the powerful trade unions.

CENTRAL ASIA: SHAPING NEW STATES

The creation of the five republics of Soviet Central Asia in 1924 and 1925: Turkmenia (now renamed Turkmenistan), Uzbekistan, Tajikistan, Kazakhstan and Kirgizia (now renamed Kyrgyzstan), was an artificial division, which ignored the traditional centres of political power. Since these new Soviet republics were given only the most limited of autonomy from centralized power in Moscow, it is hardly surprising that the process of state formation was slow and superficial. Older ties of clan or tribe, or affiliations to the earlier principalities or khanates of Bukhara, Khiva and Kokand, retained their salience and limited the emergence of specific republican nationalisms. As a result, the growth of nationalist or religio-nationalist groupings in these republics was considerably slower than their counterparts in the Baltic states or in the Transcaucasus, where nationalist sentiment has been historically more deeply rooted.

Central Asian Republics: Ethnic Breakdown

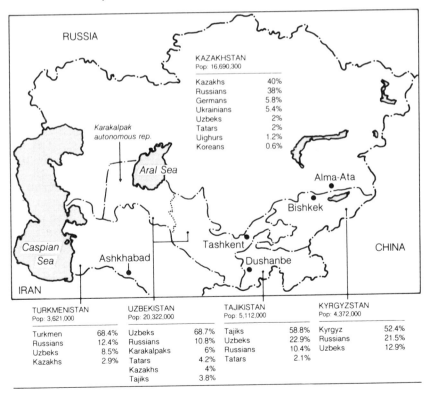

KAZAKHSTAN Pop: 16,690,300	
Kazakhs	40%
Russians	38%
Germans	5.8%
Ukrainians	5.4%
Uzbeks	2%
Tatars	2%
Uighurs	1.2%
Koreans	0.6%

TURKMENISTAN Pop: 3,621,000		UZBEKISTAN Pop: 20,322,000		TAJIKISTAN Pop: 5,112,000		KYRGYZSTAN Pop: 4,372,000	
Turkmen	68.4%	Uzbeks	68.7%	Tajiks	58.8%	Kyrgyz	52.4%
Russians	12.4%	Russians	10.8%	Uzbeks	22.9%	Russians	21.5%
Uzbeks	8.5%	Karakalpaks	6%	Russians	10.4%	Uzbeks	12.9%
Kazakhs	2.9%	Tatars	4.2%	Tatars	2.1%		
		Kazakhs	4%				
		Tajiks	3.8%				

Source: Union of Soviet Socialist Republics', *Europa World Yearbook*, vol. 2, 1991, 32nd edition, pp. 2666–750.

Yet the peoples of the Central Asian republics, albeit at a slower pace, were not immune from the processes unleashed by Gorbachev's programme of *glasnost* and *perestroika*. After 1989 grievances over the damaging effects of 70 years of Soviet imperial policy were more openly expressed, with the economic and environmental mismanagement of the region the most common focus of criticism. The excessive attention which Moscow placed on increasing cotton production in Central Asia, principally in Uzbekistan but also in Turkmenistan and Tajikistan, was widely considered a form of colonial expropriation established deliberately to create economic dependence. The ecological consequences of this cotton monoculture were vividly symbolized by the drying up of the Aral Sea and the heavy chemical pollution of water supplies. As one commentator has suggested, the Soviet authorities in Central Asia 'embarked on a long tragic experiment – to determine the capacity of monoculture to corrode not only agriculture, but also industry, education, health, and finally public morality'.

The expression of economic grievances merged rapidly with demands for greater cultural and religious freedom. Campaigns for the building of new mosques, for greater use of indigenous languages like Uzbek or Tajik, and closer ties with the rest of the Muslim world, all gained in strength. A number of informal groups were at the centre of these campaigns. In Uzbekistan, a group called Birlik actively promoted the Uzbek language and culture and forced a number of concessions on these issues from the republican leadership. In October 1991 it was finally allowed to register as a political movement, although not as a political party. Analogous groups in the other republics, like Rastokhez in Tajikistan, also had considerable success in consolidating ethnic self-awareness and national identity. On the religious front, the Islamic Renaissance Party (IRP), formed in June 1990, developed branches in all five of the republics and, although formally banned in all except Tajikistan, increased popular awareness of a common Islamic inheritance.

At first Moscow encouraged the republican communist leaderships to stifle at birth any upsurge of ethnic, nationalist and religious sentiment. In the early years of *perestroika* (1985–8) they emphasized discipline and campaigned vigorously against the large-scale corruption (much of it linked to the Uzbek cotton industry) in Central Asia, but this was popularly seen as a chauvinist Russian attempt to diminish Central Asian autonomy. The riots in Alma Ata in 1986 in protest against the replacement of an ethnic Kazakh First Secretary for Kazakhstan by a Russian, were an early warning that there were limits to the tolerance of Central Asians to Moscow's diktat. The demonstrable failure of *perestroika* to create economic growth only exacerbated tensions, which were already fuelled by the region's high level of unemployment and a far lower standard of living than the rest of the Soviet Union. During 1989 and 1990 a succession of riots, most notably in the Ferghana valley in May 1989, in Dushanbe in February 1990 and in Osh in June 1990, finally compelled Moscow and the republican leaderships to re-evaluate their policies in an effort to contain the violent expression of popular indignation over the region's economic, ethnic and religious problems.

Unlike some of their counterparts in the Baltic states or in Armenia and Georgia, the non-Russian communist *nomenklatura* of the Central Asian republics made a reasonably successful transition from being the guardians of Marxist-Leninist ideology to nationalist leadership. This was partly due to the strength of their power-base, rooted in traditional patron–client and clan affiliations, and the fact that the opposition groups had only a small following, principally from the native intelligentsia. More important, however, the republican leadership adopted many of the demands of the opposition groups into their own programme. Although insisting on the need to preserve the Soviet Union, all of the republics declared their own sovereignty during 1990 and made clear that exploitation of the natural resources of the region by the centre would have to be reversed. Similarly, the republics relaxed the constraints on cultural and linguistic expression by adopting their native language as the official republican language; some changed their names: Turkmenia became Turkmenistan, Kirghizia became Kyrgyzstan, and its capital Frunze recovered its pre-revolutionary name of Bishkek. The growth in the number of mosques built also reflected the official acceptance that Islam was an integral part of Central Asian identity.

In Uzbekistan, Islam Karimov, a former communist apparatchik, became the new republican party leader after the Ferghana valley riots in June 1989. He rapidly asserted his nationalist credentials by being the first Central Asian leader to declare his republic's sovereignty on 20 June 1990 and its independence on 31 August 1991. Karimov also openly criticized Gorbachev's November 1990 draft proposals for a union treaty, arguing that they preserved too much central power, and he was generally outspoken in demanding greater economic independence for Uzbekistan. However, Karimov has not hidden his disdain for democracy and his desire to preserve the power of the ex-communist *nomenklatura*. Opposition groups have been strongly attacked by the official media and only one small party was permitted to contest the presidential elections on 29 December 1991. This made no dent in Karimov's landslide victory.

In Turkmenistan, the old apparatchiks have been even more successful in repressing other potential claimants to power. The miniscule opposition groups, notably Agzybirlik and the Democratic Party of Turkmenistan, remained unregistered and their leaders continually harassed. As a result, the Leninist power structure has been preserved intact, and the republican president Saparmurad Niyazov continues to rule in the traditional authoritarian mould.

Democratic values have had one important success in Central
Asia. After the Osh riots in June 1990 in Kyrgyzstan, the republican
communist leadership failed to adapt itself to the new political
realities and, in the presidential elections of October 1990, a radical
anti-communist intellectual, Askar Akaev, succeeded in defeating the
ultra-conservative communist candidate, Absamat Masaliev. During
the August 1991 coup, the communists tried to oust Akaev in their
own mini-coup but were successfully outmanoeuvred and, as a result,
have been totally discredited as a force in the republic. With Akaev's
expressed admiration for liberal economic and democratic principles,
Kyrgyzstan comes closest amongst the Central Asian states to representing a Western democracy.

In Tajikistan, the opposition forces almost managed a similar
seizure of power. After the failed coup in August 1991, the communist
nomenklatura reneged on promises to abolish the party and nationalize its property. During late September, a coalition of the three major
opposition groups (Rastokhez, the Democratic Party and the IRP)
staged a popular demonstration outside the parliament building which
succeeded in enforcing these promises and even in securing the legaliz-
ation of the IRP. In the subsequent elections the communist leader
Rakhmon Nabiyev managed to secure power, but that he gained only
58% of the vote revealed the rising power of the opposition groups and
of Islam.

However, the Central Asian leader who has stolen most of the
international limelight and who has perhaps most masterfully made
the transition from communist apparatchik to nationalist leader has
been Nursultan Nazarbayev, President of Kazakhstan.

The Rise of Nursultan

Nazarbayev is by any account a survivor. He was a faithful protégé of
Brezhnev's crony, Dinmukhamed Kunaev, who held on to power from
the early 1960s to 1986. It was probably for this reason that Gorbachev
passed him over for the succession to First Secretary and imposed the
Russian, Gennady Kolbin, which led to the Alma Ata riots in 1986.
Nazarbayev, nevertheless, faithfully served under Kolbin and took
part in the widespread purges of party officials which the new administration ruthlessly implemented. When Kolbin returned to Moscow in
1989, Nazarbayev took over the republican leadership and, despite his
direct involvement in the failed and controversial policies of the previous administrations, he gained considerable respect and popularity. In the presidential elections in December 1991, he secured
98.8% of the vote, and there is no other figure in the republic whose
personal prestige is remotely close to his.

Kazakhstan crystallizes some of the most important problems of
the Soviet legacy to Central Asia. The massive influx of Slavs to the
republic pushed the Slav population (44%, including 5% of Ukrainian

origin) ahead of the native Kazakh population (40%). The northern part of Kazakhstan is predominantly Slav, which prompted Alexander Solzhenitsyn to recommend, much to the indignation of Alma Ata, that this territory should be incorporated into a wider Slavic union. The remaining 16% of the population includes every conceivable nationality (including sizeable numbers of Germans and Koreans), principally as a result of Stalin's forced deportation of peoples to the Kazakh steppes. The resulting ethnic mix is, to say the least, potentially explosive.

As well as being the favoured destination for Stalin's deportation policies, Kazakhstan has also been the dumping ground for the Soviet Union's most noxious industries. The republic's considerable natural resources were ruthlessly exploited, with little concern for the environment, and with full control remaining firmly in the hands of Moscow. For the vibrant ecological movement in Kazakhstan, the nuclear test-site of Semipalatinsk became the symbolic focus of the disastrous industrial policies of Soviet rule. After three years of rising protest, the popular campaign finally secured the closure of the site in the aftermath of the August 1991 coup.

Nazarbayev adopted a subtle and flexible strategy to overcome this Soviet legacy, promoting a non-partisan nationalism rooted in the demand for the republic's right to economic sovereignty. He insisted that economic power be devolved from the centre to the republic and the republic be able to develop its industries and to set its own prices for the resulting products. This policy was, and remains, widely supported by all sections of Kazakh society. When the Karaganda coalminers went on strike in March 1991 in support of Yeltsin's call for such an action, Nazarbayev succeeded in calling it off by agreeing to co-sponsor a letter demanding that control of the mines revert from the centre to the republic. With considerable popular support, he also initiated and developed his own radical reform programme for Kazakhstan after Gorbachev backed away from the Shatalin 500-day plan in autumn 1990.

Nazarbayev's economic radicalism is balanced by a far more cautious political outlook. As he has himself admitted, he is 'a leftist economically but a centrist politically'. This political stance is partly to be explained by his personal preference for an authoritarian mode of governance, on the model of Singapore or pre-1987 South Korea, rather than Western liberal traditions. More substantively, however, it reflects the ethnic and economic conditions of his state. To assert Kazakh independence too strongly would alienate his Slav constituency and strengthen their desire for secession. It would also open the way for wider inter-ethnic tensions from the multitude of other ethnic groupings in Kazakhstan. Nazarbayev has consistently affirmed the need for strong economic relations with the other ex-Soviet republics as the necessary precondition for the transition of the Kazakh economy to a capitalist market.

It is this astute political moderation which has made Nazarbayev such an influential figure in the wider arena, and it explains why he played a pivotal intermediary role in the power struggle between Gorbachev and Yeltsin. On the one hand, he allied himself with Yeltsin in the struggle to gain greater local economic sovereignty against the central administration. On the other, he supported Gorbachev in asserting the need for a strong union and attacked Yeltsin's statement, made shortly after the August 1991 coup, that the Russian borders might need to be revised. At first, he also attacked the agreement to form a commonwealth, since the initial signatories were the three principal Slav republics, and only acquiesced in the proposal when he realized that otherwise there would be no union left.

Nazarbayev's stature and influence has made him the most forceful spokesman and intermediary for all the former Central Asian republics. The current leaders realize that their economies are critically dependent on the wider pre-existing Soviet market and that if all economic unity were irrevocably lost they would have a very bleak future. In all the emergent states there are sizeable Slav constituencies, which represent the technocratic elite and possess an expertise that the native population has yet to acquire. It is for this reason that the leaderships have been careful to limit the growth of indigenous ethnic and religious exclusivity, so as to reassure the resident outsiders that they still have a future in Central Asia. As it is, many of the Slav population are pessimistic about their future, and the riots in Dushanbe and the Ferghana valley accelerated emigration. The relative calm in 1991, and the fact that conditions in many of the other former Soviet republics are even worse than in Central Asia, has slowed the progress of emigration. Slav fears of Islamic fundamentalism and resurgent nationalism, however, remain.

Looking Outwards

The end of centralized Soviet power in Central Asia has given the present leaders an opportunity to develop stronger inter-regional relations and to initiate economic and political relations with the outside world. In June 1990 and August 1991, when they were still five Soviet republics, their leaders met to define the appropriate structures for the development of a common market and greater political co-operation. Although the meetings failed to advance these objectives in any substantive manner, it is still clearly understood that strong economic ties are crucial, particularly for the smaller entities.

There seems little chance, however, that a strong unified Turkestan (as Russian Central Asia was known under the Czars) will emerge in the foreseeable future. Such a consolidated entity, with its connotations of pan-Turkic revivalism, would be threatening to the non-Turkic speakers such as the Tajiks or the Slavs. The smaller ethnic groups, like the Kyrgyz, Tajiks or the Turkmen, would also be fearful of Uzbek domination, since the Uzbeks constitute the largest and most powerful indigenous ethnic group in the region. Overall, there is little desire amongst the individual states to concede their recently secured political and economic independence to centralized regional control.

With regard to the outside world, the Central Asian states have been primarily driven by their need to revive their stagnant economies. They have adopted unashamed capitalist criteria for determining which countries provide the most appropriate models for economic regeneration, with South Korea and Singapore being the most popular prototypes. In November 1990, Nazarbayev visited South Korea and was clearly impressed by the Korean work ethic and its successes in encouraging rapid export-led growth. He even invited the Korean-American economist, Chan Young Bang, to act as the leading figure in a committee of economic experts, set up to oversee Kazakhstan's radical programme of economic reform. Not coincidentally, the fact that South Korean and Singaporean development was led by authoritarian governments with democratic trappings, suits the political inclinations of Nazarbayev and the other Central Asian leaders.

Turkey is another attractive model for the leaderships of the new Central Asian states. Its secular nationalism and its strong economic growth during the 1980s under Turgut Özal appeal to the local ex-communist leaders, who fear Islamic fundamentalism and want to maintain a pro-Western capitalist outlook. The Uzbek leader, Islam Karimov, has been a vigorous advocate for the 'Turkish Path' and has emphasized the strong cultural links between Turkey and the Central Asian states, and the hope that Turkey can act as the region's conduit to Europe and the West.

For the other neighbouring countries, there have been substantial efforts to increase cross-border trade. Rail links have recently been planned, connecting Xinjiang province with Alma-Ata, and Turkmenistan with Iran, so that the old Silk Road can be re-established. New trade agreements with China and Iran have been ratified, and there have been arrangements for the sale of gas and other natural resources from Central Asia in exchange for manufactured goods. All the states, except Kazakhstan, have joined the resurrected Economic Co-operation Organisation (ECO), which initially included Turkey, Iran and Pakistan. These are certainly encouraging developments, but it will be many years before they can replace the traditional trade with Russia and the other former Soviet republics.

The new Central Asian states have also not been constrained from developing their own distinctive foreign policies. This can be seen most vividly over the question of an Afghan settlement. There are sizeable Uzbek, Tajik and Turkmen ethnic groups in Afghanistan, whose interests the respective states feel a certain obligation to protect. When Alexander Rutskoi, the Russian Vice-President, set out on a mission to Iran, Pakistan and Kabul in December 1991 to seek a resolution of the Afghan problem, he was strongly attacked by Islam Karimov for 'not consulting us when there are 300,000 Uzbeks living in Afghanistan for whom we have a responsibility'. Many of these Uzbeks live immediately across the Afghan–Uzbek border.

The ex-communist leaders in Central Asia also naturally have a certain affinity with President Najibullah and are concerned about the destabilizing implications of a *Mujaheddin* government in Afghanistan. However, even on this point, there are differences of opinion. The success of the Tajik commander, Ahmad Shah Massoud, in securing wide tracts of territory adjoining Tajikistan and in imposing an Islamic system of rule in that territory, has constrained the Tajik leadership from openly supporting Najibullah. In November 1991, the Tajik foreign ministry tacitly supported Massoud's political demands by agreeing that Najibullah had to go before a settlement could be reached.

The emergent Central Asian states offer both opportunities and risks to their neighbours. For China, there is the enticement of new markets, but also the fear that nationalist sentiment might increase amongst the Turkic-speaking Uighur and other ethnic populations in Xinjiang province, which has traditionally resented Han rule and feels itself part of greater Turkestan. Iran has a very similar attitude; like China it welcomes the new opportunities for trade but it fears a possible exacerbation of its own nationalities problem, which includes the Turkic-speaking Azeris and Turkmen. In its current introspective mood, there is little desire in Iran for the export of radical Islam, which, in any case, has minimal support from the predominantly Sunni people of the Central Asian states. Iran has also consistently shown great caution over encouraging instability on its northern borders, given that it has such insecure relations with Iraq to the West and Afghanistan to the East.

Turkey has also been cautious in projecting its influence into the Central Asian states. Whilst welcoming cultural and trade links, it has only been extreme nationalist groups inside Turkey who have been openly calling for a pan-Turkic revival. The government in Turkey understands that such a revival would not only be a destabilizing factor inside the Central Asian states themselves but also be threatening to Iran and other neighbouring nations. Also, as the conference on the Black Sea states on 4 February 1992 showed, Turkey is concentrating its efforts on its immediate neighbours on or near the Black Sea. As a consequence, its penetration into the Central Asian region has been so cautious that some of the Central Asian leaders have complained that Turkey has been ignoring their economic predicament.

Although the regional powers have been slow to engage their efforts in ex-Soviet Central Asia, there is a clear realization that the new political entities have transformed the geopolitics of the region. If a strong Turkestan were to emerge, this would introduce a significant new element in the regional balance of power, recreating the old triangular balance between the Ottoman, Persian and the Bukharan empires. If the Central Asian states were to disintegrate, it cannot be long before the struggle for influence will become far more dangerous as the regional powers are drawn in.

Already, interested external actors have been active in setting markers for the future and proffering advice to the leaders in the area. The US Secretary of State, James Baker, has warned against the spread of Iranian influence and recommended that the Central Asian states look to Turkey and resist Iranian pressure to form a confederation of Muslim Central Asian states. The fear of Iranian expansionism has also affected policy-making from other countries in the Middle East. Saudi Arabia and Egypt have acted to defend Sunni Islamic traditions by building new mosques with Saudi finance and by sending Central Asian clerics to study in the al-Azhar university in Cairo. Iran is understandably disquieted by such developments and feels that it has a perfectly legitimate right to extend its political and economic influence, particularly towards the Persian-speaking Tajiks and Turkmenistan, which immediately borders Iran. Iranian concerns would be heightened if Turkey was emboldened by US policy-makers to expand its influence more aggressively in Central Asia, focusing its attention on the Turkic-speaking Uzbeks, Turkmen and Kyrgyz.

Pakistan has not been absent from the emerging struggle for influence. It has been the most active advocate for the strengthening of the ECO and the inclusion of the new Central Asian states, which it hopes would act as a forum for advancing Pakistan's regional influence. At least part of Pakistan's recent interest in an Afghan settlement is to secure trade links with the Central Asian states and to offer these landlocked countries an outlet to the sea. India, too, has not been blind to these developments and is concerned about the development of a strong new Muslim entity to its north and the disintegration of its traditional alliance with the Soviet Union. It also will be seeking good relations with the Central Asian countries to forestall an increase in Pakistan's power and influence.

Prospects for the Future

There can be no conclusive judgements over the probable evolution of the political and economic structures of power in Central Asia. The processes unleashed by the newly acquired independence of these states are still in a very early stage. The programmes they have adopted are national in orientation but not specifically *nationalistic*. The formation of distinct nation-states is far from consolidated and, as their leaderships realize, strong nationalist demands on ethnic or religious grounds can only be a destabilizing factor. It would undermine the confidence of the much-needed Slav population and aggravate interethnic tension and religious disputes. The current problems in the Transcaucasus are a salutary reminder of the inherent dangers of forceful nationalist assertion.

For the moment, however, fears of the Lebanonization of Central Asia or of Iranian-inspired Islamic revolution are somewhat overblown. The leaderships of the Central Asian states are showing considerable maturity in coming to terms with their complex environment. Following the clear example of Nazarbayev, they have initiated economic reforms, acceded to indigenous demands for ethnic, cultural and religious self-expression, and yet been careful not to permit these demands to be translated into ethnic or religious chauvinism.

The continued success of this fine balancing act depends ultimately on significant economic progress, which, in turn, is dependent on many forces outside the immediate control of the individual states. Economic introspection and a beggar-my-neighbour attitude from the other former Soviet republics, particularly Russia, would spell doom for the Central Asians. With this scenario, it is probable that the process towards nationalist ethnic and religious self-definition, at present only beginning to emerge, will be significantly quickened. The future of the embryonic Central Asian states would then be more unpredictable and far more worrying.

INDIA AND ITS NEIGHBOURS

South Asia continues to face considerable political turmoil and uncertainty. All the countries of the region face staggering political, economic and ethnic challenges that would tax any government. In the midst of these difficulties, however, a series of elections brought significant and heartening change in the political and economic realm. During 1991, new governments emerged in India, Bangladesh and Nepal. Both Bangladesh and Nepal overthrew their military and monarchical dictatorships and elected new democracies. Except for Bhutan and Myanmar (Burma) every country in South Asia is now led, if somewhat shakily, by a democratic government.

New Governments, New Democracies

In India, the minority *Janata Dal* government of prime minister V. P. Singh had been displaced in November 1990 by an even smaller faction of the party led by the succeeding Prime Minister, Chandra Shekhar. This government was not expected to last long and indeed collapsed within a few months in March 1991. The political campaign for new national elections, to be held in June 1991, was unusually violent and was shattered by the assassination of the former Congress Party prime minister, Rajiv Gandhi, by a suspected member of the Liberation Tigers of Tamil Eelam (LTTE) of Sri Lanka, operating in the Indian state of Tamil Nadu. Despite the national trauma generated by the assassination of India's third leader named Gandhi (the

Mahatma in 1948, Indira in 1984 and now Rajiv in 1991), the national elections went ahead. The Congress Party fell short of a clear majority in the 544-seat *Lok Sabha* (lower house), winning 225 seats while gaining 37% of the total votes. (Even under Nehru the Congress Party never obtained an absolute majority of the votes.) The Hindu nationalist Bharatiya Janata Party (BJP) won 119 seats, with 20% of the vote, while the previous *Janata Dal* government won only 11% and 55 seats.

The Congress Party formed a government under P. V. Narasimha Rao, a former foreign minister in Rajiv Gandhi's earlier government. Unlike the *Janata Dal*-led National Front government of V. P. Singh, whose forced reliance on legislative party support from the extreme left-wing Communist Party-Marxist (CPM) and the extreme right-wing BJP required a difficult balancing act, the government of Narasimha Rao needed only the support of the CPM to maintain a legislative majority in the *Lok Sabha*. On its economic and foreign policy objectives, however, the government has so far received the support of the BJP on the right.

In Pakistan, the *Islami Jamhoori Ittehad* (IJI), which had won 105 of the 217-seat National Assembly in the 1990 elections, remained in power under the prime ministership of Mian Mohammed Nawaz Sharif. In alliance with other smaller parties, the IJI commanded a two-thirds majority. However, the Pakistan People's Party (PPP) of former prime minister Benazir Bhutto (with 45 seats in the National Assembly), remained an angry and confrontational opposition both within the Pakistani legislature and outside, in particular in the violent politics of Sind province. Throughout 1991, power in Pakistan depended on a shaky alliance between the President, the Prime Minister and the army.

In the first major elections held in Bangladesh since its creation in December 1971, the military dictator, General Hussain Mohammed Ershad, and the *Jatiya* Party he organized to fight the national elections held in February, were defeated. Ershad, although under arrest and in detention during the elections on the grounds of widespread corruption, was overwhelmingly elected from his own constituency of Rangpur. The Bangladesh National Party (BNP), led by Begum Khaleda Zia, widow of General Zia-ur Rahman, a former military dictator of Bangladesh, garnered 138 seats in the country's parliament, well short of the 166 needed for a simple majority. The Awami League, led by Begum Hasina Shaikh Wajed, daughter of Shaikh Mujibur Rahman, the first president and leader of the liberation struggle for Bangladesh in 1971, came in a close second. Begum Zia, however, managed to secure an alliance with the *Jamiat Islami* group and was appointed Prime Minister in March.

In April 1991 the first democratic election in 32 years was held in Nepal. This was a major surprise, as just over a month earlier King Birendra Bir Bikram Shah had cracked down hard on pro-democracy demonstrators, killing perhaps as many as 300. The national election was won by the Nepali Congress, led by Girija Prasad Koirala, with 110 seats in the 205-seat parliament. The Communist Party of Nepal (the United Marxist-Leninist) formed the main opposition, winning 69 seats. The Nepali Congress had been banned until April and had operated mainly out of India. Its success was fostered by the conclusion of a favourable trade and transit agreement with India, and by the renewal of cordial ties between the two countries which had been broken in 1990. Democracy in Nepal, however, still faces the threat of overthrow from pro-palace supporters.

Adjusting to the New Global Realities

The Gulf War and the disintegration of the Soviet Union left Indian foreign policy makers groping for appropriate responses. The Gulf War initially produced hesitant and ambivalent Indian support for the US-led operation. In a significant departure from past Indian policy, the new minority government of Prime Minister Chandra Shekhar allowed American military transport planes to refuel at Bombay's Sahar airport on their way to the Gulf. This gesture in support of Western actions against Iraq was severely criticized by former prime ministers V. P. Singh and Rajiv Gandhi. Under pressure from their parties and left-wing groups, refuelling rights were quickly suspended. A major diplomatic breakthrough had already been made in Indo-American relations, however, which have continued to blossom under the new Congress government of Prime Minister Narasimha Rao.

A similar situation prevailed in Pakistan and Bangladesh. In Pakistan, the new IJI government of Mohammed Nawaz Sharif joined the Western-led allied coalition in the Gulf by sending 10,000 Pakistani soldiers to Saudi Arabia. This action was heavily censured by the opposition leader Benazir Bhutto, by the Pakistani Army Chief of Staff, Mirza Aslam Beg, and by various Islamic leaders in the country. President Ershad of Bangladesh had sent 5,000 soldiers to the Gulf by the end of 1990, but he faced severe criticism at home for supporting the allied military assault. In all three countries, the Muslim populations displayed strong emotional support for Saddam Hussein. Initial Muslim condemnation of the Iraqi invasion and annexation of a brother Arab Muslim state was displaced by anger at the massive Western assault on a fellow Muslim country. The swift defeat and destruction of Iraq, however, burst the bubble of expectations of the subcontinent's Muslims.

In the aftermath of the Gulf War, new strategic alignments between the states of South Asia and the external powers began to emerge. In what has been described by Pakistani analysts as the 'quiet revolution', the United States appeared to distance itself from Pakistan and to move closer to India. The new tilt towards India was first heralded in December 1990 with the visit of a sizeable American defence delegation led by Assistant Secretary of Defense for International Security, Henry Rowen, for talks with his Indian counterparts. This was followed in August 1991 by a visit to the US from an Indian delegation led by General Sunil Francis Rodrigues, Chief of Staff of the Indian Army. The prospect of closer military cooperation between India and America received a further boost in October 1991, when Admiral Charles Larson, Commander-in-Chief of US Pacific Command (CINCPAC) visited India. In January 1992, discussions in Delhi between Lt-Gen. John Corns, Commanding General of the US Army in the Pacific, and Admiral Frank Kelso, Chief of Naval Operations, and senior Indian military officers cleared the ground for a long-term 'forces to forces' level relationship.

In these exchanges, negotiations on a range of security areas where both sides could cooperate for mutual benefit were based on the 'Kickleighter Proposals'. These proposals, providing for defence consultations and eventually joint military exercises, were first made by the former commander of the US Army in the Pacific, Lt-Gen. Claude Kickleighter, in April 1991. Such Indo-US military cooperation, which goes well beyond anything that existed in the old Indo-Soviet military relationship, was also intended to assure Australia and the countries of South-east Asia that they need not feel threatened by India's military growth. Indeed, joint Indo-Australian naval exercises are now being discussed for 1992, a significant departure from earlier Australian criticisms of India's naval expansion.

The diplomatic changes in South Asia were a reflection of US concern over Pakistan's continuing efforts to acquire nuclear weapons, and the growing threat of Islamic fundamentalism in the Muslim crescent from Pakistan to Morocco. The growing US strategic convergence with India, and divergence from Pakistan, were also expressed in India's positive response to President Bush's request to support the US in repealing the 1975 UN resolution equating Zionism with racism, and in India's support of the US in the Security Council on the issue of the extradition from Libya of the terrorists deemed responsible for the bombing of a Pan Am and a French airliner. Pakistan, on the other hand, supported the Arab and Muslim bloc in voting against the repeal of the 1975 anti-Zionist resolution. Pakistani perceptions of an American tilt towards India has prompted it to emphasize closer ties with Muslim countries west of the subcontinent, including the newly-emerged Central Asian republics.

The disintegration of the Soviet Union destroyed the foundations of India's foreign policy, which in many ways was still trying to cling to the old world order despite India's developing ties with the United States. For example, India had at first refused to recognize the Baltic states, only to do so three weeks later; then, in August 1991, it renewed the Indo-Soviet Treaty of Peace and Friendship for another 20 years, and it was shocked, perplexed and ambivalent during the attempted coup against Gorbachev.

The US–Pakistani relationship had begun to crumble when Soviet troops were removed from Afghanistan in 1990. The disintegration of the USSR furthered this process. Pakistani support for the more extreme Afghan fundamentalist factions in the struggle to topple the government of Najibullah has now ended. Pakistan has accepted the UN proposed plan to settle the Afghanistan issue by constructing a coalition of the various groups. The United States has sought to balance its new approach to India with reassuring gestures towards Pakistan. This was signalled by the goodwill visit to Pakistan in November 1991 of General Joseph P. Hoar, the Commander-in-Chief of US Central Command. Admiral Kelso visited Pakistan *en route* to India. Such efforts have done little to assuage Pakistan's pique, however.

There was a similar shift in China's relations with Pakistan and India during the latter part of 1991. In October President Yang Shangkun paid a goodwill visit to Pakistan to express continued Chinese support. Yang's statements in Pakistan indicated a Chinese desire to counter what both states perceive to be a US-dictated new world order in the aftermath of the Gulf War and the collapse of the Soviet Union.

In December, in a belated reciprocation of Prime Minister Gandhi's 1989 visit to China, Prime Minister Li Peng visited India. Both visits were the first by the prime ministers of the two countries since they fought a war over their disputed border in October–December 1962. Although the Li Peng visit may appear to dilute the Sino-Pakistani relationship, little of substance was actually achieved between India and China except to restore confidence. Yet, now that the ex-USSR is no longer a threat to China, Sino-Indian relations may revert back to those of the 1950s. To be sure, a formal solution to the Sino-Indian border dispute that led to war in 1962 does not appear close, but an acceptance of the *status quo* may become the approved solution. China will keep the Aksai Chin plateau, which it now occupies but which India disputes, and India will keep the Northeast Frontier Agency (renamed Arunachel Pradesh) which India occupies and China disputes.

On the second major point of controversy – the status of Tibet – India reiterated the position that Tibet was an 'autonomous province' of China, first articulated by Prime Minister Jawaharlal Nehru when he and Chou En-lai finalized the Sino-Indian Treaty in 1954. Although no reciprocal Chinese statement was made on India's claim to Kashmir, the Chinese position tacitly appeared to take on the benevolent pro-Indian 'neutrality' that it had adopted on the Kashmir issue during the heyday of Sino-Indian friendship in the 1950s.

The Pakistani reaction was cautious and mixed. On the one hand, there is concern that China may be going the American way of tilting towards India. On the other, Pakistanis have noted that on the two major issues concerning Pakistan (China's stand on Kashmir and the nuclear issue), Prime Minister Li Peng had actually said nothing, suggesting thereby a continuation of Chinese support for Pakistan.

Nuclear Politics and the Proliferation Question

In 1986 the US Congress, aroused by reports on Pakistan's nuclear programme, passed the Pressler Amendment which required the suspension of all economic and military aid to Pakistan if the administration could not certify that Pakistan was not developing nuclear weapons. In late 1990 the administration felt it could no longer provide such assurances and the sanctions of the Amendment came into play. Their effect was immediate, leading to a deterioration in Pakistani–American relations during 1991 and a concomitant improvement in Indo-American relations.

Pakistani government officials and analysts have argued that the implementation of the Pressler Amendment in 1991 was blatantly discriminatory, since India had already exploded a nuclear device in 1974 and has the technological capability to produce several nuclear weapons a year. American nuclear policy in South Asia, however, was determined more by the perceived nuclear weapons motivations of India, Pakistan and other states than by the growth of nuclear technological capabilities which many non-nuclear weapons states possess. Since India tested an atomic device in 1974 there has been little clear evidence that it was actively pursuing a nuclear weapons programme. Indeed, when he visited India in January 1992, Senator Larry Pressler, the initiator of the Amendment, gave India a 'clean chit' on its nuclear programme. There are still allegations, however, that India is stockpiling plutonium.

American officials are therefore deeply concerned about the possibilities of nuclear proliferation in the area. In testimony before a Senate committee in mid-January 1992, CIA Director Robert Gates noted that while the US had no reason to believe that either India or Pakistan maintained, assembled or deployed nuclear weapons, both countries could assemble such a weapon quickly, and both have combat aircraft that could be modified to deliver such weapons in a crisis. This warning was substantiated in early February 1992 when Pakistani Foreign Secretary Shahryar Khan announced that his country had the components and knowledge to assemble a nuclear explosive device. Mr Khan was speaking after meetings with White House and Congressional officials in which he had pledged not to explode such a device or to transfer nuclear technology to other countries, Islamic or otherwise.

Mr Khan's remarks were part of an effort the Pakistani government has been making to convince the US that it is doing everything possible to meet US conditions for a resumption of aid. He noted that in 1991 Pakistan had permanently frozen production of highly enriched uranium and of weapons cores. He said that Pakistan could only meet another US condition (the destruction of weapons cores) if India would follow suit. Pakistan has for some time proposed the establishment of a nuclear-free zone in South Asia which India continues to reject.

Just as Pakistan had suffered a diplomatic setback from the shift in American policy, so India suffered from a significant shift in Moscow's policy. In mid-November 1991, the new Russian republic backed a joint Pakistani–Bangladeshi sponsored resolution presented to the UN General Assembly's Disarmament Committee, calling for the establishment of a nuclear-free zone in South Asia. The former Soviet Union had always abstained from voting on such resolutions. The resolution was passed with 104 votes in favour, 3 against, and 25 abstentions. A similar Pakistani proposal to the Political Committee of the General Assembly calling for security guarantees to non-nuclear weapons states, received 133 votes in favour (including that of France for the first time), none against. The US and the UK abstained, citing certain problems of implementing the resolution on guarantees.

As France, China and South Africa had agreed to sign the Nuclear Non-Proliferation Treaty, and as Argentina and Brazil had adhered to the Treaty of Tlatelolco, which established Latin America as a nuclear-free zone, there was greater pressure on India either to sign the NPT or to agree to a nuclear-weapons-free zone in South Asia. As a consequence, Prime Minister Rao significantly shifted India's policy when he agreed to consider the proposed 'Two Plus Three Nation' talks (India, Pakistan, China, the US and Russia). These talks are intended to establish a nuclear-weapons-free zone in South Asia.

A special meeting of Indian legislators and top foreign-policy officials in mid-February, however, made it clear that India insisted on its right to build nuclear weapons. A senior official from the Foreign Ministry noted that the meeting and its report were intended as a rebuff to Pakistan's announcement the week before that it could build a weapon, and to ensure that the Indian government safeguarded India's option to build a bomb so long as other countries continue to possess them. The adamant Indian position undercut two positive developments that had occurred in South Asia in 1991. First, both India and Pakistan took a step further in their 1990 agreement not to attack each other's nuclear installations when they exchanged information on all their nuclear facilities. Second, India and Pakistan agreed to hold talks to conclude an agreement not to produce chemical weapons. While these developments are encouraging, they do little to stem the slide towards the nuclearization of the subcontinent.

Regional and Internal Security Issues

Although an Indo-Pakistani war over Kashmir was avoided during 1991, the threat of such a war remains. With the insurgencies in both Kashmir and Punjab continuing, Pakistan's strategy has been to 'bleed' India slowly by aiding the rebels short of provoking a war. However, there have been demands by members of the BJP and other Hindu nationalists, as well as by the former Chief Minister of Kashmir, Farooq Abdullah, that India should attack bases in Pakistan where the insurgents and terrorists are being trained. In January 1992, the Indian Defence Minister, Sharad Pawar, also threatened to take retaliatory measures if Pakistan did not stop the 'proxy war' against India. India has apparently been able to produce convincing enough evidence that Pakistan has been training Kashmiri and Sikh terrorists to operate in Kashmir and Punjab to prompt the Bush administration to threaten to declare Pakistan as a state sponsoring international terrorism. Pakistan has denied these allegations, and in February it prevented by force thousands of Pakistani hotheads from marching across the cease-fire line into Indian Kashmir.

While the armed insurgency in Kashmir rumbled on throughout 1991 and into early 1992, there appear to have been some marginal shifts among the various Kashmiri organizations fighting against Indian security forces. The struggle was begun in 1989 by the Jammu and Kashmir Liberation Front (JKLF), with the encouragement and support of the Pakistani government. The JKLF insists, now as then, on an independent Jammu and Kashmir based on the boundaries of the old princely state prior to independence. This would include 'Azad' (Free) Kashmir and the 'northern territories' that had been separated from Azad Kashmir and incorporated into Pakistan proper.

By the following year, when the JKLF-led revolt was in full swing, Pakistani support for the JKLF was withdrawn and redirected towards several pro-Pakistani groups, especially the *Hizb-ul-Mujahideen* (HUM), which absorbed the *Tehrik-ul-Mujahideen* in 1991, and a new group that had united nine other pro-Pakistani splinter groups into an organization called the 'Forum Against Sell-Out' (FAS). With Pakistani support, HUM and FAS had by now eclipsed the pro-independence JKLF both in the struggle and in the search for popular support. In late 1991, however, six new pro-independence groups emerged in support of the JKLF, demanding independence from both India and Pakistan, further complicating an already messy situation.

Two other issues related to the Kashmiri problem remain unresolved. Border skirmishes between Indian and Pakistani forces continue to erupt on the Siachen Glacier along the undemarcated extension of the cease-fire line in Kashmir. The dispute has been dragging on since the early 1980s, with both sides claiming that the glacier falls on their side of the line. Pakistan has also protested about the construction of the Wuller Barrage on Wuller Lake in Kashmir on the grounds that India would be able to control the flow into Pakistan of the River Jhelum, the source of irrigation of much of Pakistani Punjab. There appears to be some movement towards a resolution of this issue, but the Siachen Glacier problem, which is much more closely tied to the Kashmiri dispute, is no nearer a solution.

In what was once East Pakistan, now Bangladesh, concern has also risen about the risks of conflict with the military rulers of Myanmar (Burma). In the closing months of 1991, and especially in the first quarter of 1992, Myanmar began a campaign of persecution of its minority Muslim population. Tens of thousands fled across the frontier into Bangladesh, an already poverty-stricken country struggling to feed its own population. Troops were mobilized on both sides of the border, but international efforts designed to pressure the military regime in Myanmar to change its policies had little effect. Myanmar also risked conflict with Thailand, when a dry-season offensive against Karen rebels based in eastern Myanmar included violations of the Thai frontier. Given the brutality of the ruling junta in Myanmar, international pressure would have to get much stronger before it changed its policies in either the east or west.

Other Indian Troubles

Armed insurgencies demanding independence from India continue unabated in Punjab and Assam. As in the case of Kashmir, these insurgencies are marked by widespread and indiscriminate killing of civilians, robberies and kidnappings, and Indian paramilitary counteractions have generated both international and domestic allegations of human rights violations. However, there is a qualitative difference between the insurgency in Kashmir, and those in Punjab and Assam. The secessionists in these two latter provinces still do not appear to have the support of much their populations. Whereas nearly all the Hindu Pandits and other Hindus who lived in Kashmir have fled, there has been no major flight of Hindus from Punjab, or Bengalis and other non-Assamese from Assam. Indeed, one of the grievances of the Assamese is that they have been reduced to a minority of about 40% in their own state, and that they are not the main beneficiaries of the state's economic wealth. In Kashmir the insurgency has crippled the tourist and handicraft industries, whereas farming and the medium industries economy of Punjab, and the oil- and tea-based industry of Assam, have continued to flourish.

As in Kashmir, several Sikh factions are involved in the insurgency in Punjab; the Khalistan Liberation Force and the Sikh Student Federation are the two main ones. Sikh militants have been more ruthless and brutal in killing fellow Sikhs in Punjab, especially those suspected of collaborating with Indian security forces, including the sizeable force of Sikh policemen in the Punjab State Police. In one episode in 1991, Sikh militants killed the families of several Sikh policemen in an effort to deter police recruitment of Sikhs. On two separate occasions in June and December, Sikh extremists halted trains, singled out Hindu passengers and massacred 50 to 100 of them. Both incidents were apparently timed to disrupt the elections in Punjab in June 1991 and February 1992. The June elections had to be postponed, but the 19 February elections were held. Not surprisingly, with calls for a boycott by several factions of the Sikh *Akali Dal* Party, and threats by Sikh militants to kill those who voted, there was only a 30% turnout. The Congress Party easily won most of the seats to the central parliament and the state legislature.

The insurgency in Assam is being conducted almost exclusively by one main organization, the United Liberation Front of Assam (ULFA), founded in 1979. In July 1991, ULFA kidnapped 14 Indian officials and a Soviet engineer, Sergei Gritchenko. Gritchenko was killed along with a kidnapped Indian journalist, Kamala Saikia. To add to the troubles of the north-east, the tribal Bodos of Assam are demanding a separate state of Bodoland within the Indian Union. Their demands led to a bloody clash between Bodos and non-Bodos in September that left more than 30 people dead and 40 villages gutted. A similar movement for the establishment of a Gurkhaland by the Gurkhas of the Darjeeling district of Assam appears to have subsided in 1991, but demands for a separate Jharkhand state, made up of parts of Bihar, Orissa and West Bengal, continue.

The somewhat quieter and more peaceful Dravidian south has not escaped the violence. There has been a rise in the 'Naxalite' movement in Andhra Pradesh. Now calling themselves the 'People's War Group' (PWG), the Naxalites are an extreme communist movement which first came to light in 1967 in the West Bengali district of Naxalbari. The PWG aims to overthrow the government of Andhra Pradesh through armed violence. A dispute between the two states of Tamil Nadu and Karnataka on the sharing of the waters of the Cauvery River led to attacks by Kannadigas on Tamil residents of Karnataka that cost the lives of several Tamils, and the exodus of almost 100,000 Tamils into refugee camps in Tamil Nadu. Violence between the upper and lower castes continues to plague the state of Bihar. Despite this grim record, overall Hindu–Muslim communal violence has eased somewhat from previous years.

Pakistan has its Troubles Too

The violent struggle between Sindhis and *Mohajirs* (Indian Muslims who settled in Pakistan after partition) rages on in Pakistan. On the one side it is led by the *Mohajir Qaumi Mahaz* under Altaf Hussain, and on the other by Benazir Bhutto and her PPP, and the extremist underground group, *Al Zulfiqar* Organization. The *Mohajir*-dominated cities of Karachi, Hyderabad and Sukkur have become battlegrounds. Demands for an independent Sindhudesh, which are becoming more widespread among Sindhis, provoked the Pakistani government to arrest the 90-year old Sindhi leader G. M. Syed. There are now fears that Sind could go the way of East Pakistan (now Bangladesh) if matters get further out of hand.

In general, Sindhis claim that they have been deprived by the *Mohajirs* of their economic and political share in their own state. The PPP has accused the MQM of organizing the murder, rape and extortion of Sindhis. The MQM's offensive against Bhutto's PPP has been joined by the new Chief Minister of Sind, Jam Sadiq Ali, and the President of Pakistan, Ghulam Ishaq Khan, who is a Pathan.

This struggle reached a rather unusual peak on 27 November 1991 when Farhat Vina Hayat, a close friend of Benazir Bhutto, was gang-raped by the alleged followers of (and on the instructions of) Irfanullah Marawat, the son-in-law of President Ghulam Ishaq Khan. It became known as the 'political rape' in Pakistan because the rapists delivered political lectures to the victim on the foolishness of being associated with Benazir Bhutto. Rather than suffering in silence, as is the usual reaction of Pakistanis shamed by rape, Farhat Vina Hayat's father, Shaukat Hayat Khan, who was a colleague of the founder of Pakistan, Mohammed Ali Jinnah, together with his other kinsmen, denounced the crime and have vowed to kill all those associated with it.

There is fresh conflict emerging between Pathans and Baluchis in Baluchistan. In October, Baluch and Pathan ethnic groups armed with Kalashnikov assault rifles fought outside the provincial capital, Quetta. This was another example of the indiscriminate violence and lawlessness Pakistan now faces as a result of the growth in the illegal heroin trade and the ready access to semi-automatic rifles, the so-called 'Kalashnikov culture'. Both are the residue of the war against the Soviet military occupation of Afghanistan. Indeed, the trade in heroin and guns in Pakistan has spilled over into India and is now part of the insurgencies in Kashmir and Punjab. Sikh and Kashmiri insurgents operating out of Pakistan receive financial support from their constituents abroad, buy drugs on the open market, and then trade them for guns to use in their struggle for independence.

The Dirty War in Sri Lanka

The Colombo government's assault against the Tamil extremist group seeking independence, the Liberation Tigers of Tamil Eelam, reached a crucial stage in 1991. In the war of attrition, the LTTE appears to be losing ground against the Sri Lankan army. This is partly because support from fellow Tamils in the Indian state of Tamil Nadu virtually ended following the assassination of former Indian Prime Minister Rajiv Gandhi by a Tamil Tiger terrorist, and partly because of the electoral defeat of the *Dravida Munnetra Kazhagham* party in Tamil Nadu and its Chief Minister, D. Karunanidhi, who had supported the separatist *Eelam* movement in Sri Lanka. Nevertheless, the continuing fierce fighting between Tamil Tigers and Sri Lankan forces, which are exclusively Sinhalese, still causes extensive casualties on both sides.

As a bloody climax to the struggle looked inevitable, the opposition Sri Lanka Freedom Party organized a select committee of all the parties in the legislature to search for a peaceful solution. The Committee's efforts were stalled in late 1991 when Saumiyamurthi Thondaman publicized a set of proposals he had made to this body before the Committee itself had a chance to report on its own peace proposals. In essence, Thondaman's proposals would grant full autonomy to Tamils in the northern and eastern provinces short of an independent Eelam. Sinhalese nationalists alleged that Thondaman, an Indian Tamil immigrant and leader of the Ceylon Workers' Congress which represents the Indian Tamil plantation workers of the central hill country, was being sponsored by India and was taking the first step in the eventual creation of an independent Tamil Eelam. The Society for the Protection of Sinhalese Interests has demanded that there should be no peace initiative at this stage, now that the LTTE are losing the war. Others, both within the select committee and outside, have pointed out that a major Sri Lankan military assault by air could result in extensive Tamil civilian casualties, while an assault on the ground could result in extensive casualties to Sri Lankan forces, especially on a terrain which is heavily mined by the LTTE and subject to deadly ambushes by the insurgents.

SAARC: The Weak Reed

Against this background it is no surprise that the summit of the heads of state of the seven-member South Asian Association of Regional Cooperation which was to have been held in November in Colombo, collapsed. The ostensible reason was that the King of Bhutan decided not to attend for fear of a coup by Bhutanese citizens of Nepali origin during his absence. Prime Minister Narasimha Rao of India immediately claimed that a summit was not possible without the presence of all the heads of state and refused to attend. President Ranasinghe Premadasa of Sri Lanka, supported by Pakistani Prime Minister Nawaz Sharif, privately stated that the Indian decision was a form of petty revenge for the sabotage of the last summit by Sri Lanka in protest against the presence of Indian Peace-Keeping Forces in Sri Lanka. Sharif visited Colombo anyway in a show of support for Premadasa.

A second attempt in December was more successful, and the heads of all the SAARC states gathered in Colombo. Surprisingly, this meeting made some headway in their efforts to cooperate. The final Colombo Declaration of 21 December 1991 called for strengthening the institutions of the Association through the setting up of various committees and groups, and for an integrated programme of action on common economic and social concerns. The debacle in November and the sudden rejuvenation of the SAARC in December, were indicative of the confused and fluctuating state of relations among the countries of the region. Democracy and the free-market economy are making strides in South Asia. The success of these two trends, however, will depend on the degree to which the indigenous governments can control the use of ethnic nationalism and contain separatist violence.

Africa

Political activity, generally considered by most African governments in the past as synonymous with subversion, reached hyperactive levels in 1991 as the democratic process on the continent lurched forward. Long starved of genuine political competition, African states indulged in a feast of national conferences, referenda and elections, with a multiplicity of parties in several states pursuing the still elusive grail of stable democratic politics. For some, the movement towards democracy took two steps forward and one step back; for others there was constant shuffling, but no clear sense of direction. In virtually all, the call for genuine democracy was the principal rallying cry; though in many, internecine disputes still took a violent rather than oratorical form.

Officially, by the beginning of 1992, only Sudan and Malawi were wholly one-party states. Nevertheless, while not all other states had fully embraced a multiparty system, political competition was widely permitted. In Zambia, Kenneth Kaunda was defeated at the polls, and in Kenya, Daniel arap Moi, one of Africa's most renowned supporters of the one-party state, finally accepted the principle of multiparty politics. The same was true of President Paul Biya of Cameroon, who permitted genuine legislative elections on 1 March 1992. Some leaders just would not let go, however. Perhaps most spectacularly, President Mobuto of Zaire, who approved the principle of a national conference but then suspended its operations, sending the country into the ungovernable chaos many had predicted (see *Strategic Survey 1990–1991*, p. 226) with no hope of any external support or assistance.

While many elections were held, and long-standing leaders were shaken in power or toppled from it, the position of the army in many states was still of great importance. This and the wild proliferation of political parties, or conversely, the stage-management of their creation, indicated that it would be some time before the form of democracy could be well entrenched in the substance. International organizations and most Western countries tried during the year to coax forward the democratic process. As a rule, however, most (including Europe's traditionally most active African power, France), felt the need to keep a certain distance, repeating the virtues of democracy, but variously unable, unwilling or uncertain as how best to advance it.

The perfect example of these sometimes contradictory trends was provided by events in Togo. Riots and strikes in April 1991 forced General Etienne Eyadéma, who had previously resisted calls for political liberalization, to convene a national conference on democracy. By 28 August the President found himself stripped of most of his power. A parliament was elected, as was a Prime Minister, Joseph Kokou Koffigoh, a lawyer who presided over a public debate about Eyadéma's human rights record and the corruption of the old regime.

Certain sectors of the army, however, were clearly opposed to the reforming tendencies and they particularly objected to the banning of Eyadéma from future presidential elections. When the transitional government banned the General's political party at the end of November, troops loyal to him sought to topple Koffigoh, who immediately appealed for French assistance to 're-establish order'. Three hundred French troops were sent to neighbouring Benin, but the direct intervention, which some in the French government supported, never materialized. Without outside support Koffigoh was forced in early December to give in to the army's demands, which included the suspension of the government created by the national conference and its replacement by a 'government of national unity'. Although the multiparty system put in place by the conference was not abolished, Eyadéma was effectively restored as the country's leader, even if Koffigoh was allowed to stay on and name a new interim government in January. While a date for elections was fixed, the stability of a democratic process which could be so easily disturbed by a few troops was put into question, as was the commitment by France unambiguously to support democratic forces in the face of resistance from old autocratic allies.

The situation in Congo was slightly better and offered a different prototype of the swings and roundabouts of democratic fortunes in Africa. A national conference assembled in February, and when its work concluded in June, President Denis Sassou-Nguesso was deprived of his control over the armed forces, and executive power was given to André Milongo, a former member of the World Bank. Ernest Kombo, a Catholic bishop who had chaired the conference, was charged with supervising the drafting of a constitution which would later be put to a referendum. Although the economic situation was dire, and many began to bemoan the tribalism that had partly contributed to the creation of over 60 political parties, Nguesso, Milongo and Kombo managed to rule for a few months as an informal triumvirate.

In early January a disaffected army made its move. Soldiers surrounded government buildings, demanding the dismissal of the secretary of state for the armed forces; a reversal of reforms of the army; and pay increases. By the middle of the month they were demanding the resignation of the prime minister. Milongo managed to hold on to power by acceding to some of these demands. If a planned referendum on the new constitution is indeed held, the way will be cleared, in principle, for legislative elections in April, and a presidential election in June.

Throughout Africa, democracy's progress in 1991 was fettered not only by the competing ambitions of opposition politicians, military officers and presidents hoping to hang on to power, but by ethnic and secessionist disputes which challenged state cohesion. In Mali, for example, the interim government of Lt Col Amadou Toumani Touré, which had come to power in March 1991 on a wave of popular protest, pledged an acceleration of the political process, but it spent more time managing the Tuareg rebellion it had inherited than managing a transition to elected politicians. Throughout the year Tuareg rebels seeking autonomy for the country's sixth and seventh regions (between Gao and Timbuktu) attacked police stations and administrative offices. The backlash against the Tuareg and Moors drove many of them into Mauritania and Algeria, thus embroiling these countries directly in the conflict. By December, Tuareg groups managed to unite under an umbrella organization, thus facilitating peace talks in Algeria in January 1992 which led to a cease-fire agreement. A precondition for holding effective legislative elections in Mali thus became linked to finding a formula for proper Tuareg representation.

An Angolan peace treaty was finally signed between the ruling MPLA and the opposition UNITA forces. As the year wore on and divisions within the MPLA rose to the surface, the government showed considerable signs of disorganization (particularly at the UN-supervised assembly camps throughout the country) and even of atrophy. Many of the government's senior members reportedly investigated the prospect of taking refuge in Portugal. UNITA appeared better organized until members who were not from the majority Ovimbundu tribe left the movement after disagreements with the leader Jonas Savimbi. This left UNITA open to the attack of being just a large tribal grouping. The elections, which are scheduled for September 1992, will depend for their success *inter alia* on a favourable merging of the two armies, an outcome still in doubt early in the year.

In Mozambique, however, the situation was not so hopeful. Despite meetings throughout the year in Rome between the government and the opposition Renamo, a cease-fire agreement could not be reached. By March 1992, a third protocol had been signed between the parties on electoral procedures, but there was still disagreement on the drawing up of a constitution and arranging a cease-fire. Outside donors expressed concern about the corrupt and inept government which President Joachim Chissano was leading, but neither was anyone much impressed by the cat-and-mouse game Renamo was playing at the peace talks.

In Western, Central and Southern Africa ethnicity and demands for autonomy were part of a hesitant political process. In the Horn of Africa in 1991 they became a major challenge to the principles of territorial integrity. The confirmed secession of Somaliland would especially create a potential precedent that few in Africa would find congenial. Perhaps ironically, of all the votes cast in Africa throughout 1991 and the early part of 1992, the most pregnant with dramatic consequences was South Africa's referendum on President de Klerk's reform process. The overwhelming 'yes' that the white voters produced offered the pessimist the prospect of a violent rearguard action by the extreme right, while it gave the optimist hope that Africa's most disliked regime could now move ahead to produce a power-sharing agreement with the majority black population which would be a model of political compromise.

THE HORN OF AFRICA

For many years the Horn has been an extremely volatile region, with only the superpowers able to restrain the worst excesses. When these outside powers cut most of their links with the region in January 1991 the security situation deteriorated rapidly. Middle Eastern powers, which had shown an interest in the late 1980s, were too preoccupied with the post-Gulf War developments to give much attention to the Horn. Iran, focusing on Sudan, was perhaps the only Gulf power keen to establish influence in the region.

All four countries of the region – Ethiopia, Djibouti, Somalia and Sudan – suffered heightened political turbulence and they face increased uncertainty. The old political order gave way in Ethiopia and Somalia, but the successor regimes are unable to establish stability in either country, and there is no end in sight to their political and economic misery. Somalia slid fast into anarchy, as clan-based factions fought for political control in the capital, Mogadishu, and throughout the country. In Ethiopia, the long-running civil wars in Eritrea and Tigray came to an end when the central government collapsed, but fighting broke out again in other parts of the country. Adding to these problems were the declarations of de facto independence by Eritrea from Ethiopia and by the Somaliland Republic from Somalia which are certain to exacerbate existing difficulties in Ethiopia, Somalia and Djibouti.

While other countries in the region made some moves towards political pluralism, Sudan remained firmly under a fundamentalist military dictatorship. Members of the Islamic fundamentalist National Islamic Front dominated virtually every facet of public life, reducing the military leader, Omar Hassan al-Bashir, to a figurehead. Fighting between government forces and the Sudan People's Liberation Army continued, and neither side appeared willing to negotiate peace. The SPLA position, however, was weakened when the organization broke apart in August 1991 and its two rival factions engaged in fierce inter-ethnic fighting.

In late 1991 major guerrilla attacks shook even Djibouti, which had enjoyed peace since independence in 1977. President Hassan Gouled's leadership came under serious challenge as a section of the Afar ethnic community, which formed the Front for the Restoration of Unity and Democracy, demanded radical changes in the country's political system. The outbreak of fighting in this last peaceful enclave epitomized the disasters that had engulfed the region.

Ethiopia

On 21 May 1991 the 14-year rule of Ethiopian dictator Mengistu Haile Mariam came to an end. As Mengistu fled the country, Ethiopia appeared to be ripping apart at the seams. The US sponsored the peace talks in London on 27–28 May 1991, attended by representatives of the Mengistu regime, the Eritrean People's Liberation Front, the Oromo Liberation Front and the Ethiopian People's Revolutionary Democratic Front. Before the talks were over, US Assistant Secretary of State for African Affairs, Herman Cohen, invited the EPRDF to occupy Addis Ababa 'to stabilize the situation'. The EPRDF formed a government under President Meles Zenawi, a former guerrilla leader.

Mengistu's escape to Zimbabwe was seen by some as a great opportunity for Ethiopians to establish peace and stability, but that reaction reflected a narrow interpretation of the causes of Ethiopia's problems. Mengistu's centralized and dictatorial rule, and his misguided macroeconomic policies no doubt intensified these problems, but most of them predated his leadership. For centuries, Ethiopia's original Amhara and Tigray inhabitants had conquered, assimilated and oppressed other ethnic groups; long before Mengistu, Ethiopia had an authoritarian and centralized political structure.

Throughout the 1980s Mengistu had come under considerable pressure from Western powers to show respect for human rights and to liberalize his political system. In March 1990, when his defence perimeter was shrinking, and again in early 1991, when it had almost disappeared, he had announced a package of measures to encourage political pluralism, but these moves granted too little and came too late.

The post-Mengistu Meles government is based on the National Charter, which was approved at a peace conference held in Addis Ababa in July 1991. The conference agreed that the important posts of President, Vice-President, Prime Minister and Secretary to the Council of Representatives should be held by people from different ethnic backgrounds or political groups. An 87-member Council of Representatives, responsible for drafting the new Ethiopian constitution, was also elected.

The absence of discord at the July conference raised hopes for Ethiopia's future. But the surface impression of harmony was no accident; the meeting had been carefully stage-managed by Meles. The EPRDF called the conference, prepared the agenda, drew up the Charter, made agreements with key delegations over seat allocations prior to the meeting and created several of the groups that participated. Although the EPRDF has only 32 seats in the Council, the seat allocation was manipulated to give the EPRDF and its allies a built-in majority. In the final analysis, the smooth functioning of the Council will depend on the durability of unity within the EPRDF and cooperation between the EPRDF and its allies.

The leading group within the EPRDF, the Tigrayan People's Liberation Front, was established in 1975 with the help of the EPLF. The TPLF, dominated by Tigrinya-speakers, sought to modify its image and goals in the early 1980s. In 1981, it played a leading role in the formation of the Amhara-dominated Ethiopian People's Democratic Movement, and eight years later merged with the EPDM to form the now-ruling EPRDF; by 1991, the EPRDF included several other resistance groups. There has never been any doubt, however, that the TPLF, by virtue of its superior military force, was the senior partner in the coalition. It was not surprising, therefore, that when the EPRDF captured Addis Ababa in May 1991, it was Meles, a TPLF leader, who emerged as Ethiopia's interim president.

As events unfolded, it was clear that one factor Meles needed to take seriously was self-determination for the Afars. The Afar ethnic group, which occupies the original Afar province, also spreads into Djibouti, Eritrea and several Ethiopian provinces. Their main political group, the Afar Liberation Front, was formed in the mid-1970s by the son of Ali Mirah, the traditional Afar leader. In 1987 the Afar-inhabited Assab province was separated from the rest of Eritrea and given autonomous status, but that did not appease the Afars, because the most fertile land in the Awash valley remained under Amhara control. In 1991, Meles tried to deal with the recently-reconstituted ALF as the only legitimate representative of the Afar people. His plan was to try to marginalize other Afar groups whose leaders had held senior positions under Mengistu.

Meles tried to encourage a return to feudal rule in Afar society, with Ali Mirah as leader, but that merely heightened tensions between Mirah and anti-feudal elements in the Afar community. By mid-1991, members of Ali Mirah's family and other groups were seeking alliances with leading Djibouti Afar politicians. In Eritrea, the EPLF, which had traditionally supported self-determination for the Afar, insisted that Assab province, which incorporates about 60% of Eritrea's coastline, remain part of Eritrea. This would give Eritrea exclusive control of the Red Sea coastline from Sudan to Djibouti.

Meles also had to deal with the Oromos, Somalis and other ethnic groups which wanted more freedom. The OLF virtually disappeared from the political scene until the late 1980s. It now includes four other Oromo groups that signed an agreement for unity and cooperation on 17 July 1991. Yahannes Lata Wagayo, the OLF leader, attended the London peace conference in May 1991, but was unhappy with the way the US pre-empted its results. The OLF had hoped to play a bigger role in the post-Mengistu government, but the US unilaterally encouraged the EPRDF to occupy Addis Ababa. The OLF, which has 12 seats in the Council of Representatives, said on 29 May 1991 that it would seek a referendum on the future of the Oromo people.

The fall of Mengistu and the proliferation of political groups made governing very difficult. The EPRDF had originally been fascinated by an Albanian-type of communism, but when an opportunity for leadership was dangled before it in 1991, the Front made a dramatic switch and accepted US-engineered democratic programmes. It was not clear, however, how well Meles and his associates understood democratic ideals and multiparty democracy. As late as 1990, the EPRDF was still condemning multiparty democracy as 'dangerous, confusing, anti-democratic and bourgeois'.

The dislocation caused by the fighting in the final days of the Mengistu regime aggravated Ethiopia's economic problems. The challenge for Meles was to liberalize the economy and establish conditions conducive to foreign investment. By early 1992, however, the new government had still not passed the necessary legislation to encourage such investment.

Independence for Eritrea

The Eritrean People's Liberation Front, established in 1971, had always sought full independence for the former Italian colony that was federated with Ethiopia under UN auspices in 1952. With Mengistu's ouster, the road to Eritrean independence under EPLF leadership became clear. The EPLF's Secretary-General, Issaias Afewerki, who is also head of the interim administration in Eritrea, said on 29 May 1991 that he planned to organize a referendum (now slated for 1993) to determine the views of Eritreans on full independence or federation with Ethiopia. This appears a tactical ploy only, because the EPLF will accept nothing short of independence. Although the Eritrean leadership has pledged that Ethiopia can use the ports of Assab and Massawa now in Eritrea's territory, many Ethiopians find it difficult to see how their country could do without Eritrea.

Eritrean independence has both national and regional implications. Eritreans are not a homogeneous group; there are several ethnic groups and two major religions (Islam and Christianity) in Eritrea. Moreover, along with the social diversity, these have in the past led to violent conflicts and major differences are likely to resurface. The territory's independence also poses problems for Ethiopia, Djibouti and the OAU. Meles will find it hard to refuse autonomy for other parts of Ethiopia if Eritrean secession is accepted. The position Eritrea takes on the Afar problem will affect Djibouti: self-determination for the Afar in Ethiopia and Eritrea could complicate Djibouti's ethnic problems. The OAU is worried that Eritrean independence might encourage secession in other parts of Africa.

The Israelis are also troubled. If Eritrea sought closer relations with the Arab world or joined the Arab League, it would confirm Israel's fears of the Red Sea becoming an 'Arab' lake. Israel's air routes to Eastern and Southern Africa could also be affected, because the Israeli national airline to Nairobi and Johannesburg overflies Eritrean airspace.

Even Greater Problems in Somalia

President Siad Barre, who had ruled Somalia from October 1969, was toppled in January 1991. He had headed an authoritarian regime that literally ruined the country: the economy was in a shambles, political institutions had collapsed, corruption was rampant and morale in the civil and armed services was non-existent. The situation was so appalling that few people had any illusion that Barre's fall would bring an immediate end to the suffering. In the confusion before and after his departure, government offices and foreign embassies were looted, and water and electricity were cut off in Mogadishu for months.

Moreover, the opposition forces were every bit as chaotic as the Barre regime, thereby ensuring that the immediate post-Barre era would be chaotic. The main resistance forces were clan-based: the Somali National Movement, established in 1981 by the Issaq of northern Somalia; the United Somali Congress, formed in 1989 by the Hawiye of central Somalia; and the Somali Patriotic Movement, created in 1989 by the Ogadenis. Increasingly, every public issue came to be defined in clan terms. It was, therefore, not surprising that when Barre was ousted by the USC the country was plunged into deeper problems.

Barre's successor, Ali Mahdi Mohammed, who belongs to the Hawiye (Abgal) clan, was promptly installed in office in controversial circumstances, without the approval of some USC factions or the support of other resistance movements. The Hawiye clan has about six sub-clans or lineages, two of which – Abgal and Habr Gedir – are bitterly divided. His appointment was accordingly contested by the USC faction aligned with General Mohammed Farah 'Aideed' of the Hawiye (Habr Gedir) clan, as well as by the SNM and the SPM, with whom Aideed had signed an agreement in August 1990. In these circumstances Somalia was ungovernable throughout 1991. Mahdi controlled Mogadishu for only a few months, and in May northern Somalia, the former British Somaliland, seceded.

Somalia's relative stability in the 1970s and early 1980s depended on Barre's skilful manipulation of domestic politics. He maintained power by suppressing critics and detaining opponents; by playing on clan interests and rivalries; and, occasionally, by buying off opposition groups with cash. By the late 1980s, however, it had become obvious that he no longer had the skill to manipulate sectional interests nor the vision to lead the country out of its political quagmire.

Barre had relied on his Marehan clan to rule, but his main power base until the late 1980s had been the army, which was dominated by Ogadenis. Although all Somalis belong to one ethnic group, clan loyalty often undercuts the sense of shared nationhood. Barre had prohibited any reference to clans in the early 1970s, but lineages continued to determine the course of the country's political development. Clan and lineage affiliations were vital in obtaining jobs, services and favours. Clan rivalry was so strong when Mahdi took office that there appeared little common ground left.

By early 1992 intra-clan fighting had left Mogadishu without a government and thousands of people dead. President Mahdi controlled only the northern sector of the capital. His embattled government is dominated by the Hawiye, although the Ogadenis and the Issaqs were also given important cabinet posts. Mahdi had promised to maintain a broad-based government of national reconciliation and a multiparty system, but persistent political squabbles prevented the realization of these objectives.

Barre's defeat in late January 1991 merely accelerated the disintegration of Somalia. First, the anti-Barre opposition forces had only one thing in common: the defeat of Barre. Second, when Barre was overthrown, power was assumed by the Hawiye, a clan that had played virtually no role in the anti-Barre struggle until just before his fall. Third, by appointing an interim president without consulting other groups, the USC contravened the August 1990 agreement to consult.

Since the overthrow of Barre, there have been several clan-based civil wars in Somalia, but it has been hard to gauge the direction of the fighting. One of the guerrilla groups includes Barre's forces, which regrouped in southern Somalia and have been trying to topple the Mahdi regime. In early 1991, some reports suggested that the SPM, which continued to occupy the countryside near Kismayu, had amalgamated with other groups from the Darod clan-family, including some Barre supporters, to form the Somali National Front.

Around Mogadishu, the USC continued to fight on several fronts, including fierce battles with its own breakaway groups. Factions within the USC, especially the Habr Gedir group led by Aideed and the Abgal group of President Mahdi, do not agree on several issues and the uneasy relations between them were exacerbated in July 1991. At the USC annual congress earlier that month, Aideed was elected chairman; later in the month, the national reconciliation conference in Djibouti confirmed Mahdi as Somali President for two years; Aideed apparently wanted both jobs. In November–December 1991, factional fighting was so intense that Mahdi's supporters had to withdraw from southern Mogadishu. According to international aid workers, the number of deaths from the unrestrained fighting in the city in these months alone was more than 4,000.

Issaq Secession

The Issaq clan, which comprises about 20% of Somalia's population, presented the strongest challenge to Barre's leadership from 1988 on. Their main political organization, the Somali National Movement, was formed in 1981 and nurtured by the Ethiopian government. The aim of the SNM was to overthrow Barre and establish a more democratic system in Somalia, but it was not heavily involved in the final assault against Mogadishu and thus denied a chance to form the immediate post-Barre government. Rather than continue the civil war against a new regime, the SNM leader, Abdurahman Ahmed Ali, proclaimed the 'Somaliland Republic' on 18 May 1991, with himself as president. Secession was not unanimously supported by the SNM leadership, however. Like most Somali groups, the SNM has been divided along ideological lines, with differences between the liberals,

Islamic fundamentalists and traditionalists. Some SNM leaders regarded the secessionist move not as final, but as merely a step towards renegotiating the 1960 unification arrangement.

The secession has serious national and regional implications. An independent 'Somaliland Republic', dominated by Issaqs or the SNM, will be resented by other northern clans, especially the Dolbahante and Gadabursi. Ahmed Ali formed a 17-member interim government in 1991 and promised multiparty elections within two years. Although 13 out of 17 members of the interim government were Issaqs, its membership appeared to have been carefully balanced between the main Issaq sub-clans and other clans in the territory. It would not be surprising, however, if the 'Somaliland Republic' mirrored the anarchic conditions of the rest of Somalia.

As of early 1992, the 'Somaliland Republic' had not been formally recognized by any country. Its immediate neighbours, Ethiopia and Djibouti, were worried about the possible effects secession would have on their internal stability. In particular, both Djibouti and Somalia have campaigned against the international recognition of the territory. Because the secession was contrary to Article III of the Charter of the OAU and appeared to set a precedent for other contentious problems in the rest of Africa, the new republic is unlikely to find allies on the continent.

Since Barre's fall, several parties, including the UN, Italy, Djibouti and Egypt have tried to mediate the conflicts in Somalia. The new UN Secretary-General, Boutros Ghali, has had a long-standing interest in the Horn, and early in 1992 he sent Under Secretary-General James Jonah to try to persuade the warring factions to negotiate peace, but to no avail. The various clans and sub-clans still hate each other vehemently, clan leaders have virtually no legitimacy and their supporters can abandon them at any time, and the number of clan militias keeps rising. The uncontrollable Somali factions have no common ground for negotiating and there is little hope that the fighting will end soon.

The War in the Sudan

The antagonists in Sudan have even greater differences than those in Somalia. Sudan's difficulties in 1991 included the increased influence of Muslim fanatics in the government, a deteriorating economy, a continuing civil war and a major split within the Sudan People's Liberation Army.

Sudan's military leader, Omar Hassan al-Bashir, who has been under the influence of Islamic fundamentalists since taking power in June 1989, appears to be a convenient figurehead for the National Islamic Front, which in fact runs the country. The NIF controls the civil service, the economy, the media, financial institutions and the military. Muslim moderates in the civil service and the army have been sidelined and replaced by fundamentalists. The soaring influence

of fanatics and their hostility to external advice has accelerated
Sudan's political and economic decline.

Sudan is unable to feed its people, a predicament aggravated by
the increase in the number of refugees in the country. The traditional
food security structures have collapsed, most Sudanese families no
longer grow enough food for themselves, and poverty and malnu-
trition are widespread. According to UN estimates, more than eight
million Sudanese faced starvation in 1991 unless urgent relief
measures were undertaken.

The food crisis in 1990 and 1991 was compounded by the arrogance of the Bashir government, which refused until December 1990
to admit to the extent and gravity of the famine. The Sudanese government also sought to maintain sole control of the transportation and
distribution of aid. The UN World Food Programme, the US Agency
for International Development and UNICEF provided much of the
badly-needed relief to Sudan in 1991, but by the end of the year the food
situation still remained critical in some parts of the country. There was
no doubt that the government's resistance to external, especially Western, assistance exacerbated Sudan's economic problems.

Sudan's relations with some Arab states in 1991 were fluid and
unstable, partly because of Bashir's dependence on support from
Muslim fanatics, and partly because of the changing alignments in the
Arab world after the 1991 Gulf War. Egyptian leaders feared that success for Sudan's Muslim Brotherhood would encourage fundamentalist Muslims in Egypt. Accordingly, in 1991 Egypt sought to influence
Sudan's domestic politics. Along with the US, Egypt quietly supported
a coalition of anti-Bashir forces in the National Democratic Alliance.
These included General Ali Ahmed Fathi, former Commander-in-
Chief of Sudan's Armed Forces, some SPLA supporters, and some
members of the traditional parties, especially the Democratic Union-
ist Party, which is affiliated to the pro-Egyptian Khatmiyya sect.
Egypt wanted to see the DUP leader, Ahmad al-Mirghani, assume a
bigger role in Sudanese politics, but given the predominance of NIF
supporters in key positions, the DUP/Khatmiyya alliance had
virtually no chance of taking on important roles in the government,
save through a military coup.

Sudan's support for Iraq during the Gulf crisis alienated Saudi
Arabia and Kuwait. Prior to this, Iraq's involvement in Sudan was low
key, and its main interest was to help moderate Muslims maintain
some influence, because of the fear that a fundamentalist-dominated
government might drift towards Iran. During the crisis, Iraq increased
its aid to Sudan, which reciprocated by offering diplomatic support.
The Bashir regime saw no problem in being close to both Iraq and
Iran, and its vacillating relationship with Iran improved dramatically
in 1991. By late 1991, there were reports that Iran had sent arms and a
number of Revolutionary Guards to train the Sudanese. The visit by
Iranian President Ali Rafsanjani to Khartoum in December 1991 was

an indication of the close rapport between the two states. This has complicated both the Bashir government dealings with internal forces opposed to fundamentalist influence, and Sudan's relations with some of its neighbours.

One of the internal forces strongly opposed to fundamentalist influence in the government was the SPLA, which has been fighting a civil war against various Sudanese governments since 1983. It was largely because of fundamentalist influence that Bashir was unwilling to negotiate seriously with the SPLA over whether the *Sharia* (Islamic law) would be extended to the south of the country which is largely Christian. Some of Bashir's supporters would prefer secession by the south to a modification of the *Sharia*. During 1991 Bashir's policy on the civil war was erratic: government declarations of war were often followed by calls for peace. After the Meles government in Ethiopia had expelled the SPLA in mid-1991, Bashir launched an offensive against southerners, but his forces suffered badly.

From mid-1991, Nigerian President Ibrahim Babangida tried to negotiate peace on behalf of the OAU, but the two sides had little in common. The US government also talked to the SPLA leader John Garang and some Sudanese officials separately, but there was no enthusiasm for a settlement on either side. The US plan required both to accept a cease-fire and to permit the passage of relief supplies to areas where they were needed. As of early 1992, prospects for ending the conflict were dim. Although both sides talked of peace, neither was ready to make the compromises necessary to achieve it.

The SPLA's stand against the Khartoum government was weakened considerably by internal divisions in 1991. The movement claimed to speak for the entire southern region, but some ethnic groups resented the fact that it was dominated by the Dinka. The smaller tribes feared that the secession of the region would lead to Dinka overlordship. Some began to view the SPLA as an instrument through which the Dinka hoped to control other tribes. Their resentment, in addition to policy and personality differences, caused a major split within the SPLA in August 1991. A faction of non-Dinkas, known as the Nasir group, accused Garang, a Dinka himself, of autocratic rule and arrogance, and demanded his resignation before it could consider rejoining the SPLA.

At the policy level, the Garang faction insisted that the SPLA's principal aim was the creation of a pluralist, united and secular Sudan, while the breakaway faction felt the grand plan of transforming the whole country was no longer feasible. It felt that recent changes in the international climate dictated a change in their objectives. The US also tried to persuade Garang to back away from a comprehensive blueprint for the whole country. The split in the SPLA led to fierce fighting between the two factions, resulting in many civilian casualties, with the Bashir government benefiting the most.

Upset in Djibouti

Until 1991 Djibouti was the most stable and peaceful country in the Horn. Yet beneath the surface problems were developing. These revolved around the centralization of power by President Hassan Gouled, the issue of succession, and ethnic tensions. In 1991, these issues bubbled to the surface.

Since independence in 1977, Djibouti's stability had been due largely to Gouled's acute political skill in balancing this ethnically divided society, and to the French commitment to provide aid and to guard Djibouti's independence. Guerrilla attacks in the north by members of the Afar-dominated FRUD in late 1991, however, considerably changed Djibouti's image as an oasis of stability in the Horn, and suggested that Gouled's ability to balance ethnic interests was diminishing. Increased violence, demands for more freedom, and political changes in neighbouring states all had an impact on the stability of the country.

The most politically destabilizing element, however, remained the centralization of political power and decision-making. President Gouled has, over the years, arrogated enormous political power to his office, both as head of state and as president of the ruling party, the *Rassemblement pour le progrès*. He governs the territory as his personal fiefdom, with a few of his Issa cronies controlling the judiciary, the police, the civil service, the army and the economy. Behind the appearance of political stability has been a one-man show growing weaker because of rampant corruption and the impotence of Djibouti's public institutions.

In anticipation of Gouled stepping down in 1993, when his second term expires, some senior politicians started to position themselves in 1991 for succession. The most senior politician in Gouled's cabinet is Prime Minister Hamadou, but as an Afar he has little chance of becoming president. Elders from the Issa clan will nominate Gouled's successor. One of the front-runners among the Issa politicians is Foreign Minister Moumin Bahdon Farah, who is a close ally of Ismail Omar Guelleh, secretary to the cabinet and Gouled's nephew. In 1991, Farah and Guelleh targeted a group of Issa personalities, who were also gearing up for the presidency: Ismail Guedi Hared, a senior presidential adviser, and his allies, including Army Commander-in-Chief, General Ali Meidal Waiss.

In a political manoeuvre attributed to Farah's camp, General Waiss's powers were reduced in early 1991 by the creation of a National Defence Council charged with devising, analysing and initiating national defence strategy. In an attempt to marginalize General Waiss further, the government established a ministerial commission of inquiry in mid-1991 to investigate charges that he had misappropriated funds. While there might be some merit in investigating corruption by the Commander-in-Chief, corruption was so widespread in the Gouled government that the decision to single out General Waiss was viewed as just part of the race for the presidency. While the attention of senior politicians was focused on the uncertainties of presidential succession, the country faced its most serious ethnic problems since independence.

A long-standing rivalry between the major ethnic groups, the Issa and the Afar erupted in November 1991. The Issa, a Somali people of the Dir clan-family, make up about 40% of the total population, while the Afars form about 35% of the total. Although the Issa and Afar have co-existed without major conflicts, there have always been latent tensions between them.

On several occasions the Afar, who feel they have lost out since independence, have accused the Issa of nepotism and tribalism. The resulting animosity between the two groups has been amplified by the fact that the principal anti-government opposition has been largely Afar. In January 1991, the government claimed there had been an abortive coup, following which they detained more than 60 Afars, including Ali Aref, Chief Minister of the territory before independence in 1977. The authorities claimed Aref was the financial backer of the rebels, and that if the plot had succeeded, there would have been a civil war between the Afar and Issa communities.

FRUD, which was launched in April 1991 by Mohammed Adoyta Youssef, was also Afar-dominated, but the government persistently portrayed it as a group of 'Ethiopian mercenaries'. Adoyta argued that his movement aimed at replacing 'President Gouled's tribalist government' with one of national union and demanded a dialogue with the government, but Gouled refused to recognize the movement. Nevertheless, FRUD appears to have become a symbol of resistance and salvation for the people of the northern towns of Obock and Tadjourah. It claimed to have more than 2,000 guerrilla fighters deployed to the north and south of the capital, but it was hard to verify its strength and other claims the movement made in relation to its successes. One of FRUD's biggest problems was a lack of even rudimentary communications equipment. The only way in which the mobile units operating to the west of Obock could send messages to the reinforcements waiting out in the north was by camel.

The first clashes between government troops and FRUD took place at Alayli Dada in June 1991, but there were no large-scale attacks against government troops until 12–13 November when FRUD killed 28 soldiers and captured more than 50 others. The Gouled government responded by deploying more than 300 troops from the Issa-dominated National Security Forces (*Force Nationale de Sécurité* - FNS), but this may have made the problem worse. The brutality of the FNS forced about one-third of Obock's 10,000 inhabitants to flee to other areas, including Ethiopia. By early 1992, fighting between government forces and the rebels was still going on near Tadjourah.

The Djibouti government sought help from France in its fight against the rebels. France refused to intervene directly against the anti-government forces. It viewed the fighting in northern Djibouti as an internal revolt and thus not covered by the military agreements it had reached with Djibouti in February 1991. These agreements gave the French forces responsibility for surveillance of air and maritime traffic, and Paris saw them as a response to the Gulf crisis and the consequent use of Djibouti as a training ground for French helicopter crews. In early 1992, however, the French military in Djibouti, the foreign ministry and the Elysée Palace were sending conflicting signals over Djibouti's internal crisis.

Prospects

The outlook is for more unpredictable changes in Ethiopia, Somalia, Sudan and Djibouti. Yet even those that occurred during 1991 and early 1992 were of a kind and a magnitude to create serious difficulties for the rest of Africa. The exercise of ethnic self-determination and prospective border changes could challenge the long-standing OAU dictum which insists that the borders inherited from the colonial period, no matter how arbitrary, must stand. The immediate risk for the neighbouring states of the Horn consists largely in managing the consequences for their own security of instability in the Horn, particularly when this produces a large influx of refugees. For the remainder of the OAU, however, the fact that the use of armed force in the Horn may result in the creation of new states along language, ethnic and tribal lines is an unwelcome development. Despite their wish to remain aloof from the problems in the Horn, outside states may find that position difficult to maintain. Unless the OAU becomes engaged in managing their disputes around principles which it has upheld over time, both the principles and the OAU itself risk becoming marginalized, and African security becomes threatened by ever more parochial disputes.

SOUTH AFRICA: DISOWNING APARTHEID

On 17 March 1992 white South Africans defied their history, their fears and the gloomier expectations of a watching world to become that rarest of all political phenomena: a ruling tribe willing to shed its exclusive hold on power. By voting two to one in favour of continuing negotiations with their black fellow countrymen for a new democratic constitution, they also and almost incidentally 'closed the book on apartheid', as President F. W. de Klerk said as he welcomed the result of the whites-only referendum.

The referendum was South Africa's second great watershed in an eventful year. The first was undoubtedly the historic gathering in Johannesburg on December 20–21 when 19 delegations, representing not only the ruling National Party and the African National Congress, but a host of smaller parties and homeland leaders, attended the Convention for a Democratic South Africa (Codesa). These long delayed all-party talks grappled with the problem of how to move from minority rule to a democratic South Africa which, nevertheless, guaranteed the rights of minorities. At the end of one-and-a-half days, 17 of the delegations committed themselves to an undivided South Africa, free of discrimination; a sovereign constitution enshrining the separation of powers of the executive, legislature and the judiciary; and a multiparty democracy based on universal adult suffrage and a justiciable bill of rights.

Making a Positive Choice

If Codesa marked the true beginnings of the new South Africa, however, the referendum signalled a complete and final break with the past. De Klerk's decision to hold the referendum had been prompted by a string of by-election defeats inflicted on his government by the extreme rightwing Conservative Party, culminating in the loss of the highly symbolic Nationalist stronghold of Potchefstroom in mid-February.

It appeared at first to be a high-risk gamble. Although de Klerk had long committed himself to seeking a mandate from the white electorate before introducing major constitutional change, the timing of this sudden test of white opinion seemed at first glance to be singularly inopportune. Significant advances had been made during the course of another turbulent year in negotiations with the ANC, which remains the government's main opponent and negotiating partner, but there was little visible agreement on the outline of the new constitution. There was instead continuing brutal political violence in the black townships (which claimed a further 2,672 lives in 1991), a soaring crime rate in the white suburbs and a continuing decline in real incomes as South Africa failed to lift itself out of a deep and persistent economic recession. Coupling these disabilities with the white electorate's reputation for having moved, throughout its history, consistently to the right pushed up the odds against de Klerk and in favour of the racist – and populist – Conservative Party.

The sense that white South Africa was facing its own 'High Noon' was compounded by the President's promise that if he lost the referendum he would call an immediate election – which he would have found difficult to win in the face of a referendum defeat. In the event his decision was revealed to be a master stroke by a canny political tactician. Unsettled by the speed of his challenge, the CP, led by Dr Andries Treurnicht, first dithered over whether or not to accept it, then made the fatal mistake of aligning itself with the neo-Nazi paramilitarist Afrikaner Resistance Movement (AWB), thus repelling many potential supporters.

The government, for its part, was supported by its long-time opponents, the liberal Democratic Party and by the business community which, dreading South Africa's return to the international

isolation ward, ploughed hundreds of thousands of rand into an adver-
tising campaign which spelt out the stark consequences of a 'no' vote.
Despite some mild expressions of annoyance that, once again, white
South Africans were voting unilaterally to decide the future of the
country, the ANC played its part by delivering an agreement with the
government on the structure of the interim government. ANC President Nelson Mandela reminded white South Africans that if they
turned their backs on reform they would be voting not for a return to
apartheid, but for civil war. Almost as persuasive was the undertaking
by a leading cricket official to withdraw South Africa from the World
Cup where its triumphs had become a potent symbol of the country's
emergence from its long and lonely isolation from the rest of the world.

In the end, white South Africa peered into the abyss towards
which Dr Treurnicht beckoned and drew back, recognizing that the
momentum of change could not be stopped without consequences far
more frightening than the prospect of sharing power with their black
compatriots. In an 85% poll they gave de Klerk an overwhelming
68.6% mandate to continue down a path of reform which, before the
end of the present parliament in 1994, will create a new democratic
constitution in which black South Africans will participate fully.

The vote also effectively pulled the teeth of the right-wing tiger.
Although in the immediate aftermath of the referendum, the Conservative Party papered over the divisions within its own ranks, an
eventual split appeared inevitable. A number of its more moderate
politicians are expected to defy the CP's boycott of the all-party constitutional talks. Others are expected to throw their weight behind the
AWB, while Dr Treurnicht presides over a dwindling rump. At the
same time, de Klerk, having mobilized the white electorate behind
him in the referendum, has emerged in a far more powerful position
from which to negotiate with the ANC.

A Shaky Economy

If the referendum closed the book on apartheid, the final chapters had
been written earlier in the year when the government finally scrapped
the Group Areas Act, which imposed residential apartheid; the Land
Acts which, since 1913, had deprived black South Africans of rights of
ownership to all but 13% of the country; and the Population Registration Act, which colour coded all South Africans at birth.

The scrapping of this law on 12 July 1991 was itself the key to
lifting most of the US sanctions against South Africa in terms of the
Comprehensive Anti-Apartheid Act of 1986 (CAAA). The removal of
the CAAA sanctions (despite continued protestations from the ANC
that this was premature) led to a crumbling of anti-South African
measures around the world, with Japan and Israel rapidly following
the US lead. The last EC sanctions were finally lifted at the end of January 1992, after Denmark's minority government won the approval

of its parliament. Even the Commonwealth Heads of Government meeting in Harare on 2 October lifted 'people to people' sanctions (air links, visa restrictions and cultural boycotts) and said that the trade and investment sanctions would soon be phased out.

The most visible sign of South Africa's readmission to the world community in 1991, however, was not an immediate increase in trade and investment, but the welcoming back of its sports teams on to the world scene and the ability of South African Airways to secure new routes to countries which had long denied the South African carrier over-flight or landing rights. There was also a stream of businessmen and politicians from both Eastern Europe and African states to South Africa in search of trading agreements, diplomatic representation and investment. Many African states which had long covertly traded with South Africa were now willing openly to ignore the OAU ban on trade and diplomatic ties, as they saw in South Africa's relative economic strength the source of much desperately needed help. By the year's end South Africa had opened diplomatic missions in 16 African states.

The same considerations were the spur to a heightened level of interest in the capitals of Eastern Europe. A visit by President de Klerk to Moscow planned for late 1991 was postponed because of the turbulence in the Russian Republic, but 'offices of interest' which had been opened in Pretoria and Moscow were upgraded to full diplomatic status following a visit by Russian Foreign Minister Andrei Kozyrev to South Africa early in 1992.

Although the oil and arms embargo will remain until all the constitutional reforms are in place, the most important remaining sanction is the Gramm Amendment in the US which imposes a *de facto* veto on South African access to IMF loans. As South Africa maintains a strong current account surplus on its balance of payments it is not yet eligible for IMF funds. The repeal of the Gramm Amendment provisions, however, would be an important signal to international banks to resume long-term loans to South Africa, thus reversing the net capital outflow which has partially crippled the economy since international banks effectively foreclosed on the country in 1985.

Although it is widely expected that the Gramm Amendment will not be revoked until the ANC gives the nod, the US State Department indicated during the referendum campaign that it was preparing the way for such an eventuality. For its part, the ANC, which has failed to prevent the roll back of trade and investment sanctions, had given a clear sign that it will finally abandon this strategy following the creation of an interim government.

South Africa's desperate need for large injections of foreign capital and investment was underscored again last year by its persistent inability to lift itself out of its longest recession since World War II. Once again it registered negative growth of 0.5%, hampered at least in part by swingeing real interest rates which, nevertheless, failed to bring inflation down to less than 16%. With population growth of 2.3% a year and unemployment estimated at 45% of the adult population, the country's economic performance bodes ill for the hopes and aspirations of those who believe that their political liberation will bring an immediate economic dividend.

There is a widespread perception that mineral-rich South Africa is a wealthy country, but in fact it falls somewhere between Mexico and Argentina in terms of per capita GDP. Nevertheless, because of the 1985 debt freeze, it remains substantially under-borrowed compared to other developing countries (19.4% of GDP). With the erosion of sanctions it has begun to return to international capital markets on a significant scale, with four major European bond issues in the past year, despite the fact that the ANC sent a shiver through capital markets with its threat to 'review' all loans to the 'apartheid regime'.

It is now largely acknowledged by the international community that without direct foreign investment South Africa's downward economic spiral could cripple any successor government. For the time being foreign investors are sitting on their wallets, deterred at least in part by continuing confusion over the economic policies which may be adopted by a future black majority government.

Although the ANC has shed much of its socialist rhetoric and has begun to accept the imperative of economic growth and the need to retain white skills, capital and expertise, it remains under pressure from its supporters to embrace draconian redistributive policies and has periodically repeated its threat to nationalize 'the commanding heights of the economy'. Given the different strains of economic thinking within the ANC, and the possible, though ill-defined, influence of the South African Communist Party, investors remain unsure as to whether to accept assurances by more pragmatic officials that nationalization is simply one of the 'many options' currently being considered.

The need for some redistribution of national income is obvious in an economy which has been grossly skewed by apartheid. In 1991 and again in his 1992 budget, Finance Minister Barend du Plessis attempted to address this through substantial increases in government spending on black education, pensions, housing, health and welfare. Nevertheless, with 70% of South Africa's tax burden borne by the heavily taxed top 5% of income earners and with a budget deficit of 4.5% of GDP, he had little room for manoeuvre.

Indeed, the government's attempt last year to spread the tax burden by introducing 10% VAT on goods and services led to an immediate and direct clash with the ANC-backed Congress of South African Trade Unions and the Pan Africanist Congress's National Council of Trade Unions. The unions, offended as much by the fact that the government had not consulted them as by the fact that the tax had been imposed on basic foods, organized a successful two-day national strike. The government's response was to 'suspend' VAT on eight basic foods, but its lapse in 1992 could easily lead to a resumption of hostilities. The strike was marred by violent deaths and union intimidation, but the government's maladroit handling of the affair and the unions' response highlighted the way in which effective power could no longer be wielded by government alone.

Bombast and Bloodshed

While nagging doubt about the country's future economic policies is one factor inhibiting overseas investment, political violence and instability remain the most important brake on the inflow of foreign capital. The brutal civil war between ANC supporters and Chief Mangosuthu Buthelezi's Inkatha Freedom Party continued to rage in Natal and in the black townships of South Africa's industrial heartland.

A much trumpeted peace meeting between Nelson Mandela and Chief Buthelezi in January had little effect in dampening the violence. At the same time, allegations of security force involvement (the so-called Third Force) eroded the trust that had been built up between Mandela and de Klerk and threatened to derail the negotiating process itself. On 5 April 1991 the ANC issued a seven-point ultimatum, threatening to suspend negotiations unless the government met its demands by 9 May. These included the banning of all 'traditional weapons' – mainly the spears and axes carried by Chief Buthelezi's Inkatha *impis*; the dismissal of the Ministers of Police and Defence, Adriaan Vlok and General Magnus Malan; the appointment of a Commission of Enquiry into alleged misdeeds by the security establishment; and the phasing out of migrant workers hostels which had been the site of much of the violence.

The government moved rapidly to prevent the collapse of the peace process with the appointment of a liberal judge, Richard Goldstone, as a one-man commission of enquiry, and promised to ban most traditional weapons. But de Klerk, unwilling to face the hostility of a traditionally right-wing security establishment, refused to dismiss Malan and Vlok. The violence continued as allegations mounted of Third Force involvement in acts ranging from the assassination of political officials to the random massacres of mourners and train commuters. Former policemen and soldiers alleged that elements within the police and particularly the South African Defence Force were applying the same destabilization tactics to the internal political process as they had once employed with such devastating effect in Mozambique and other 'Frontline States'.

The key question was whether or not these were merely rogue elements of the now disbanded Civil Co-operation Bureau (the security forces' dirty-tricks brigade), or whether the campaign was being orchestrated by senior figures within the defence and police establishment. In July the issue plunged the government into its deepest crisis since de Klerk took office with disclosures that the police had provided Inkatha and its trade union affiliate with secret funds. For the first time the disclosures directly implicated government ministers and the scandal threatened to undermine de Klerk's international reputation, as well as his standing with the ANC. The President resolved this crisis by demoting Vlok and Malan. This failed to resolve the violence, however, largely because it could not be ascribed to one single cause. However much elements within the security forces may wish to destabilize the settlement process for their own ends, they could not do so without the long-standing hostility between the ANC and Inkatha, which had been further inflamed by Chief Buthelezi's growing conviction that he would be marginalized by any agreement that the ANC and the government reached. If this were to occur, he threatened, he would 'tear the agreement down in pieces and trample on it'. The conflict in black townships and the growing lawlessness in the white suburbs was further aggravated by a flood of weapons, mainly AK-47s, into South Africa from Mozambique.

As the ANC and the government traded accusations on who bore the main burden of responsibility for the violence, the bloodshed continued to threaten the peace process. In an effort to recover the momentum, 29 political, homeland, trade union and business organizations signed a National Peace Accord on 14 September. The Accord bound all the signatories to promote peace, drew up codes of conduct for both the police and political parties and set up a number of monitoring committees. The code of conduct for the police held it accountable to society rather than to the government and was backed up by the undertaking to establish a police board to advise on future policing policy; a unit to investigate alleged misconduct; and regional ombudsmen to ensure the investigation of all complaints against the police. Political parties were committed to instilling a spirit of democratic tolerance among their supporters.

On The Negotiating Track

While the National Peace Accord did little to curb the violence – more than 200 people died in the following month – the conference provided a negotiating model for Codesa, which was finally held in December. Despite initial heated exchanges between Mandela and de Klerk on the ANC's refusal to disband its armed wing, *Umkhonto we Sizwe* (MK), the Convention was remarkable for the broad consensus it achieved on the declaration of intent. Only two parties refused to sign: Inkatha, on the basis that it appeared to rule out a federal system of government, and the 'independent homeland' of Bophuthatswana, on the basis that it appeared to 'undermine its sovereignty'.

Codesa established five committees, charged with: creating a climate for free political participation, including a possible role for the international community; establishing constitutional principles; finding an acceptable formula for transition; examining the future of the homelands; and deciding on a timetable for reform. The most important development at Codesa, however, was President de Klerk's sudden concession to the ANC on its demand for a form of interim government. Within two months ANC and government representatives on the Codesa working committees had agreed the broad shape of the 'interim executive' and the principle of an elected, multiracial 'transitional parliament' which would provide both a broad-based transitional government and the forum in which the final constitution would be negotiated. In the first phase Codesa will appoint multiparty councils to oversee key areas of government, including preparations for the elections to the transitional parliament, government finance and regional and local government and, possibly, also international relations, housing, health and education. It is expected to be completed by mid-year. Although the ANC and the government still differ on the timing of elections for the transitional parliament, which could be held in 1993, and the life of the transitional government (de Klerk's opening bid was ten years, the ANC's five), neither is expected to be a major stumbling block. Indeed, South Africans in the past year have become used to the fact that the hottest rhetorical exchanges between the two are the surest sign that the spirit of compromise is abroad.

There are deeper divisions on the shape of the transitional parliament, with the government pushing for the adoption of its constitutional proposal floated at last year's National Party congresses. This called for a bicameral legislature based on a national assembly and a regionally-based Senate, a rotating three to five man presidency and a cabinet appointed by consensus of the presidency. These are more difficult issues, but with the ANC accepting some devolution of power to regional government level – a major government goal – its acceptance of a regionally-based senate and of the need in the initial stages at least for coalition government, compromise is closer than much of the rhetoric suggests. Codesa could well have completed its work on the interim constitution by the end of 1992.

There's Still a Long Trail Awinding

The fact that the transitional councils exclude, for the time being, oversight of the two most sensitive areas of government – law and order, and defence – serves as mute testimony to the most potent threat to the negotiating process: the seemingly incurable and spreading contagion of violence. The government has adamantly refused to give the ANC oversight of the police and the defence force until it disbands its military wing. For its part, Inkatha has suspended peace talks with the ANC until the future of *Umkhonto we Sizwe* is resolved. There have been reports that Buthelezi, increasingly alienated by the apparent collusion between the ANC and the government, had made common cause with the CP – although allegations of an Inkatha–AWB alliance have been vigorously denied.

Nevertheless, the danger remains that marginalized groups, including white right-wingers, radical black parties such as the PAC and the Azanian People's Organisation – who together with the Conservative Party have boycotted Codesa – and Inkatha may all take matters into their own hands. Right-wing violence erupted in the run-up to the referendum with the bombing of National Party offices, multiracial schools and repatriation centres for former ANC exiles.

Although the government has grown tougher in coping with the AWB – ten members were arrested after the bombings and police have not hesitated to open fire on right-wing extremists – its attempts to control the violence are severely compromised by renegade elements in the police and a seriously demoralized defence force. The defence force's resentments are many: its diminished political role; its withdrawal from Namibia and Angola; the deep and continuing cuts in the defence budget; and its growing inability to enforce conscription on white youths. Certain generals have made no attempt to conceal their contempt for de Klerk's reforms.

Any threat of direct military intervention in the political process, however, has been averted by de Klerk's resounding victory in the referendum. The positive vote has also strengthened him for his long-delayed confrontation with those in the security establishment who have been stoking black-on-black violence for their own purposes. As negotiations move into the final stage, however, the most immediate and important task facing both de Klerk and Mandela is the need to involve Buthelezi more closely in the process, to allay his fears of exclusion and to accommodate at least some of his ambitions in the interim government and beyond. Failure to do so will almost certainly condemn South Africa to continuing instability and violence.

On 17 March 1992 President de Klerk persuaded white South Africa finally to turn its back on the country's apartheid past. His – and Mandela's – biggest remaining challenge could be to avoid a Zulu veto on its future.

Strategic Policy Issues

ARMS CONTROL: THE AGENDA TRANSFORMED

The attempted coup in Moscow in August 1991 had profound implications for arms control. The East–West arms race, which had already been slowed down by the events of 1989–90, was shifted into reverse. Sweeping cuts in nuclear and conventional forces were announced, weapons modernization programmes were halted, and defence spending was reduced sharply. In the former Soviet Union, the military–industrial complex ground to a halt alongside the rest of the economy. Most strikingly, unilateralism – long dismissed by the Western establishment as dangerous and unrealistic given the conditions prevailing during the Cold War – became fashionable, as first the United States and then other nuclear powers announced significant reductions in their respective nuclear forces.

At the same time, it became evident that the non-proliferation concerns that had emerged in the wake of the Gulf War would increasingly dominate the arms control agenda. Testifying before the US Congress in January 1992, the directors of the Central and Defense Intelligence Agencies focused on the threat posed by the growing proliferation of nuclear, chemical and biological weapons. Worries about nuclear developments in North Korea and the UN inspections of Iraq's military and nuclear establishments dominated the headlines. With the collapse of the Soviet Union in December 1991, an additional worry emerged: the possibility of nuclear weapons, technology and know-how proliferating from the new Commonwealth of Independent States to other unstable regions.

Completing the Old Agenda

Before the August coup, the old agenda still dominated much of the arms control discourse. In June 1991, the Soviet Union finally accepted the interpretation of its obligations under the Conventional Forces in Europe Treaty that the other 21 signatories had insisted upon: all treaty-limited equipment deployed within the Atlantic-to-the-Urals zone in November 1990 would count against the treaty ceilings. One month later, Presidents Bush and Gorbachev finally signed the Strategic Arms Reduction Treaty, which had been under negotiation since 1982. (For details on these treaties, see the Arms Control sections of *Strategic Survey 1989–90* and *Strategic Survey 1990–91*.)

The unravelling of the Soviet Union in late 1991, however, called into question the relevance of these treaties. In a number of instances, nuclear and conventional force levels were in the process of coming down well below treaty-mandated limits, even though the treaties had not entered fully into force. Moreover, the weapons affected by the

START Treaty were deployed in four newly independent states: Belarus, Kazakhstan, Russia and the Ukraine. Having the non-Russian republics sign the treaty would anoint them as nuclear weapons states, clearly an undesirable precedent of instantaneous nuclear proliferation. Yet, with almost 30% of the former Soviet Union's strategic forces deployed outside Russia, not applying START to these systems posed equally formidable problems. In the end, it was decided that Russia would sign START and the other three republics would approve its terms in writing and commit to applying its provisions to forces deployed on their territory.

The CFE Treaty posed perhaps even more complex challenges. The intricate zonal limits of the Treaty were based on the boundaries of Soviet military districts, which, in some cases, failed to coincide with newly established international borders. Moreover, instead of force limits applying to one signatory state, limits were now to apply to at least eight new republics. Under heavy Western pressure, all agreed to abide by the terms of the Treaty and to ensure that their national equipment holdings would not in the aggregate exceed those of the Soviet Union. Dividing the spoils of the Soviet conventional military among the former republics, however, was sure to be a difficult task. It is also unclear whether it is entirely sensible to fix equipment ceilings for the newly independent republics at the levels flowing from the Treaty, possibly entitling Belarus to more MBTs than France, and the Ukraine more MBTs than Germany.

With START and CFE on the road to ratification and eventual entry into force, few items remained on the old arms-control agenda. A new agreement on confidence-and security-building measures was signed in March 1992. Under the terms of the Vienna Document, CSCE members will for the first time constrain their military activities involving more than 40,000 troops or 900 tanks, as well as limit the number of activities involving smaller forces. Activation of personnel will be subject to prior notification, and new weapon systems deployed within the ATTU will be subject to on-site inspections by all participants. In addition, an Open Skies Treaty which will allow periodic overflights of CFE signatories was signed in Helsinki in March 1992. Finally, a CFE-1A agreement setting national limits on manpower levels was expected to enter into force alongside the first CFE Treaty.

The transformation of the arms control agenda is also evident from the discussions in Helsinki on follow-on negotiations. In addition to discussing proposals for further reduction and confidence-building measures, attention was increasingly drawn to devising mechanisms for conflict prevention, crisis management and, even, security-building. The last item includes issues such as defence conversion, civil-military relations, defence budgeting and transparency, and legislative and civilian control. In short, European arms control is being redefined: the goal is no longer the management of adversarial relations; it is increasingly the building of cooperative, secure and stable relations in peace.

The Advent of Denuclearization

Nowhere is this new direction more evident than in the nuclear arena, where the focus since the failed Moscow coup is no longer on stabilizing the military balance through mutually agreed and verifiable steps. Instead, the emphasis is on steep, unilateral and reciprocated reductions designed to enhance prospects for safe and secure control over dwindling arsenals of weapons. This new approach to nuclear arms control first became apparent a month after the coup when, on 27 September 1991, President Bush announced sweeping changes in the American tactical nuclear inventory. One week later, President Gorbachev matched the US initiative.

Under the Bush/Gorbachev initiatives on non-strategic nuclear forces, all US and Soviet ground-based weapons will be destroyed, approximately 50% of all sea-based weapons will be destroyed and the remainder stored on land, and air-based weapon inventories will be reduced by half. The UK announced that it would implement similar measures. France scaled back its tactical missile modernization programme and pledged not to deploy the new missiles in active units.

Bush and Gorbachev also took important steps to limit strategic nuclear forces. They took all strategic bombers off 24-hour alert and removed those ICBMs and SLBMs slated for elimination under START from alert as well. The two leaders cancelled the mobile basing portions of their ICBM programmes, as well as their short-range attack missile programmes. Bush repeated his call for a ban on land-based, multiple-warhead (MIRVed) missiles, while Gorbachev announced that Soviet forces would be reduced to 5,000 (1,000 below nominal START levels). Finally, Gorbachev announced a one-year unilateral moratorium on nuclear testing, and he called on the other nuclear powers to negotiate a comprehensive test ban.

Following the collapse of the Soviet Union in December, the US again took the lead in proposing significant nuclear reductions. On 28 January 1992, Bush proposed that the Slavic republics, Kazakhstan and the US negotiate a ban on MIRVed ICBM. As an inducement, Bush offered to cut America's post-START inventory by approximately half, to 4,700 weapons; he would accomplish this by eliminating the MX missile, removing two of the three warheads on all *Minuteman* III missiles, removing one-third of all SLBM warheads, and converting a 'substantial portion' of US strategic bombers to conventional roles. Bush also cancelled – on a unilateral basis – the *Midgetman* missile, the advanced cruise missile, and a new warhead for the *Trident* D5 missile, thus, for the moment, terminating all US nuclear modernization programmes.

One day later, Russian President Boris Yeltsin responded by detailing reductions which would effectively implement the Gorbachev cuts announced the previous October. He also proposed to reduce US and Russian forces to 2,000–2,500 weapons on each side (thus implicitly accepting a ban on land-based MIRVed missiles), and, picking up on American suggestions, he proposed that the US and the new republics develop a jointly operated, global missile defence system.

In the spirit of the times, both sides agreed to forego formal negotiations on these various proposals and, instead, work out the details at frequent ministerial sessions in time for the June 1992 summit in Washington. Given both opposition in the Pentagon to reductions below those proposed by Bush in January and the absence of substantial Russian leverage, it seems likely that Russia will agree to a modified version of the Bush proposal, implying a 50% reduction in post-START force levels to around 4,500 weapons on each side.

Equally noteworthy are the various cooperative efforts directed at the safe transportation, dismantlement and secure storage of nuclear weapons and materials. In November 1991, the US Congress appropriated $400m of Defense Department funds for the purpose of helping Russia to disable and dismantle its nuclear and chemical weapons. The US, the EC and Japan plan to spend up to $75m on a German-proposed international science centre in Moscow which will provide work for Russian nuclear and weapons scientists. The US and the UK also plan to provide transportation equipment to ensure the safe removal of nuclear weapons from active units in the former Soviet Union to central storage locations, and to help ensure the safe storage of fissile materials recovered from dismantled nuclear weapons.

Non-Proliferation: Renewed Urgency

When, on 16 January 1991, the US-led coalition in the Gulf found itself face-to-face with a country of 17 million people that had fielded the fourth largest army in the world, equipped with 5,000 tanks, hundreds of ballistic missiles, large stockpiles of chemical and possibly biological weapons, and an incipient nuclear weapons capability, the international community knew that something had gone terribly wrong. As subsequent inspections by the UN Special Commission showed, not only had pre-war estimates vastly understated Iraq's capabilities, but Baghdad had been able to amass these largely through purchases from Western countries and the Soviet Union. The question that immediately arose was: how many other Iraqs exist? The answer was not long in coming: North Korea appeared to be on the brink of developing nuclear weapons; Pakistan admitted for the first time that it possessed all the components for nuclear weapons; and similar statements followed from India. The list of countries with chemical weapons programmes gave no sign of shrinking, while a number of countries were busily trying to acquire ballistic missiles.

However, this new and well-founded attention to proliferation has obscured an equally noteworthy trend towards what Julian Perry Robinson has termed 'deproliferation'. For example, in Iraq, the April 1991 cease-fire resolution passed by the UN Security Council mandated the elimination of Baghdad's inventory and capacity to produce weapons of mass destruction and ballistic missiles with ranges over 150 km. South Africa may be the first country to have given up a viable nuclear option when it decided to sign the Non-Proliferation Treaty (NPT) in 1991; Argentina and Brazil signed an agreement, subject to bilateral and international inspections, renouncing the non-peaceful use of nuclear energy, and Brazil began to dismantle a prospective nuclear test site; North and South Korea agreed, on paper at least, to a nuclear-free peninsula; and France and China finally joined the NPT regime. In the chemical area, the United States and Russia remained committed to destroying 80% of their chemical weapons stockpiles; and nearly every country in Latin America has signed a declaration renouncing chemical and biological weapons. Finally, in the missile area, Argentina and Brazil abandoned their efforts to develop long-range capabilities for military purposes, while the US successfully cajoled Israel and China to abide by the Missile Technology Control Regime's guidelines on ballistic missile technology exports.

Welcome as this deproliferation trend is, developments in North Korea, South Asia, the ex-USSR and throughout the Middle East make clear that the battle to halt and reverse proliferation has only begun. In 1991–92, non-proliferation efforts in the chemical and biological, nuclear and missile, and conventional arms transfer areas have focused on a variety of global, regional and other ad hoc arrangements.

On chemical weapons, negotiations in Geneva have progressed to the point where a final convention banning the possession, acquisition, production, stockpiling, transfer and use of these weapons may be concluded in 1992. Prospects for the convention improved in May 1991 when President Bush declared that the United States would agree to destroy its entire chemical stockpile under the terms of the convention. Previously, the US had reserved the right to retain 2% of its stockpile until all countries with chemical weapons had joined. The US also abandoned its position on retaining the right to retaliate in case of CW use, declaring that the Gulf War had demonstrated that the ability to retaliate in kind was no longer necessary. Among the obstacles remaining before the convention can be finalized is the issue of challenge inspections. In July, the US reversed itself on this issue by proposing a challenge-inspection regime that, in practice, could deny access to international inspectors to any undeclared site. Though welcomed in parts of the developing world, European opposition to the US shift away from 'anytime, anywhere' inspections or even from guaranteed, though managed, access to suspect sites needs to be addressed before final agreement is reached.

On nuclear weapons and ballistic missiles, non-proliferation measures have emphasized a strengthening of the IAEA inspection regime, tighter export controls, and regional efforts. Regional efforts are particularly noteworthy in view of the failure of inspections and export controls to prevent what happened in Iraq. In the Middle East, the Bush administration has taken the lead in reducing to politically more realistic proportions the overambitious efforts by Egypt and other Arab states to create a zone free of all weapons of mass destruction. While calling on all Middle Eastern countries to abide by or sign the biological weapons convention and become original signatories to the CWC, the Bush administration has proposed that these countries agree to freeze the production of fissile materials as well as the production, acquisition and testing of ballistic missiles.

Significant changes are also evident on the Korean Peninsula, where North and South signed a non-aggression agreement in December 1991 and a declaration on the establishment of a non-nuclear peninsula the following January. The latter provides for a ban on nuclear weapons and fissile material production facilities, to be inspected bilaterally and on site. North Korea also signed a full-scope safeguards agreement, opening the way for IAEA inspections in June 1992. Suspicions remain, however, that Pyongyang will seek to stall meaningful inspections until after it has fabricated a sufficient amount of plutonium for weapons purposes.

In South Asia, the Soviet collapse has led India to reassess its relations with the US. Frequent bilateral contacts have resulted in intense discussions on nuclear and CW issues. As a result, there now appears to be a possibility that regional talks on nuclear proliferation between India, Pakistan, the US, China and Russia (which the latter three have urged India to accept since these were first proposed by Pakistan in June 1991) may be convened this year. In the meantime, India and Pakistan have begun to discuss the chemical weapons issue bilaterally, with an eye towards agreeing to simultaneous accession to the CWC.

Finally, the issue of controlling conventional arms transfers has for the first time been considered in detail by the UN Security Council, as well as by the G-7. In December 1991, the UN General Assembly approved the establishment of an arms transfer register, in which states are encouraged to record their annual weapons imports and exports. In January 1992, the CSCE countries, which are responsible for over 90% of the world's arms trade, agreed to discuss arms sales as a matter of priority in the post-Helsinki arms control discussions.

Perhaps the most significant development in this area, however, have been the meetings of the Permanent Five: China, France, the UK, Russia, and the US. Although there has been no agreement to halt, reduce or even to control the sale of arms to the Middle East or elsewhere, the five have made some progress in making sales more transparent. They are now committed to exchanging information on the sale of major weapons systems for the purpose of consultation. They have also adopted guidelines for arms transfers in which they pledge to avoid transfers that would increase tensions or contribute to instability, introduce destabilizing capabilities, or be incompatible with strengthening legitimate security and defence needs. Although perhaps not very significant in practice, these guidelines may lay the basis for more concrete efforts at limiting the transfer of conventional arms to the Middle East and elsewhere among the five countries responsible for some 85% of armament exports.

RESPONSES TO WEAPONS PROLIFERATION

The end of the Cold War dramatically changed perceptions of Third World weapons proliferation. Previously regarded as a somewhat abstract and essentially regional problem, it has emerged as possibly the most serious threat to international security today. Regional efforts to acquire nuclear, chemical and biological weapons, ballistic missiles and advanced conventional forces increasingly threaten not just regional stability, but even the global stability brought about by the end of the superpower rivalry.

The proliferation problem is now high on the international security agenda, the subject of closer strategic assessment and higher level action than ever before. But its inherent complexity continues to pose an exceptional challenge. It is not a single, coherent problem comparable to superpower deterrence. Instead, proliferation is a diverse set of issues, involving dozens of different supplier and recipient countries with a wide range of motives and aims, several types of weaponry and individual weapons projects, each with unique prospects and potential consequence. Forging strong and coherent policies to deal with this complex area will be taxing.

The nature of current proliferation dangers was amply illustrated by the extent of Iraq's programmes, revealed after its military defeat in February 1991. Although much had been known, neither the scale or number of individual projects was appreciated until the United Nations Special Commission undertook its investigations. Iraq's chemical weapons programme was the best known due to use against Iran, but the scale of the biological weapons effort came as a surprise.

Even more shocking was the scale of the nuclear weapons programme, conducted in secret defiance of Iraq's adherence to the 1968 Nuclear Non-Proliferation Treaty. This included large-scale uranium mining, enrichment with calutrons (up to 180 were planned) and at least 1,500 gas centrifuges, and design work on boosted or fusion bombs. Even by conservative estimates, Iraq could have produced 3–5 bombs annually by the mid-1990s. By that time Iraq's missile programme, which was built on 819 *Scud* missiles imported from the Soviet Union during the Iran–Iraq War, probably could have advanced to mass production. It was not special genius that made Iraqi progress possible, but determination, willingness to spend vast amounts of money, and the cooperation of hundreds of Western firms.

North Korea, which has weapons projects still operating under heavy secrecy, is engaged in an equally ambitious effort. This includes a suspect nuclear programme at Yongbyon, 90km north of Pyongyang, a large-scale chemical weapons programme, production of improved *Scud* missiles and development of a 1,000-km range version. North Korean weapons programmes rely on aging – but tried and proven – technology. Although it signed the NPT in 1985, North Korea refused to sign the required IAEA safeguards agreement until 30 January 1992 and continues to delay ratification, apparently hoping to buy enough time to complete its first nuclear weapons. Despite the country's diplomatic isolation, it has found ready clients, especially Iran and Syria, for its ballistic missiles.

Other regional powers have made considerable progress. Israel almost certainly has a complete strategic and tactical nuclear arsenal, while India and Pakistan can assemble nuclear weapons virtually at will. Aiding would-be proliferators are governments like China, Israel and North Korea which knowingly export destabilizing weapon systems. Other support has come from firms in Europe, Japan and the US, who have been only too willing to furnish advanced components, manufacturing technology and technical assistance.

Although proliferation problems increasingly constitute a cumulative threat, there is no single international forum for dealing with them collectively short of the UN Security Council. Diplomatic responses to proliferation have been channelled along several independent paths. The most prominent of these are export control regimes and the IAEA's safeguards regime. For outside powers, proliferation is dealt with above all as a problem of technology transfer control; Western responses to proliferation naturally stress established institutions for export control and safeguards on existing nuclear installations.

During 1991 major non-proliferation regimes made significant strides to improve their scope and strength. As they become more comprehensive and effective, however, they may be reaching the limits of their potential. There is growing awareness that the spread of technology can be slowed, but never completely stopped. Ultimately export controls only win time. In the long run they must be replaced by regional arms control, universal treaties banning the most destabilizing armaments, based on a degree of common understanding of the place and role of weapons of mass destruction and power-projection in the international system. At its heart, non-proliferation is a political issue – most modern industrial states have renounced the possession of nuclear (and chemical and biological) weapons voluntarily, not as a result of technical constraints.

The Rebirth of CoCom

The only regime that attempts to control a wide spectrum of strategically relevant technology is the Coordinating Committee for Multilateral Export Control. Created in 1949 to deal with the Soviet Union and its allies, CoCom has undergone great changes since the end of the Cold War. Although it has only a residual role to play, the major challenge is to adapt it into an instrument against Third World proliferation.

CoCom has had a chequered history for 40 years. Ironically, at the end of the Cold War it was stronger than it had ever been. Although still an informal agreement lacking the legal authority of a treaty, CoCom's work by then reflected a vigorous Western consensus. Its critical 'International List' of restricted dual-use technologies had been streamlined, leading to more effective regulation of the most advanced Western technologies. The organization's Paris secretariat was refinanced during the 1980s and expanded to cope with the growth of East–West trade. Its official membership had slowly grown to include all NATO governments (except Iceland) plus Australia and Japan. In the late 1980s ten other governments began applying CoCom restrictions unilaterally: in Europe: Austria, Finland, Sweden and Switzerland; and in Asia: Hong Kong, Indonesia, Malaysia, New Zealand, Singapore and South Korea. Advanced technologies continued to reach the Soviet Union, but in an increasingly random and unreliable way.

Many CoCom participants thought the democratic revolutions of 1989 foreshadowed the organization's demise. With the end of East–West antagonism, CoCom's original justification was gone. The end of the Warsaw Pact on 1 April 1991 made it appear simply as one more superannuated Cold War relic. In place of restraint, the West suddenly discovered an interest in accelerating the transfer of computers, industrial and environmental technology to the new democracies. It was no longer unrestricted technology transfers to the East that threatened Western interests; the danger of economic and political instability came from insufficient technology transfer.

These changing perceptions led to substantial changes agreed at the high-level CoCom Consultative Group meeting in Paris on 24 May 1991. The International List of 116 categories was cut by roughly 65% and restructured into a new 'Core List' of nine categories which stress advanced electronics, materials, computers and propulsion technology. Czechoslovakia, Hungary and Poland received further dispensations and are setting up their own export control systems along CoCom lines. The new Core List also recognizes for the first time that CoCom restrictions can help prevent the spread of destabilizing technologies to the Third World, especially by blocking efforts by potential proliferators to acquire proscribed technology through third parties. The need for CoCom was reaffirmed by the rise of nationalist warfare in Yugoslavia and Azerbaijan, and by fears that ex-Soviet republics might be preparing to sell militarily-relevant technology to virtually anyone with hard currency.

CoCom's successful adaptation has not yet altered its essential asymmetry; it still focuses on East–West technology transfer although the most explicit threats now arise from North–South trade. Many observers argue that with its unique organization and superior experience, CoCom should be reoriented to address contemporary priorities. It could be particularly valuable because it is the only organization which does not focus not on a specific proliferation problem but tries to restrict the entire spectrum of nuclear, military and militarily-relevant (dual-use) technologies.

There are several fundamental barriers to reorienting CoCom, however. Some members object to the creation of an overall export control system to deal with the Third World, preferring instead to rely on tailored regimes which minimize their losses in trade and leave them with greater political manoeuvring room. Objections among CoCom members are of extreme importance; since CoCom decisions are made unanimously, any of the participating governments can easily block the organization's growth or reorientation.

A second problem is the need to include within a reoriented CoCom additional suppliers of technology to the Third World, especially China, Eastern European countries and ex-Soviet republics. Although they have a strong interest in non-proliferation, CoCom is the wrong forum in which to expect their cooperation. These countries will insist on the elimination of controls targeted against themselves as a precondition to joining, something CoCom members will find hard to swallow. Indeed, to be fully effective, a global CoCom would eventually need the cooperation of regional powers like Brazil, Israel, India, South Korea and Taiwan at the same time as it tries to enforce export prohibitions against them.

Finally, such a scheme would arouse the hostility of the newly targeted countries themselves. After watching powerlessly while other non-proliferation regimes were established without their consent or cooperation, regional leaders are now more outspoken in their criticism of even the most tailored and refined export controls. The reorientation of an overarching control system like CoCom would arouse organized opposition. Whatever its actual intent or effect, they could plausibly argue that it amounted to illegitimate restraint of their civilian economic development.

The barriers to changing CoCom make it unlikely that it can serve as the leading non-proliferation instrument. Non-proliferation efforts in the foreseeable future will tend to stress the existing network of specific proliferation regimes. The latter have the advantage of greater Western and Eastern support, they are easier to expand in membership and technology coverage, and most of them hold greater potential for North-South cooperation.

Controlling Nuclear Proliferation

The strongest and most successful non-proliferation regime remains that against the spread of nuclear weapons. It is based on the 1968 Nuclear Non-Proliferation Treaty (NPT) and the safeguards and inspections authority of the Vienna-based International Atomic Energy Agency (IAEA). Over the years it has been subject to serious criticism from Western observers suspicious of its weaknesses and from regional spokesmen resentful of its strengths, yet it remains the most widely accepted non-proliferation regime, the standard by which others are measured.

Since the August 1990 NPT Review Conference failed to agree on a final document, there has been concern regarding the future of the treaty. The Extension Conference due in 1995 will determine whether the treaty continues in force for perpetuity or for an indeterminate fixed period. Standing in the way of a long or permanent extension is a vocal bloc of treaty members, led by Mexico, which insist on completion of a Comprehensive Test Ban (CTB) as a precondition. This measure is opposed by the US and UK who find it unacceptable so long as nuclear weapons remain important elements of their forces. A UN conference in January 1991 to consider amending the 1976 Peaceful Nuclear Explosions Treaty into an outright CTBT not only failed to resolve, but further polarized, the issue.

Despite the pressure on the NPT as 1995 approaches, the treaty has been gaining adherents. In 1992, the last of the declared nuclear powers, China and France, joined. Other new signatories in 1991 and 1992 include Algeria, South Africa and, as a result, the Southern African Frontline States. Syria concluded an IAEA Safeguards Agreement bringing its NPT obligations into force. Nuclear proliferation worries now centre on the regional powers outside the treaty and IAEA safeguards (principally India, Israel and Pakistan and possibly Cuba) and a handful of 'suspect parties' to the treaty (Iran, Iraq, Libya and especially North Korea). Having absorbed almost all of the likely signatories, NPT enforcement must now stress not only better export control and safeguards, but the respective duties of nuclear and non-nuclear states as well as the status of those non-signatories which have crossed over the nuclear threshold: Israel, India and Pakistan.

In July 1974, hoping to restrict access to technology that could lead directly to nuclear weapons, ten nuclear suppliers agreed to the Zangger Committee 'trigger list' of items to be exported only under IAEA safeguards. This was reinforced by the creation of a second organization, the London Nuclear Suppliers Agreement of 1978, with wider membership and restrictions. Like other technology transfer control agreements these are not treaties, but they create bodies to coordinate national export policies. Membership has grown to 19 and 14 countries respectively. The London Group has become particularly active since 1991 when it resumed regular meetings. Special efforts are in progress to broaden its membership to include emerging nuclear suppliers such as Argentina, Brazil and South Korea.

A fundamental nuclear export control issue of the 1970s and 1980s was partially resolved in 1990–91 as key European suppliers agreed to insist on 'full scope safeguards' requiring IAEA inspection of all a recipient's nuclear facilities as a precondition for relevant exports. The addition of the UK, France, Germany, Italy, Japan, Netherlands and Switzerland has made it increasingly difficult for a country to acquire nuclear technology without safeguards on all its nuclear facilities. There are continuing problems, however, with emerging nuclear exporters such as Argentina, China, India and the ex-Soviet republics, all hesitant to sacrifice export opportunities.

The case of Iraq illustrates the enormous challenge of properly safeguarding nuclear technology, and has encouraged greater efforts to strengthen the monitoring abilities of the IAEA. In the past, its inspectors only could go where they were invited. To be more effective, the organization needs easier access to commercial data and military intelligence so that it can more aggressively use its right to conduct 'special inspections' on un-safeguarded facilities. More ambitious reforms, however, would require renegotiation of the IAEA statutes and its numerous bilateral agreements.

Even limited improvements will not be easy to implement. The organization is seriously overburdened and underfunded. Its annual safeguards budget is only a paltry $62m, and 60% of it goes to inspecting Western countries where there are the smallest proliferation risks. Safeguarding programmes were cut this year by 13% due to a financial crisis triggered by the loss of the annual Soviet contribution of $20m.

Another area of recent progress has been regional confidence building and arms control. Regional initiatives are the most effective way of dealing with countries outside the NPT. Yet to be effective, such initiatives require the advocacy of governments within the region. This lesson was pointed out by the experience of President Bush's Middle East arms-control initiative on 29 May 1991, calling for a regional freeze on weapons of mass destruction and talks towards an outright ban; with a poor reception from regional governments it was dropped in favour of the more sweeping Middle East peace process.

There has been a mixed picture elsewhere. Brazil and Argentina, building on their Foz do Iguaçú Declaration of 28 November 1990 renouncing acquisition of nuclear weapons, agreed on 13 December 1991 to set up a joint nuclear information-sharing agency and to put all their nuclear sites under full IAEA safeguards. Although neither country has joined the NPT, the new agreement involves basically the same obligations. On 20 January 1992 North and South Korea signed an accord banning nuclear weapons from the Korean Peninsula, but it is complicated by North Korean stalling and the painful politics of reunification. Progress has been even slower in South Asia, despite the proposal from Pakistan in June 1991 for a meeting between India, Pakistan, China, the US and the USSR to devise ways of keeping nuclear weapons out of the region. The Indian government dismissed the plan but in response to unprecedented criticism and to subsequent US overtures, agreed on 16 March 1992 to hold talks with Washington on proliferation.

Chemical Weapons

There has been enough progress towards a Chemical Weapons Convention that a completed document can be expected by the end of 1992. Although the 1925 Geneva Protocol prohibits the use of CW, it permits possession and lacks any means of verification. The proposed Convention is to overcome these shortcomings by banning CW production and possession. The negotiations in Geneva received a boost in May 1991 when President Bush announced that the US would renounce the use of chemical weapons and would destroy all its stockpiles within ten years after the Convention comes into force. There are still serious obstacles, however, some inherent in CW technology, others due to last minute uncertainty among leading negotiators.

The major unresolved issue is the extent and powers of the verification system to assure compliance with the ban. Because almost any chemicals factory can be used to produce CW, the verification system will have to be larger than for any previous treaty. It also requires more intrusive inspection powers to ensure that factories are not suddenly switched from legitimate uses to CW production. Nonetheless, the previous verification doctrine of 'anytime, anywhere' disturbed several governments. The dispute involves two conflicting Western interests: the need for effective verification to prevent CW cheating, and the need to keep other national security interests secret. The UK, Japan and the US introduced a proposal in July 1991 which constrains challenge inspections of undeclared CW facilities to preserve the secrecy of other areas of military R&D. This was criticized for undermining the credibility of the Convention, but it has become increasingly accepted as an unavoidable compromise.

After the confirmation of Iraqi CW use in the mid-1980s, Western governments slapped controls on the sale of chemicals related to CW production. In 1985 17 countries established the Australian Group to coordinate these export controls. Membership now includes 22 Western governments plus the European Commission. Another 12 governments are formally consulted on the Group's 'Core List'. Efforts are being made to extend controls to cover production equipment, but the prevalence of such technology and its essential civilian applications make this difficult.

The Australian Group has become a vital instrument inhibiting CW proliferation, but its future is obscure. Many governments expect it to cease operating soon after the CWC comes into force, which will occur after it is signed and ratified by 60 to 75 countries (the exact number is undetermined). Some Third World countries are likely to make their signatures contingent on the end of related trade curbs. Yet there is growing recognition that the Convention will not make export controls obsolete; key countries will refuse to join the Convention and some signatories will remain suspect.

Regional agreements are helping to overcome some of these problems. In September 1991 Argentina, Brazil and Chile signed a declaration banning the production or use of CW. Even India and Pakistan have been able to conduct successful talks on the issue, most recently in November 1991 when they declared that they will be among the first signatories of the Convention. The Middle Eastern situation is more intractable; several Arab governments insist that Middle Eastern proliferation problems must be resolved together, linking their signature of the Convention to Israeli acceptance of the NPT.

Biological Weapons

The third review conference of the 1972 Biological and Toxin Weapons Convention met in September 1991, in the wake of new evidence of the spread of biological weapons research. Just three weeks earlier, the UN reported that Iraq had undertaken 'biological research for military purposes', and was 'capable of producing vast quantities of biological warfare agents'. This came after confirmation that the USSR had continued illicit work for years after signing the Convention, which prohibits development and production of biological weapons (BW). In all, US government sources maintain, about ten countries have BW programmes. The limited progress of the review conference, however, showed up the difficulties of strengthening this particular non-proliferation regime significantly.

Despite the signatures of 119 countries the BW Convention lacks any means of verification. Washington maintains that the nature of the technology prevents the Convention from being effectively verifiable. Nor is there great interest in establishing a system which would have to deal with the fact that virtually every modern hospital and brewery has equipment which can be used to breed BW agents. This also has inhibited efforts to coordinate BW export controls through the Australian Group. As a first step a group of experts was established during the review meeting under a British plan to identify possible verification measures by the end of 1993. The review meeting itself concentrated on measures to build confidence by encouraging openness about biological activity and preventing the transfer of relevant agents and equipment that might be used for illegal purposes.

Ballistic Missiles

Recent trends in ballistic missile proliferation are moving in two directions. On the one hand, some of the programmes of greatest concern in the late 1980s (such as those of Argentina, Brazil, Egypt and India) have slowed or stopped entirely. Iraq's vast missile stocks and facilities are being destroyed by the UN. Technology from Western sources is increasingly unavailable. On the other hand, a new breed of suppliers is emerging; North Korea began shipping improved *Scud*-type missiles to Iran and Syria in early 1992, and China has outstanding missile contracts with Pakistan and Syria.

Unlike nuclear, chemical or biological weapons, there is no treaty (except the purely bilateral INF Treaty) prohibiting ballistic missiles. Instead, control efforts focus on the Missile Technology Control Regime, whose 18 members cooperate to halt transfers of long-range missiles and missile-production technology. An early shortcoming was its failure to include several key suppliers; this problem was alleviated in 1991. In October, Israel, a supplier of missile technology to China and South Africa, agreed to accept MTCR restrictions. In exchange, the US dropped the threat of sanctions against suspect Israeli firms. Russia stopped supplying armaments to Afghanistan on 1 January 1992, including *Scud* missiles. Other countries, including Argentina, Brazil and several in Eastern Europe have indicated a willingness to abide by MTCR guidelines.

Aside from obdurate North Korea, the biggest question remains China. Washington imposed sanctions on China in June 1991 following confirmation that missile components had reached Pakistan. Secretary of State Baker visited Beijing in November 1991, where he discussed suspected sales of Chinese M-9 and M-11 missiles (with ranges variously described as from 180 to 360 km), and apparently won China's commitment to accept MTCR restrictions. China's policy was formalized in a letter from Foreign Minister Qian Qichen early in 1992. Washington responded by dropping its sanctions on the Chinese space programme. It remains to be seen, however, how China interprets the MTCR guidelines.

More also can be done to strengthen the MTCR by widening its membership and reducing its thresholds for permitted technology exports, items on the agenda of its summer 1992 Oslo meeting. As a regime, however, it remains seriously disadvantaged without a major treaty justifying its work and clarifying its goals. Proposals for a ballistic missile test ban or even a global treaty prohibiting long-range ballistic missiles have been suggested. A major barrier for such proposals is the difficulty of separating ballistic missiles from space launch vehicles relying on much the same technology. Nor are the established nuclear powers likely to agree to such proposals so long as ballistic missiles constitute major components of their armed forces.

Human Talent

The role of engineers and scientists in the weapons proliferation process is not a new problem. Indeed, after World War II, ex-patriot German engineers and scientists were instrumental in military R&D in the USSR, the US and France. They also helped establish modern arms industries in Argentina, Egypt, India and Spain. More recently Western 'techno-mercenaries', such as the late Gerald Bull who designed Iraq's long-range 'supergun', have created major weapons for several regional powers. Despite its overwhelming importance in the proliferation process, the spread of skilled workers poses an extreme test for proliferation control. It may be largely uncontrollable.

Of most immediate concern are the thousands of scientists and engineers left with little work or pay after the collapse of the Soviet Union. The USSR employed some 100,000 people in nuclear weapons establishments. According to CIA Director Gates, approximately 1,000–2,000 have detailed knowledge of weapons design and 3,000–5,000 others were directly involved in related manufacturing processes. Russian sources put the number of nuclear technicians with high-level security clearances at 15,000. Ex-Soviet nuclear weapons experts, especially those associated with the prestigious Kurchatov Institute of Atomic Energy in Moscow, report employment offers from Brazil, China, India, Iraq and Libya, raising fears of an international auction for their talents. Veterans of the Soviet chemical weapons and ballistic missile programmes may be in a similar position.

The dangers of the new situation are very real, but they must be qualified. Ex-Soviet weapons experts clearly have an interest in drawing outside attention to their plight. Some potential proliferators also need foreign technical assistance more than others. India has more brilliant engineers than it can use, but a lack of talented people has kept Libya from successfully acquiring nuclear weapons and long-range rockets, despite 20 years of effort. However, for potential proliferators with a growing technical infrastructure like Iraq and Iran, qualified personnel can greatly improve the learning curve involved in a budding nuclear programme.

There are limits to what other countries can do to discourage scientists from leaving their home country. Channelling Western R&D funds to ex-Soviet weapons laboratories, the only tangible response so far, has the advantage of avoiding the sort of exile which 'white-collar mercenary' status would imply. However, huge salaries in return for expatriation will inevitably tempt some. Restrictions on travel may be a hindrance, but cannot eliminate the problem. A control regime, in any case, cannot rely on a systematic challenge to civil liberties.

At Best, Cautious Optimism

The various non-proliferation regimes all share important characteristics, but they also have major differences. All have gained support in recent years as recognition of the risks rose, but none has reduced the dangers to manageable proportions. The more formal regimes, those based on universal membership treaties like the NPT, tend to be strongest. This points to the need to reinforce the legal and moral basis of other regimes like ballistic missiles. They also gain strength when supported by clear export controls targeting as few technologies as possible but involving as many suppliers as can be recruited. But proliferation problems involving widely available technology (biological weapons) or no physical technology at all (human talent) may be beyond the bounds of effective outside control.

Although proliferation threats are severe, there is ground for cautious optimism. In most cases control regimes already exist and can be made better, and solutions exist even to some of the most difficult proliferation dangers. The real route to proliferation control, however, involves regional conflict resolution, crisis prevention, confidence building and arms control. When regional actors resolve the disputes that motivate their most destabilizing weapons projects they accomplish more than the most elaborate non-proliferation systems. This is especially true for the most difficult proliferation problems, which virtually defy solution any other way. It also is the only approach that addresses all proliferation risks simultaneously.

RETHINKING EAST ASIAN SECURITY

Now that the overlay of the Cold War is being lifted from East Asia, the states of the region face complex choices about their future security arrangements. To be sure, the conflict between East and West never did fit East Asia as well as it fit Europe, notwithstanding the bloody wars that were fought in East Asia in the name of the Cold War. The perceived threat from communism was felt more acutely in Washington than anywhere in East Asia, with the exception of South Korea, and the fragmentation of the communist world, first by the Sino-Soviet split and then by conflicts between communist states in Indochina, made it far harder to sustain an image of a single ideological threat. Even now, East Asia is different, for while Soviet and European communism has died, an ideological variant lives on in Asia.

Although the perceived communist threat was more undefined and less worrying in most of the region than it was in Europe, the demise of the Soviet Union and its ideology is having a profound impact in Asia. It has begun to melt the glue that held non-communist East Asians together. The melting process has been limited by the fact that many East Asians see the United States as the only power able to fill a strategic vacuum that otherwise might be filled by local powers. In addition, the US remains a vital trade and investment partner for most states in East Asia, and the bonds of alliance were often more based on economic self-interest than on any real fear of the Soviet Union.

From an American perspective, the change in the global situation has accentuated the different ways in which the US has always viewed East Asians and Europeans. This was not only true in the sense that there have been less intense cultural and ethnic ties to East Asia, but that East Asians were seen as more of a military burden. Now that the threat, so sharply discerned in the US, has receded, much more is made of the fact that many states in East Asia have grown richer and run ever larger trade surpluses with the United States. It is thus not surprising that many Americans question the need for a military commitment in the region. At a time when the US economy is struggling to compete with other market economies, it is appealing for some Americans to feel that the reasons for their own problems and for other people's successes is the heavier defence burden borne by the United States.

When these sentiments are coupled with far less worry about a threat from the former USSR, a reduction in US military presence in East Asia is foreordained. Already US bases in the Philippines are being liquidated, American ships spend fewer days at sea in the Pacific, and some US troops are being pulled out of South Korea and Japan. It is not far-fetched to think that in a decade or so there will be no American troops in Asia. In January 1992 President Bush made the first trip to Japan by an American President in nine years and talked mainly of American jobs. It is not surprising that concern has grown that domestic American priorities may well lead the United States to leave Asians to their own devices.

To a certain degree, that Asians must now begin to sort out their own problems can be a healthy development, not least because the Cold War was often a distorting lens through which to view local issues. So far, however, there has been little serious thought in the region about how security might be handled in the post-Cold War world. There are good reasons for some uncertainty on the subject, if only because Asia is so vast and its problems so diverse. There is little reason, apart from the convenience of geopolitical terminology, why Asia, let alone the Pacific, should be considered a coherent unit. And if historical legacy is anything to go by, then there is no reason to dwell on Asian or even East Asian security as if it were something as organized as Western European security was during the Cold War. There have been no all-Asian multilateral organizations or agreements spanning the region, and even most of the organizations which were specific to parts of the area have had a very patchy record of success. No significant multilateral security arrangements, such as the South East Asian Treaty Organization, have survived, and the political and economic groupings that now exist are, at best, tentative.

Such difficulties might be cause for dismissing the prospects of developing coherent security arrangements for East Asia. It would be a mistake to do so blithely. The region has had a remarkable record of economic success in recent years, and its combined GDP is rapidly approaching that of Europe or North America. What happens in East Asia is simply too important to the prosperity of other parts of the global market economy for anyone to be sanguine about rising insecurity in the region. What does seem increasingly clear is that, unlike Europeans, who will continue to see their problems as best resolved by region-wide multilateralism, East Asians may find it easier to think in subregional and often ad hoc ways. Such *à la carte* multilateralism has its risks, but it may well be better suited to the diverse problems in the region.

Challenges to Security

The disintegration of the Soviet Union has not generated the same pressing security concern in East Asia as it has in Europe. As East Asian governments see it, Russia is the clear successor state to the Soviet Union, and only in Central Asia are there disputes over military forces, including nuclear weapons, of potential significance to Asia. What seems most likely in East Asia is that Russian military power there will simply rust. East Asian security benefited most in the Gorbachev era: the Soviet Union cut troops and ships from their order of battle; pressed Vietnam to withdraw from Cambodia, opened relations with South Korea; and normalized relations with China. As far as East Asians are concerned, the most important change since the second Russian revolution is the death of European communism and the unsettling effect it has had on the remaining adherents to the creed in China, Vietnam and North Korea. However, even this can be exaggerated. The earlier splits in the communist movement had already provided sufficient ground for Asian communists to discount the loss of their Soviet comrades.

Even a successfully reforming Russia seems headed for the status of an Australia with nuclear weapons. With a population of only some eight million spread thinly over its vast Far Eastern region, Russia is unlikely to make a major contribution to the regional economy or to pose a threat by virtue of population movement in the course of an economic collapse. The dire economic problems in Russia may mean that local authorities have greater freedom to determine their own policies, but it is hard to imagine Russia as a military threat to anyone in East Asia.

That said, Russia remains an important influence on North Korea, and continues to play a role in North-east Asia, the most vital security zone in the region. Indeed, antagonism on the Korean Peninsula is the only remnant of the East–West conflict in the region. Managing the process of Korean reunification would seem to be an obvious case for multilateral cooperation, but the great powers are wary of getting too closely involved. In addition, neither North nor South Korea fully trusts its allies; both believe that they would do best to sort out their own problems. With North Korea feeling more pressed into a corner by reforms in China and by the Russian revolution, and South Korea feeling more confident because of its growing economic prosperity and suspicious of the intentions of the US and even more so of Japan, there is an added incentive to try to resolve the problem of unification on an intra-Korean basis.

North Korea remains one of the world's most bizarre regimes, and as its allies desert it, North Korea is pursuing a nuclear weapons capability as a way to ensure its own survival. South Korea may also be hard to handle if greater democratization leads to more rows with the United States over trade and to demands for a more rapid American military withdrawal. It is difficult to envisage a variety of the 'Two-plus-Four' arrangement that was so successful in Germany working in Korea. In Germany, the assistance of the major powers that provided the basis for reunification was rooted in historical and legal realities with regard to Berlin that do not exist in Korea. The Koreans may be left to their own deadly devices.

Nevertheless, it is hard for the great powers to stay aloof when the most imminent risk of conflict in East Asia comes from North Korea's attempt to shore up its weakening position by developing nuclear weapons. Thus the US, Japan, China and South Korea are cooperating in bringing pressure to bear on North Korea to prevent this proliferation. If diplomatic and economic pressure fails, the Americans might feel that a military option must be considered, even though all those involved know that North Korea will have no problem in causing major damage in the South in retaliation with conventional weapons. The risks of allowing North Korea to develop nuclear weapons, however, are huge. South Korea, and even Japan, may feel it necessary to follow suit; given Korean–Japanese mutual distrust the destabilizing effects are self-evident. If the danger of nuclear proliferation is one of the major items on the post-Cold War agenda, Korea may become the first testing ground.

The Korean conflict demonstrates one of the main features of security in East Asia: that nationalism long distorted by imperialism and then the Cold War may well be beyond control because there is no multilateral 'habit of dialogue'. The question of unsettled nationalism is nowhere more evident than in the case of China which claims Hong Kong and Taiwan as its own, as well as the Spratly and Paracel Islands in the South China Sea. China has demonstrated that it is prepared to be a ruthless bargainer (as seen in the case of Hong Kong) and even to use military force (as it did in the Spratly operation of March 1988).

As China expands its blue-water fleet and as its economic interests become more integrated with the regional and global economy, the question arises whether China will choose irredentism or greater interdependence. China will be faced with increasing internal tension between communist political power in Beijing and the rapidly developing provinces along the Chinese 'Gold Coast'. A China that feels itself under pressure because of domestic difficulties and the shrinking of the communist world may lean to the more mercantilist and irredentist option. It may also become a China that sells arms and transfers dangerous technology more indiscriminately and blocks efforts for international collective security through the UN or some of its specialized agencies, such as the IAEA.

China's choice – independence or interdependence – is made more difficult by the fact that it is far more a military than an economic power, in a region where Japan is far more an economic than a military power. As the military power of the former superpowers is removed from the immediate scene, the most important choices about the future shape of East Asian security will be taken in China and Japan. To an important extent, because of its ponderous and consensual decision-making process and because of its scandal-ridden parochial political system, Japan has enormous trouble developing a vision of the role it should play in the post-Cold War world. Therefore, it may well find itself having to react to China's choices; for example, if Beijing were to pursue territorial claims in the South China Sea or press Taiwan not to become more independent.

To some extent, Taiwan and South-east Asian nations may welcome a more forthright Japanese response to China, and this despite the legacy of Japan's behaviour during World War II. Japanese investment in these countries, and the economic interdependence that has developed over the past decade, certainly provides a basis for more coherent and cooperative efforts in the security sphere. That Japan failed to support the Cambodian peace settlement by providing troops for a UN peace-keeping operation is due more to domestic Japanese politics than to any objection from the international community. Not surprisingly, Japan has regularly failed to take a leading role in shaping either a multilateral economic or military arrangement in the region, and certainly nothing that might be construed as being anti-Chinese. For the moment, Japan's strategy is to rely on bilateral arrangements, avoiding multilateral structures that might allow others to tie Japan down.

Yet Japan might be forced into seeking greater regional cooperation if its relations with the US deteriorated and the international market economy did break up into three more distinct large trading blocks. For the time being, most of the rhetoric about either a coming war between Japan and the US, or the emergence of three exclusive trade areas, has been overblown. The reality of very complex interdependence between parts of the global market economy make either scenario unlikely, albeit not impossible. When over 50% of trade among OECD states takes place within single multinationals, such state-centric talk of trade wars seems out of date. The greatest impact on trade and investment flows across the Pacific (and around the world) results from changes in the priorities of domestic policies and shifts in currency rates.

Even if there is more cause for optimism about international economics not leading to military threats, it is fair to say that the US, although now the largest market for nearly all the East Asian states, will decline in relative economic importance for most of them. Japan, now the largest investor in East Asia and the most important exporter to other East Asian countries, will rise in significance. Thus some, like Prime Minister Mahathir of Malaysia, who now support notions of greater East Asian economic cooperation because it is a way to limit the influence of the United States, may find that a more confident Japan might try to lead such a group so that they are merely made part of a larger Japan Inc International.

As the US retreats militarily from the region, it cannot afford to sever its economic links there. These two elements could come together if America finds that one of its most lucrative exports to East Asia is weapons. Increasingly wealthy East Asian nations, worried about unchecked great power rivalries and simmering local disputes, are already becoming one of the most promising export markets for sophisticated weaponry. East Asia is now second to the Middle East as an arms-importing region. Few countries, apart from China, are anywhere near self-sufficient in major arms production, and with their fast pace of economic growth, ability to handle high technology, and antipathy to domestic arms production, the states of East Asia are likely to sustain a significant arms race for years. What is perhaps most worrying about such a contest is that it will take place in a region whose diversity, and possibly its disputes, are not mitigated by multilateral cooperation. A fundamental question for the region's security thus revolves around the prospects for multilateralism in East Asia.

The Search for Structure

It is striking that the only multilateral security network in East Asia is the Five Power Defence Arrangement (the UK, Australia, New Zealand, Malaysia and Singapore) – a surprisingly resilient left-over from Britain's Commonwealth connections in the region. Apart from building confidence by getting Malaysia and Singapore to undertake joint exercises, however, the FPDA contributes little to resolving the far more important uncertainties about security in the region. The more far-reaching SEATO died in the 1970s and proposals for a North-east Asian equivalent never lifted very far off the drawing board.

Until recently, regional economic cooperation has also been paltry; the most promising of the economic groups in East Asia is APEC, which has emerged since 1989 as the first official attempt to organize the governments of the Pacific into a forum where they could think about the region's economic problems. As talking shops go, this one is in the early stages of construction, with membership still being sorted out. In 1991 'the Three Chinas' (Taiwan, Hong Kong and the People's Republic) were included. No substantive policy decisions have been taken and none are foreseen for some time to come. Nearly all of the major economic issues in the Pacific are part of broader global processes and often GATT, or even the G-7, is a better level at which such problems can be resolved. For those who hope to create similar structures in the security field, however, even this limited progress is cheering.

Only the Association of South-east Asian Nations has had any success, but even in this case it is easy, although perhaps unfair, to be dismissive of its security role. It was established much later and for different purposes than the highly successful European security structures and thus suffers when compared to European multilateralism. Although ASEAN is one of the most successful organizations in the developing world, much of that success can be attributed to the particular circumstance of having to face powerful communists in nearby Indochina. Despite recognizing the danger of a communist overspill into ASEAN countries, there has been no attempt at military cooperation.

To be sure, in the 25 years since its establishment ASEAN has helped to keep peace between its own potentially antagonistic members. Political declarations have helped to build confidence and to shape a habit of dialogue, but it remains to be seen if this process can survive the passing of the old order. ASEAN played a role in arranging a settlement of the Cambodian conflict, but this very settlement may well mean that the shared concern with expanding communism will fade. With Indochinese states likely to seek membership of ASEAN, the organization will have to take on the more difficult task of building more positive cooperation without the luxury of a shared threat.

There are territorial disputes in the region that require consideration, such as settling claims to the South China Sea. There are economic rationales for greater cooperation as a way of coping with a rising Japan. There might even be a reason to act more in concert as a way of keeping the US active in the region as a balancer to Japanese, Chinese or even Indian interests. Thus far, however, most actions on these matters have been handled bilaterally. Some South-east Asians, most notably Singapore, are anxious about the implications of an American military withdrawal from the Philippines and East Asia generally, and have offered the US facilities in order to keep them engaged.

It can be argued that, to some extent, the lack of initiative on the part of ASEAN is due to Japanese and American uncertainty about their objectives. What is unquestioned, however, is that ASEAN has failed to take a lead where others have faltered or balked. The habit of dialogue – best seen at ASEAN ministerial summits and subsequent meetings with 'dialogue partners' from the US, Japan and the EC – must become more of a habit of cooperative action.

There have been some proposals for multilateral structures to deal with security issues, and, curiously, the most discussed ideas have come from two of the more peripheral states – Australia and Canada. On 27 July 1990, Australian officials advanced the grandiose notion of a Conference on Security and Cooperation in Asia, but were immediately rebuffed by those who pointed out that the CSCE process would not translate well to the more diffuse Asian context. As Australia backed off to think again, the Canadian Minister for External Affairs, Joe Clark, jumped in with a proposal in April 1991 for less ambitious efforts to build security and confidence in the north Pacific. As in the case of APEC, such proposals have first to deal with the problems of membership and agenda before they can even begin to think about dealing with serious problems. Nevertheless, these proposals indicate that the impetus and interest are present for an exploration of the possibilities of building security on a multilateral basis.

A La Carte Security

In the past, opposition to multilateralism was led by the US and Japan, who feared it would merely provide a way for the Soviet Union to undermine the complex web of bilateral Western alliances. But the end of the Cold War and the uncertainty about what will follow it has led even those who had the deepest doubts to look again at proposals for multilateral security. Japanese officials, seeking something less than a CSCA, are now discussing the construction of a security 'multiplex' which will add multilateral efforts to the already existing bilateral arrangements. What this term reflects is an unwillingness to focus more specifically on the new features of the post-Cold War world and the risks in need of most attention.

The more general risk is that the United States will leave East Asian security to the East Asians, as it did in the 1920s and 1930s, and this despite continuing economic interests. In such circumstances, the danger of conflict will grow both because the US will not be there to keep local antagonists apart, and because local states, such as Japan in the 1930s or China and Japan in the 1990s, may be tempted to fill the vacuum. The challenge for the region will be to find a variety of multilateral arrangements that will demonstrate that a habit of dialogue builds more common security, and will allow America a lower-cost way of remaining a major player in regional security.

Although there is a general risk to the region of unchecked local antagonisms, thinking about a CSCA or even a multiplex may be too vague or too grandiose; an à la carte approach to multilateral security may be simpler and more effective. Instead of laboriously negotiating on a set menu of security, the à la carte approach would focus on the most attractive items for the most dangerous conflicts. Some of the specific CSCE measures to build confidence through mutual visits and inspections, and the sharing of data can help to control the process of creating a new security order in the Pacific.

Building confidence on the Korean Peninsula must be the most likely place to start, and the question of agreeing how not to let conflicting claims in the South China Sea escalate into more open conflict must be a close second on the menu. In neither of these cases does it make sense for the United States to leave the parties to sort it out themselves. Unless the East Asians can agree to work together and to limit their national interests, however, the risk must be that the 1930s will provide the pattern for the future of East Asia.

WATER RESOURCES: SCARCITY AND CONFLICT

Water resource management and allocation may well be the most salient of the environmental issues which have gained increasing prominence in political debate and strategic thinking. Water is more than an emotive issue of individual survival; it is often perceived as a problem of national and international security. The administration of water resources has sparked intense competition among domestic interest groups in many countries and control over transnational water resources has been a frequent cause of interstate tension.

There is no dearth of examples. In several cities in Latin America the provision of clean drinking water and efficient sewage systems is in the hands of public institutions burdened by bureaucratic and financial constraints; water theft, shortages and pollution result from lack of accountability and the failure of long-term policy co-ordination. In India governments have pursued costly and often grandiose dam-building projects on the basis that hydro-electric power (HEP) generation will accelerate regional economic development. The Narmada River Project in the State of Gujarat, for example, is designed to provide flood control, generate HEP and divert water for irrigation, but its benefits are strenuously disputed. Not only has it been estimated that 80% of the villages in the Project's catchment area will not be supplied with irrigation water, but that the Project will displace many people, perhaps as many as 1.5 million. The Cauvery Waters dispute has led to violent clashes between farmers in the states of Karnatake and Tamil Nadu in southern India.

In the Canadian province of Québec, following complaints by environmental groups, the Federal Court has placed a moratorium on the James Bay II HEP project. This was designed to supply low-cost electricity to the United States, but it threatened to flood large areas of Cree hunting grounds. Prolonged drought in the African Sahel countries, especially in 1968–73 and 1984–5, combined with the failure of large-scale irrigation schemes, led to widespread displacement of rural populations. In order to maintain internal political stability the governments of the countries concerned have tried to give priority food and water allocations to urban consumers. The Sahel drought has also contributed to the perhaps irrevocable intervention by international aid agencies and non-governmental organizations into the region.

Clearly, the location of surface and ground-water resources does not conveniently coincide with international boundaries and control over shared water is often disputed, depending on the overall level of relations between the states in question. For example, disputes over the Senegal river and the Shatt al-Arab waterway have aggravated existing ethnic, religious and ideological tensions between Mauritania and Senegal, and Iran and Iraq respectively.

In the case of international or trans-boundary rivers, because downstream riparian states are vulnerable to the effects of upstream hydraulic works, disputes over water rights call into question the legal definition of absolute sovereignty and territorial integrity. In South Asia, the long-standing India–Bangladesh dispute over the management of the Ganges and Brahmaputra rivers reflects concern over territorial integrity which bilateral agreements, such as the 1977 accord (which lapsed in 1982), have done little to alleviate. Should the flow of the Ganges be regulated by a single dam, the Farraka Barrage in India, or by a series of dams, as advocated by Bangladesh? Should water flowing through a proposed canal to link the Brahmaputra and the Ganges, crossing Bangladeshi territory, be controlled by India or Bangladesh? Should discussion of this and other proposals involve other states in the region: Nepal, Bhutan and China? Although India has repeatedly stated its opposition to multilateral talks of this nature, pressures continue to mount.

In almost all the disputed areas there is agreement that the most desirable and efficient method to follow is that of co-operative management of international or transboundary water resources. In the absence of political goodwill, however, this remains a fanciful dream. Furthermore, there are no comprehensive guidelines in international law on the non-navigational use of international rivers or groundwater beyond the general principles of 'equitable utilisation' and *sic utere tuo ut alienam non laedas* (states must not permit the use of their territory to cause injury to other states) enshrined in the Helsinki Rules of 1966. Whilst upstream states may claim priority over river usage, the doctrine of absolute sovereignty over portions of international river basins has never been a generally recognized principle of international law. Since 1974 the United Nations International Law Commission has been trying to draft general principles on consulation between riparian states; it has not yet been able to establish any binding framework which could be ratified internationally. Bilateral or multilateral treaties are still the only means of establishing rights of usage. Such lacunae and ambiguities do nothing to facilitate conflict resolution.

Water and Politics in the Middle East

Population growth and ambitious agricultural policies place enormous pressure on local water resources in the Middle East – an arena of such political mistrust that control over water supply is regarded, rightly or wrongly, as a strategic asset, a bargaining tool or a political weapon with a significant influence on the regional balance of power. The question of equitable allocation of the region's water resources has become an important element in any future peace settlement.

In the overblown cadences of Middle Eastern political rhetoric the 'water weapon' has on occasion made the 'oil weapon' look puny. President Turgut Özal of Turkey has spoken of the inevitability of water wars; Dr Boutros Ghali, when he was Egyptian Deputy Prime Minister for Foreign Affairs, repeatedly stated that Egypt was prepared to go to war to safeguard the flow of Nile waters; King Hussein has declared that Jordan would be prepared to fight Israel in defence of water rights on the Jordan river. These views have attracted widespread attention, although it would be a mistake to assume from them that conflict is imminent. Such statements do not necessarily reflect political realities or even current practice at a technical level. Yet ultimately the region's water resources can only be allocated within the framework of a political settlement, and thus far Middle Eastern politics have prevented any formal multilateral agreements on water use or the establishment of international water commissions to adjudicate disputes.

In the Nile Basin, for example, there is a relatively impressive record of cooperation and regular meetings between Sudan and Egypt. Nile waters are allocated on the basis of a Sudanese–Egyptian agreement signed in 1959. The long-term development of the Nile waters, however, hinges on projects on the Upper White Nile and on the Blue Nile, hence on the cooperation of the East African riparian states (Tanzania, Kenya, Uganda, Burundi, Ruanda, Zaire) and of Ethiopia which supplies 86% of the Nile's average annual flow. There are, as yet, no formal treaties between all nine Nile riparians on the equitable allocation of Nile waters and the development of the Upper White Nile in southern Sudan has been postponed indefinitely because of civil war, jeopardizing Egypt's water planning programme.

Discussions on Middle Eastern water supplies within the context of the Madrid peace process are overshadowed by political considerations. At the multilateral discussions in Moscow in January 1992 it was felt that water issues could not be satisfactorily discussed while the Syrian and Palestinian delegations were boycotting the talks. Even hydrological data has become politically sensitive and thus difficult to verify.

Water has always been a scarce commodity in the arid countries of the Middle East. The present crisis, however, has resulted from the disparity between available supplies and the insistence of governments on a policy of food security, policies made more difficult by rapid population growth. Although the agricultural sector in arid zones uses 70–80% of available water supplies, fear of dependence on food imports has prompted Middle Eastern governments to invest in ambitious irrigation and land reclamation schemes which cannot be justified on strict cost-benefit criteria. It has been estimated that extensive agriculture in arid areas uses ten times as much water as industry for each dollar of income created. Reallocation of water to non-agricultural uses, however, has profound social consequences which can influence political stability.

In the hydrocarbon-rich states in the region, particularly in the Gulf, desalination is an affordable answer to increasing water consumption and relieves pressure on ground-water reserves. Most of this water is used for domestic purposes but, in the case of Saudi Arabia for example, some of this expensive water, is used in capital-intensive agriculture to produce cereals for export and to ensure self-sufficiency in food production at a cost far higher than that of imports would be.

Water in the Arab–Israeli Conflict

Control over transnational water resources in the Jordan basin is one of the leading features of the security situation of the region, especially as it faces serious shortfalls in supply. Those supplies will be further strained by the swelling populations of the riparian states. By the year 2000 it is estimated that the population of Jordan (1991 estimate 3.4m plus approximately 300,000 returnees from the Gulf states) will increase to 4.8m, that of Israel and the Occupied Territories (1990 estimate 6.276m) will reach 8.5–9m (assuming an influx of about 1m immigrants expected from the former Soviet Union), Lebanon (in 1987–8 2.76m) may rise as high as 4.7m and Syria (1991 estimate 12.8m) will have 18m people within its borders. All attempts to create multilateral agreements in the Jordan basin have failed. Instead, the four riparian states have pursued unilateral development policies which their neighbours have considered detrimental. The main sources of tension are: conflicting Israeli and Jordanian demands on the river Jordan, Jordanian–Syrian plans to develop the river Yarmouk, and Israeli water policies in the Occupied Territories and in southern Lebanon. Arab accusations of Israeli 'water theft' stand alongside Israel's anxieties that a key proportion of its water supply might fall into inexpert and, worse, hostile hands.

Patterns of Consumption and Future Requirements

Israeli water consumption has outpaced supply from renewable sources for some time. Average annual consumption is estimated at 2,100 million cubic metres (mcm) and supply at 1,950 mcm, although droughts in the past few years have reduced these figures to 1,820 mcm and 1650 mcm respectively in 1991. In 1991 Israeli's cumulative water deficit was equivalent to a year's supply. In 1990–91 average rainfall levels were at their lowest for 20 years and the heavy and unusual rainfall levels of early 1992 will largely be needed to make good this deficit.

Only 3% of the Jordan basin area lies inside the Green Line, or Israel's pre-1967 boundaries. The Jordan river, whose headwaters are in Lebanon and Syria, is the source of 40% of Israel's water supply. Israeli annexation of the Golan Heights has ensured control over the Banias, one of the main sources of the Upper Jordan, and all shores of the Lake Tiberias reservoir. In addition, Israel uses 15% of the waters of the river Yarmouk, equivalent to 3% of its water supply.

The Occupied Territories have also been affected by drought, and in 1990–91 water supply there was 100–150 mcm below the annual average of 650 mcm. The West Bank accounts for 30–40% of Israel's annual water budget; it is estimated that 80–95% of the West Bank aquifers (notably the Yarkon-Taninim or mountain aquifer) service Israelis on both sides of the Green Line. The aquifers have been overpumped 15–20% beyond their safe yield. Palestinian farmers have been refused permits for well-digging on the grounds of potential aquifer depletion, whilst deep-bore artesian wells drilled by Israelis inside the Green Line and on the West Bank have caused some Arab wells to dry up. Restrictions on well drilling have only recently been applied to Israeli farmers. Water allocation quotas and pricing policies for Israeli and Palestinian inhabitants of the West Bank and the Gaza Strip differ markedly. In the Gaza Strip the water supply picture is grim: the coastal aquifer has been severely overpumped and contaminated by seawater intrusion to such an extent that plans have been drawn up to supply Israeli settlers in the Katif bloc by pipeline from inside the Green Line.

Water shortages in Jordan have become acute. Jordan's water deficit is forecast at a minimum of 200 mcm per annum by the end of the 1990s. Although 71% of its water supplies go to the agricultural sector the country is still heavily dependent on food imports; in 1990 such imports totalled $493m, 19% of Jordan's total import budget. It was estimated in 1991 that in the long term, demand for water in Israel, Jordan and the Occupied Territories could exceed supply by up to 50%.

Lebanon is the only state in this region which is relatively well-endowed with surface and ground-water resources. The Litani river in the south of the country, with its high quality water, has been developed primarily for HEP generation, with most of its flow diverted into the Awali river. The lower Litani, the Awali and the headwaters of the Upper Jordan lie within the Israeli-controlled South Lebanon Security Zone.

Hydropolitical issues

The history of interstate negotiations over the allocation of the Jordan, Yarmouk, Litani waters and aquifers is depressing. None of the multilateral packages proposed since the 1940s has ever gone beyond the theoretical stage. All foundered on the issues of water quotas, incompatible river diversion plans, and on the question of whether or not to include the Litani river in development schemes (as was advocated by all Israeli-backed plans). Significantly, the most comprehensive scheme, the Johnston Plan of 1955, failed to be ratified by any of the parties. Jordanian Prime Minister Fawzi al-Mulki's response ('Jordan is fully prepared to continue bearing economic hardships rather than participate in any project with Israel, either directly or indirectly') typified reactions of the Arab states to the plan; Israeli officials were disappointed with their water quotas and that the Litani was not included.

Yet the dispute over water resources has provoked limited military action in the region: in April 1967 Israel, ostensibly fearing reduction in Upper Jordan flows, bombed installations forming part of the Arab League-sponsored Jordan Headwaters diversion project in Syria. Between 1967 and 1970 Israel repeatedly bombed Jordan's East Ghor (King Abdallah) canal in retaliation for incursions by the Palestine Liberation Organisation (PLO) into Israeli territory from bases in Jordan.

In the absence of a basin-wide consensus, Israel, Jordan, Syria and Lebanon pressed ahead with unilateral hydraulic projects: these include Jordan's East Ghor canal (1957) and Israel's National Water Carrier (1964). Nor have recent developments presented a more encouraging picture of cooperation. According to a treaty signed between Syria and Jordan in September 1987, a jointly-built al-Wahda (Unity) dam on the Yarmouk would supply HEP to Syria and Jordan (3:1 division) and 180 mcm of irrigation water to Jordan. Syria controls the headwaters, and the project's site is on Syrian territory; Jordan, on the other hand, will be paying the costs and has applied for a World Bank loan. Israel has, however, refused to make any formal statement of non-objection to the project, thereby blocking World Bank funding, as the Bank will not fund any hydraulic works in dispute.

The lack of an agreement led Syria in March 1990 to begin the construction of a number of small dams in the Yarmouk basin which will reduce the water available for storage in the al-Wahda dam, if it is

ever built, and belies repeated Syrian claims that this dam would provide the answer to Jordan's water shortage. Any joint ventures
between the states of this region, such as joint management of aquifers
in the Arava and Yarmouk basins or storage of Yarmouk waters in
Lake Tiberias could only be envisaged after a political settlement.
There are a number of alternatives to basin-wide cooperation.
Conservation, through the reduction of irrigated areas, waste water
recycling and changes in water pricing structures would substantially
reduce annual water requirements, or more capital-intensive schemes
such as silver iodide cloud seeding, salt-water cultivation or
desalination of seawater could be tried. Israel and Jordan, to a lesser
extent, have already invested in such projects. There are even indications that agricultural priorities are being questioned. Although
agriculture accounted for only 3.1% of Israeli GDP and 3–4% of its
exports, the sector consumed 75% of water supplies in the 1980s. The
agricultural water quota was reduced by 10% in 1986 and 25% in 1991;
water prices to farmers were increased by 50% in summer 1991. Water
rationing in all sectors was introduced in Jordan in summer 1991 and
the irrigated area in the Jordan Valley, Jordan's agricultural
showpiece, is to be reduced by 33% in the coming season.

A successful conclusion to the present Middle East peace process
is the precondition for any solution to the water question. At present
Israel will not contemplate territorial concessions without guarantees
that its water supply will be safeguarded. Rafael Eitan, the former
Israeli Minister of Agriculture, claimed in newspaper advertisements
in 1991 that territorial concessions would lead to Palestinian 'mismanagement, poor planning, lack of knowledge or plain neglect of the
shared aquifer'. If Israel does concede territory on the West Bank it has
been suggested that it should retain control of a 2–6km strip on the hill
ridge overlooking the West Bank to safeguard its supplies from the
Yarkon-Taninim aquifer. Syria maintains that negotiations over water
and other environmental matters are inconceivable without territorial
concessions by Israel.

Controversy also surrounds reported plans by Israel to divert
Litani waters into the northern Galilee, although there is no evidence
of actual diversions. On 11 May 1991 the Israeli government
announced that Israel would not withdraw from the South Lebanon
Security Zone unless it were guaranteed a share in the Lebanese water
supplies (a sentiment echoed by Antoine Lahad, commander of the
South Lebanese milita, in October 1991). The Lebanese government
has described these supplies as essential to economic reconstruction
and therefore non-negotiable.

The Tigris–Euphrates Region

A proliferation of multi-purpose dam projects, combined with competition for regional political and economic leadership is a perennial

source of tension in the Tigris-Euphrates basin. This tension has been sharpened as a result of the differently-perceived environmental implications and economic motivations of Turkey's South-East Anatolia Project (GAP – *Güneydogu Anadolu Projesi*) and its influence on relations with Syria and Iraq. The long-standing rivalry between Iraq and Syria has also at times been influenced by the issue of riparian rights. Pressure on the region's water resources will intensify; populations are expected to increase sharply to 114m from the estimated 1990 level of 88m by the year 2000. There is neither sufficient water in the Euphrates river in particular to supply planned irrigation projects in all the riparian states without sweeping modernization of existing irrigation systems, nor any consensus between Turkey and Syria on the desirability of basin-wide allocation agreements.

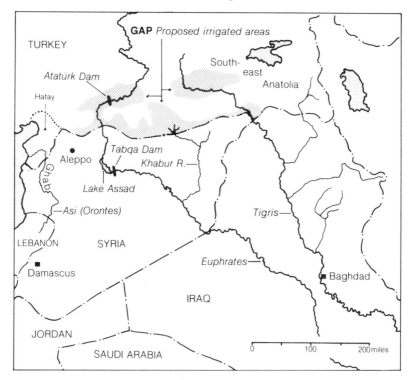

Patterns of Water Consumption and Future Requirements

Turkey enjoys a water surplus and controls 98.8% of the discharge of the Euphrates as well as approximately 50% of the discharge of the Tigris. In water terms it is well off. GAP, originally conceived of as a domestic project to raise the level of development in the Kurdish areas of the south-east, aims to increase agricultural production, create local growth poles by attracting investment from all economic sectors and, above all, generate HEP to reduce Turkey's dependence on imported oil (and its average annual fuel bill of over $2bn). The scheme involves 21 dams, 17 HEP plants and 13 major development projects; the centrepiece is the Atatürk dam and Urfa tunnels designed eventually to irrigate over 1m hectares (ha) in the Euphrates Basin. In addition, Turkey plans to irrigate 600,000 ha and generate HEP from eight dams on the Tigris. GAP should eventually irrigate 1.6 million hectares in the six provinces which it covers, boost Turkey's agricultural export potential, particularly towards Europe, and generate 53% of Turkey's electricity requirements. Although the key Ataturk dam has been built, the overall project is unlikely to be completed before the middle of the twenty-first century. Nevertheless, serious fears have already been expressed by Syrian and Iraqi planners over the likely depletion of Euphrates waters. Depletion rates in the region of 10,000–11,000 mcm per annum at the Syrian border have been forecast for 2010, but there is greater concern over the possible deterioration in the quality of downstream water.

The Euphrates supplies 85% of Syria's surface waters. Syria has long been planning to increase its area of irrigated farmland in the Euphrates and Khabur valleys, but land reclamation has fallen well short of targets. Should existing plans come to fruition, the flow of Euphrates water into Iraq might drop to 8,000–11,000 mcm per year from the present average of 21,000 mcm.

Syria has been able to develop additional irrigated farmland elsewhere: in the Ghab region on the Asi (Orontes) river, which flows into the Turkish province of Hatay, and also in the upper Yarmouk region in the south-east. On the basis of current consumption levels, Syria faces a water deficit of up to 1,000 mcm by the end of the 1990s, and the inhabitants of the main cities of Damascus and Aleppo already suffer frequent water and power shutdowns. Spending priorities have been allotted for further agricultural projects in recent economic development plans, with substantial subsidies for cereal growers, but because productivity is still sluggish, food imports, especially cereals, are still buoyant.

Before the 1990–91 Gulf War, Iraq had been planning to increase its area of irrigated farmland by 2m ha in the Euphrates and Tigris basins but feared that Syrian and Turkish projects would cut the Euphrates flow by two-thirds, to 11,000 mcm per annum. Although salinity (65% of irrigated land) and waterlogging are long-standing problems, some observers had thought that the outlook for Iraqi agriculture was promising compared with that for other states in the region. By August 1989, however, despite a self-sufficiency drive that was prompted by the Iran–Iraq War, Iraq was importing 80% of its food requirements by value. In the circumstances this was economically advisable, but politically embarrassing. In September 1990, at the beginning of the Gulf crisis, Iraqi farmers were ordered to allocate 80% of farmland to cereal production to counteract the effects of UN embargoes. Given the widespread damage to agricultural, hydrological and other infrastructure during the course of the Gulf War, the medium-term future of Iraqi agricultural schemes can only be considered very uncertain.

Hydropolitical Issues

Since the 1970s there have been several clashes between Turkey, Syria and Iraq over riparian rights: a serious dispute arose in 1975 between Iraq and Syria over alleged reductions in Euphrates flow as the result of the completion of Syria's Tabqa (ath-Thawra) dam. Armed conflict was averted only by the mediation of Saudi Arabia and the Arab League. In January 1990 closure of the last diversion tunnel on the Ataturk dam temporarily reduced the flow of the Euphrates into Syria and Iraq for one month and triggered an outcry throughout the Arab world, despite Turkish claims that it had supplied the relevant technical information about its plans and released compensatory flows down the Euphrates for two months beforehand. Syria and Iraq claimed that large areas in the Euphrates valley suffered water shortages which damaged irrigated farmland. In February 1991 the Syrian Foreign Minister, Farouk al-Sharaa, accused the Turkish government of reducing the flow of the Euphrates for ten days without warning; Turkey claimed that the shortfall had occurred for technical reasons.

Cooperation at a technical level has not proved politically useful. A joint Turkish–Iraqi technical committee was established in 1980 (Syria joined in 1983) and has met 15 times, but it has not reached any comprehensive agreements as Turkey and Syria differ widely in their definition of the legal status of the Tigris and Euphrates rivers and consequently of riparian rights. Furthermore, the conflict over water between Turkey and Syria is influenced by wider political considerations: Syria's support for the PKK rebels in the Kurdish regions of South East Anatolia; Turkey's harbouring of Islamic opponents of the Assad regime; Syrian irredentist claims to the Turkish province of Hatay (Alexandretta, ceded to Turkey in 1939) and Syrian unease over the extent of Turkish–Iraqi economic cooperation before the Gulf crisis.

The history of Turkish–Syrian negotiations over water rights illustrates the linkage between water issues and discussions on border security and extradition of political opponents which is evident in policy statements made by both countries. Under the provisions of the July 1987 Turkish–Syrian protocol, Turkey guaranteed Syria a minimum discharge of 500 cubic metres per second from the Euphrates until a permanent settlement was reached; in another protocol, both parties agreed not to harbour each other's opposition movements. A number of PKK bases were transferred from Syria, but only into the Beqaa valley in Lebanon, and incursions into Turkey continued.

In October 1989 President Özal announced that Turkey would withhold Euphrates waters from Syria unless support for the PKK ceased forthwith; in the same month Syrian forces shot down a Turkish civilian airliner inside Turkish territory in Hatay. One of President Assad's immediate moves following the Atatürk dam episode in January 1990 was to attend a ceremony for PKK officers in the Beqaa valley.

Turkey has adopted an assertive approach to the subject of Euphrates water rights, as exemplified in a recent statement by Prime Minister Süleyman Demirel: 'I do not believe in worrying about threats of war resulting from development projects in Turkey. If there is a threat we will repel it. Turkey has deterrence, it will have more deterrence in the coming period. Turkey will build more such works. The more it builds, the fewer threats it will be faced with'. According to Demirel, if Turkey accepts its downstream position in the region with regard to oil supplies it is justified in taking advantage of its position as an upstream user of water resources. Turkey is opposed to a multilateral agreement on the allocation of Tigris and Euphrates waters, claiming sovereignty over its portion of the rivers but also a willingness to cooperate on joint ventures with its downstream neighbours. Furthermore, Turkey has tried, unsuccessfully, to link a deal on the Euphrates to one on the Asi, which would imply Syrian recognition of Turkish jurisdiction over the province of Hatay. Syria, conversely, insists on a system of water quotas and the establishment of a Euphrates River Authority.

Close economic ties were built up between Turkey and Iraq during the 1980s when Turkey became an important transit route for Iraqi oil and other goods, as well as a major trading partner. In 1984 the two countries concluded a 'hot pursuit' agreement whereby Turkish forces were able to raid PKK positions in Northern Iraq.

Relations deteriorated in late 1989, however, because of Iraqi disquiet over interruption in Euphrates flows; as a result Iraq became less cooperative on matters of border security and PKK raids were launched into Turkey from bases in Northern Iraq. In the post-Gulf War period, although PKK raids into Turkey from Iraq and Turkish retaliatory strikes continue, a future food-for-oil agreement cannot be ruled out. In April 1990 Syria and Iraq signed an agreement on the allocation of Euphrates waters, and in June called on Turkey to reconsider its position on a tripartite accord.

Despite the clear links between water rights and political issues it must be emphasized that the water crisis in the Tigris–Euphrates region relates above all to the way in which priority has been given in all three states to irrigated agriculture. Yet it is oil, not agriculture, which holds the key to the economic future of Syria and Iraq.

The Way Forward: Implications For Regional Security

Recently there has been a proliferation of proposals for tackling the 'Middle East water crisis', based on the general theme of inter-basin transfers of water and/or regional economic cooperation. These include Turkey's 'peace pipelines' which would pump 3.5 mcm of water per day from the Seyhan and Ceyhan rivers to Jordan, Israel and the Occupied Territories, Syria and the Red Sea coast of Saudi Arabia, and 2.5 mcm per day to the east coast of Saudi Arabia and to the other peninsula states. The scheme was coolly received by its proposed beneficiaries on the grounds that Israeli involvement was controversial, the pipeline could easily be shut down or sabotaged, and that Turkey would profit from a life-giving resource. In November 1991, Iran offered to construct a rival water pipeline from the Karun river to Qatar and to other Gulf states, but this has not been followed through.

Other proposals include pumping Nile water into Gaza, and possibly beyond; storing Yarmouk waters in Lake Tiberias for use by Israel and Jordan, joint Israeli–Lebanese diversion of the Litani into the river Jordan to generate HEP, and the establishment of a water committee with extensive powers within a confederal Israeli–Palestinian–Jordanian framework. None of these proposals has made any headway. The only positive indications of inter-state cooperation are Syrian–Egyptian–Libyan agreements on the establishment on paper of an Arab Authority for Agricultural Production to coordinate the production of cereal crops, and on the creation of a joint electrical grid to be supplied by HEP generated on the Upper Nile and in East Africa.

Israel, which has been acting as a *de facto* upstream state, and Turkey regard control over water supply as a strategic imperative. In the Middle East and elsewhere, however, the notion that water is a national strategic asset to be monopolized at all cost is misconceived and unconstructive.

Because riparian states are interdependent in many ways and have different forms of political and economic leverage at their disposal, unilateral action by an upstream riparian state, while a serious cause of regional instability, is unlikely to lead to full-scale conflict. Concern over water shortage, a consequence of demographic pressure, distorted economic priorities and the failure, hitherto, to regulate and conserve supplies undoubtedly contribute to interstate tension but in the Middle East cannot be considered the principal *casus belli*. The long-term solution to the problem of inequitable allocation of water might be the creation of fluvial commissions or regulating authorities, but the process must begin on a much smaller scale with cooperation on the exchange of data and the pursuit of more efficient water management at a national level. This will be difficult to obtain while overarching regional settlements remain elusive, but it is not impossible. Such efforts can only strengthen the mechanisms for cooperation on which a more general settlement of the water problem depends.

Chronologies: 1991

USSR

January

2–   In Latvia, Soviet troops surround newspaper building in Riga; Latvians barricade main streets as Soviet troops open fire (14); Soviet troops seize Interior Ministry (20); Gorbachev meets Latvian leader Anatolijs Gorbunovs (22); Gorbunovs recommends referendum on independence (23).

4–5   At meeting in Moscow COMECON agrees to dissolve.

7–   Moscow orders paratroopers into Baltic states to enforce draft; Moldovans revoke laws punishing deserters and draft-dodgers (12).

8–   Soviet troops surround Lithuanian parliament (9); impose curfew in Vilnius (13); Lithuanian Foreign Minister flees with authorization to form exile government (11); troops seize national security department and radio station (12, 14); Gorbachev disclaims responsibility for attack (14).

9–   Georgia refuses to withdraw police and armed forces from South Ossetia; Georgian police storm Ossete barricades in Tskhinvali (13).

21–   Gorbachev summons 15-republic meeting on Baltic crisis (21); paratroopers and two-thirds of troops withdraw from Baltic (30).

February

4–   Russia, Ukraine, Belorussia and Kazakhstan begin talks; republics pledge to press ahead with own referenda (6).

5–   Gorbachev declares Lithuanian independence referendum invalid; majority vote for independence (9); Lithuanian parliament declares independence (12).

25   Georgian President Gamsakhurdia proposes talks to end ethnic conflict.

March

3–   Ukrainian miners stage 24-hour strike; strikes spread to west Siberia (11–12); then to Urals (19); miners reject call to return to work (24).

4   Soviet Parliament ratifies German reunification treaty.

4   In local referendums Latvia and Estonia vote in favour of secession.

6   In union-wide referendum, eight out of 15 republics, including Russia, vote in favour of preserving the country as renewed federation.

10–   Demonstrations in Russian Republic call for Gorbachev's resignation; Soviet government bans rallies in Moscow from 26 March to 15 April as Interior Ministry takes over law enforcement in capital (26).

April

1–   Georgians back independence in referendum; Georgia declares independence. (9).

3–   Gorbachev offers coalminers doubling of wages to end strike; miners reject offer (10); Yeltsin and Gorbachev announce strike agreement (24); Yeltsin visits Siberia and persuades miners to return to work (29–30).

4   Russian parliament gives Yeltsin emergency powers to run republic.

23   Central Committee backs Gorbachev's economic rescue package.

May

1–   Yeltsin places mines under Russian control; Donbass miners end 9-week strike (3).

1–   Fighting breaks out on Armenian/Azerbaijani border; Armenian and Azerbaijani leaders begin talks (3); talks break down (8).

15–   CCP General Secretary Jiang Zemin begins 5-day visit to Moscow;
        Foreign Ministers Bessmertnykh and Qian Qichen sign border agreement
        (16).
20   Russian Parliament votes for free foreign travel and emigration.
24–   Armed forces destroy Lithuanian guard post on Latvian border; 4 other
        border checkpoints burned down (25); 3 Baltic leaders meet in Lithuania
        to discuss border attacks by Soviet troops (30).
June
3–   Soviet troops surround parliament, railway station, airport and Interior
        Ministry buildings in Vilnius; protestors converge on parliamentary
        buildings (4); Gorbachev rebuffs Lithuanian leader's call to renounce
        force and begin independence negotiations (5); Soviet troops seize tele-
        phone exchange (26).
9–   Troops burn border post between Latvia and Russian Federation; break
        into customs post in Riga and confiscate documents (17).
12   Boris Yeltsin wins Russian presidential elections.
July
14   Soviet and Azeri troops attack 3 Armenian villages on northern border of
        Nagorno-Karabakh in Azerbaijan.
20   Yeltsin bans CP activity in Russian workplaces.
24   Gorbachev and 10 republics agree on new union treaty.
30–31   At summit in Moscow attended by Yeltsin and Kazakh President
        Nazarbayev, Bush promises MFN status if USSR carries out reforms.
August
1–   Lithuania temporarily withdraws armed police from border posts; gov-
        ernment takes charge of CP headquarters (23); ends conscription of
        Lithuanians (28).
19–   Gorbachev ousted in coup; Boris Yeltsin opposes coup plotters (20); coup
        collapses and Gorbachev returns to Moscow from Crimea (22);
        Gorbachev resigns as General Secretary of CP and announces
        confiscation of Party property (24); committee of radical reformers
        announced as interim government (25); 13 charged with coup attempt;
        Boris Pankin replaces Bessmertnykh as foreign minister (28); government
        dismissed and KGB ruling body disbanded (28); Supreme Soviet votes to
        suspend all CP activities (29).
20–   Estonia, Latvia and Lithuania, Belorussia and Ukraine (25) Azerbaijan
        (30) Uzbekistan and Kirgizia (31) declare independence.
29–   Russia and Ukraine form economic alliance; Russia signs economic coop-
        eration agreement with Kazakhstan (30).
September
1–   Baltic republics apply for membership of UN (3); Gorbachev and 10
        Republican leaders recognize Baltic independence (6).
2–   6 shot dead by police in Georgia; demonstrations mounted in Tbilisi (3);
        Gamsakhurdia's resignation demanded (5); supporters rally to his
        defence (12); he agrees to emergency session of parliament to discuss new
        elections as opponents seize TV station; state of emergency declared (24).
3   Boris Yeltsin announces all Soviet nuclear weapons stationed in republics
        to be moved to Russia.
8–   Ayaz Mutalibov wins Azerbaijani presidential elections; Azeris clash
        with Armenians near Nagorno-Karabakh (16).
9–   Tadzhikistan declares independence; crowds defy state of emergency
        when ban lifted on CP (24); state of emergency cancelled (30).
11   Gorbachev says USSR will withdraw 11,000 military personnel from
        Cuba.

October

1–   Georgian president Gamsakhurdia gives opponents 2 days to disarm; government and rebel troops fight outside capital (5).

1–   At meeting in Khazakhstan 12 republics sign common market plan; 11 republics agree to maintain unified army (9); Ukraine refuses to sign economic pact (17); 12 republics agrees to pay national debt (29).

9–   Soviet Union establishes diplomatic ties with Estonia and Lithuania; with Latvia (15); Estonia, Latvia and Lithuania join CSCE (15).

9–   Jokhar Dudayev stages successful coup in Russian autonomous region of Chechen-Ingushetia; wins disputed elections as President (27).

11   Soviet State Council dissolves KGB.

22–   Ukraine authorizes creation of own army; parliament accepts central control of nuclear arms on its territory (24); votes to close Chernobyl plant (29).

27   Turkmenistan declares independence.

November

4–   Ukraine establishes own national guard; parliament agrees to sign interrepublic economic treaty (6).

8–   Yeltsin imposes state of emergency in Chechen-Ingushetia and sends troops; troops forced to retreat (10); Russian parliament rescinds emergency (11).

18   G-7 resumes talks with Soviet republics over debt repayments; agrees to 1-year deferral of debt repayments (21).

19   Eduard Shevardnadze replaces Boris Pankin as Soviet Foreign Minister.

25   Russia, Belorussia, Kazakhstan, Tajikistan, Turkmenistan, Uzbekistan and Kirghizia refuse to sign new confederal treaty.

26–   Azerbaijani parliament votes to seize control of Nagorno-Karabakh; Armenia and Azerbaijan agree to resume peace talks in Moscow (27).

December

1–   Leonid Kravchuk wins Ukrainian presidential elections; proposes Ukraine, Russia, Belorussia and Kazakhstan place nuclear weapons under collective control (2); Ukraine and Russia agree all tactical nuclear weapons deployed in Ukraine will be moved to Russia (19).

2–   Nursultan Nazarbayev wins Kazakh presidential election.

8–   Russia, Ukraine and Belorussia declare USSR ceases to exist and establish Commonwealth of Independent States (CIS); Armenia and Kyrgyzstan agree to join CIS (11); Central Asian Republics agree to join (13); Norway recognizes Russian independence (16); 11 republics sign CIS treaty in Alma-Alta (21); EC recognizes Russia (25); US establishes diplomatic relations with Russia, Ukraine, Armenia, Kazakhstan, Belarus and Kyrgyzstan; Germany recognizes Russia and Ukraine (26); UK and EC recognize Ukraine (31).

10–   In Nagorno-Karabakh 7 killed during independence referendum; state of emergency introduced in Armenia (16).

18–   Russia, Kazakhstan, Belarus and Ukraine agree to uphold all arms-control agreements; Gorbachev hands control of nuclear weapons to Russia (25).

22   In Georgia, street battles break out in Tbilisi; opponents of President Gamsakhurdia attack parliament with rockets (23); rebels storm Tbilisi prison and release opposition leaders (27); cease-fire agreed (28); troops oust rebels from parliament, retake main square (29); fighting continues (30).

25   Gorbachev resigns as president.

UNITED STATES AND CANADA

January
7   Secretary of Defense Cheney cancels Navy's A-12 'stealth' bomber.
9   President Bush resumes $42.5-m military aid to El Salvador.
12   US Congress authorizes use of military force against Iraq.
February
4   Bush submits general FY 1992 budget proposal of $1.45 trillion.
14   130-nation meeting on global warming ends in Virginia, agrees to reduce carbon monoxide levels, aid developing nations which forgo use of polluting fuels.
23   Bush announces beginning of ground offensive in Kuwait; tells nation Kuwait is liberated (27).
March
1   In Montreal 39 countries sign treaty to introduce measures to make plastic explosives easier to detect at airports.
6   Bush declares Gulf War over.
20   Bush announces at start of President Lech Walesa's week-long visit that US will forgive at least $33bn of Polish debt.
26   Canadian Belanger-Campeau Commission on Québec's sovereignty recommends sovereignty referendum for 1992.
April
10   Bush cancels military and economic aid to Jordan.
12   Cheney announces plan to close 31 major military bases in the US.
17   Congress passes proposed $1.45 trillion budget resolution.
28   G-7 finance ministers meet in Washington, agree medium-term strategy to promote world growth.
May
6   US suspends $5m aid to Yugoslavia.
21–   US House of Representatives rejects proposed military budget for FY 1992; approves own defence bill (22).
June
6   Gen. Robert RisCassi announces US plans to turn over combined ground forces command in S. Korea to a Korean general.
11   Bush approves $1.5bn in agricultural credit guarantees to USSR.
11   Pakistan and US begin talks in Washington on suspension of US aid.
July
2   S. Korean President Roh Tae-Woo visits US, says N. Korean nuclear development is East Asia's most serious security problem.
10   Bush ends economic sanctions against South Africa.
30   Pentagon announces plans to cut ⅓ of 1,600 overseas bases by 1996.
September
5   Former Panamanian president, Gen. Manuel Noriega, appears on drug trafficking charges in Florida.
17   Canada announces intention to close 2 German air-bases and reduce troops in Europe from 6,600 to 1,100 by 1995.
17   46th UN General Assembly accepts memberships of Estonia, Latvia, Lithuania, North and South Korea, Micronesia and Marshall Islands.
26   Bush resumes $21-m aid programme to Jordan.
October
1   Bush announces $400-m loan guarantees for USSR.
November
20   Bush authorizes $1.5-bn grain credits to USSR.

25   US Senate approves transfer of up to $500m from defence budget to help dismantle Soviet nuclear weapons.

December

3–   In New York Boutros Ghali of Egypt sworn in as UN Secretary-General; UN repeals 1975 resolution equating Zionism with racism (16).

EUROPE

January

2–   Greek Premier Mitsotakis declares state of emergency on border following Albanian exodus; asserts Greek Albanians are free to cross border (14).

4   Polish parliament approves Jan Krzysztof Bielecki as premier.

4   45 Islamic countries including Iraq and Kuwait meet in Turkey.

9–   Yugoslav army ordered to disarm paramilitary groups countrywide; 6 republics begin talks on federation's future (10); Croatian Serbs begin disarming (16); Yugoslav army demands disbandment of Croatian forces and goes on alert (23); Croatian leader, Franjo Tudjman, agrees to demobilize police reserves if Yugoslav army ends combat alert (27); Yugoslav army orders arrest of Martin Spegelj, Croatian defence minister (30).

13   Portuguese president, Mario Soares, wins another term.

29   In France, Pierre Joxe, replaces defence minister, J. P. Chevenèment.

February

4–   Croatia refuses to take part in further federal talks (13); Slovenian parliament adopts constitutional amendments severing links with federal government (20); Croatia invalidates all federal laws within its territory (21).

6   EC grants £100-m loan to Syria; France, Germany and Italy submit defence proposals; £710m aid given to sub-Saharan Africa (12).

9–   Riots in Durres as Albanians flee country; factory workers join student protest in Tirana (11); students and teachers begin hunger strike as troops surround university (18); President Ramiz Alia takes over all powers (20); armed battle erupts outside military academy (22); army tanks withdrawn from government buildings in Tirana after 3-days of violence (25).

22   European ministers agree on WEU as central vehicle for European defence.

27   Polish and Czech defence ministers sign military cooperation pacts.

March

3–   Krajina announces secession from Croatia; heavy fighting in Belgrade (9–11); Yugoslav presidency holds emergency meeting (12); federal president Borisav Jovic resigns, but later rescinds (15, 20); Serbian president Milosevic leaves multirepublic presidency (16); Milosevic orders mobilization of security forces in Serbia as Montenegro and Vojvodina withdraw from presidency (17–18); Yugoslav army pledges non-interference in politics (19); anti-government demonstrations in Belgrade (27).

6–   Albanian refugees converge on Italian port of Brindisi and Albanian port of Vlore; Italy imposes naval blockade (8); Italy forces refugees to sail home (10); US resumes diplomatic relations with Albania (15).

11–   Czechoslovakian separatist demonstrations take place in Bratislava; President Vaclav Havel visits NATO (21).

14   Erich Honecker, former East German leader, flees to Soviet Union.

29   Italian premier Giulio Andreotti resigns and coalition collapses.

April

1–   Krajina announces intention to join Serbia; federal presidency holds emergency meeting over imminent military takeover in Croatia (3); Slovenia announces secession from federation (11); army moves into Croatian villages (28); talks fail to agree formula to end ethnic conflict (29).

1–   Albanian ruling CP wins legislative elections; army fires on anti-Communist demonstrators in Shkoder (2); general strike called by democratic opposition (4); Ramiz Alia renamed President (30).
22   Meeting of 39 Antarctic Treaty nations begins in Madrid.
25   NATO meets with ex-Warsaw Pact members in Prague.
May
2–   Clash in Borovo, Croatia results in 12 deaths; army seals off area (3); demands emergency powers as federal government orders police in Croatia to disarm (8); army granted emergency powers (9); nationalists refuse to disarm (10); federal presidency fails to agree replacement for ex-president Stipe Mesic (15); Croatia votes for independence in referendum (19); announces formation of separate army (29).
14   Poland restores diplomatic relations with South Africa.
28   NATO defence ministers agree establishment of RRC in 2-day meeting.
29   UK restores diplomatic relations with Albania after 50-year rift.
June
2–   Albanian parliament dissolved; government resigns (4); Ylli Bufi named premier (5); 3-week general strike disbanded (7); coalition government instated (12); EC restores relations with Albania (21); US Secretary of State, James Baker, makes 1-day visit to Tirana (22).
6–7   NATO foreign ministers meet in Copenhagen discuss European defence.
19   Last Soviet soldier leaves Hungary.
19   CSCE foreign ministers begin 2-day conference in Berlin, accept Albanian membership.
25   Croatia and Slovenia adopt declaration of independence; troops put on alert in Slovenia (26); ethnic Albanian students demonstrate in Kosovo (27); cease-fire agreed between premier Ante Makovic and Slovenia, and Croat Stipe Mesic elected head of state (31).
30   Last Soviet troops leave Czechoslovakia.
July
8–   Yugoslavian factions agree EC-sponsored cease-fire; Slovenian parliament accepts peace plan (10); state presidency accepts plan (13); Cease-fire breaks down (14); army shells Croatian village as EC monitors arrive (15); peace talks in Brioni fail as fighting continues (16); Slovenia cuts power supplies to 5 army bases (17); summit of feuding leaders agrees new peace pact (22); talks collapse and fighting intensifies (23); EC agrees to send monitoring mission to Croatia if all parties agree to cease-fire (29); Croatian leader, Stipe Mesic, rejects federal presidency proposal to establish peace plan commission (30).
15–17   Gorbachev attends G-7 summit in London; G-7 recommends special status for USSR in IMF and World Bank.
August
4   Yugoslav federal presidency proclaims new cease-fire (4); Serbian separatists bomb Croatian villages (7); CSCE begins 2-day meeting to end fighting (8); federal presidency holds emergency session to prop up fragile Croatian truce (13); Zagreb bombed (19); Serbs assault Croatian town of Vukovar (26–28); Croatian and federal army agree new cease-fire (27).
8–   Italy declares state of emergency as 1,300 Albanian refugees besiege coast near Bari; Rome begins forced repatriation (9); Italy increases emergency food aid to Albania (12).
8   Shah of Iran's last premier, Shapour Bakhtiar, assassinated in Paris.
20–   EC suspends economic aid to Soviet Union due to coup; recognizes Lithuania, Latvia and Estonia as independent states (27).
26–   Denmark resumes diplomatic relations with Estonia, Latvia and

Lithuania; as does Germany (28); and Finland (29).

27 Israeli premier Shamir begins 4-day visit to Bulgaria.

29 Speaking in US, UK premier John Major announces accelerated 6-point package to USSR, including IMF and World Bank help.

29 Romania and Moldova establish diplomatic relations.

September

1– Yugoslavian EC-backed peace plan signed by 6 republics; Serbs and federal army seal off Slovenia (4); 150 EC monitors arrive in Zagreb (5); EC-sponsored peace conference reconvenes in Hague (7); Macedonia votes to become independent (8); Croatia orders overnight curfew as fighting spreads southwards (9); Croats capture 20 federal army barracks (15); new cease-fire agreement signed (17); fighting in Croatia and on Adriatic coast continues (18); new cease-fire agreed (22); UN imposes arms embargo on all factions (25); EC agrees to double number of cease-fire monitors as fresh army columns sent to Croatia (30).

17 Albania signs Paris Charter of CSCE.

25– Fighting between Romanian security forces and miners break out; Premier Petre Roman and government resign (27–28).

October

1– Yugoslavian army launches new offensive against Croatia; attack Dubrovnik from air, sea and land (2): federal troops attack Zagreb (7); Croats sign new cease-fire, Slovenia and Croatia sever all ties with federation (8); Serbian president Milosevic and Croatian counterpart Tudjman call for immediate cease-fire, state will begin peace negotiations within 1 month in Moscow (15); Bosnia-Herzegovina declares its independence (15); Soviet-brokered truce collapses (16); federal army assaults Dubrovnik (23); federal presidency boycotts EC Hague peace talks (25); federal army advances on Dubrovnik, EC threatens sanctions against Serbia (28); federal president Stipe Mesic joins attempt to break naval blockade of Dubrovnik (29); flotilla fails as shelling continues (30).

2– USSR foreign minister arrives in Czechoslovakia to sign bilateral treaty; Czechoslovakia and Germany sign cooperation treaty (7).

7– EC finance ministers pledge one third of £4.2-bn credit to USSR for food and medicines; France and Germany propose European army (15); EC and EFTA agree 19-nation European Economic Area (EEA) (22).

7 Bulgaria and Greece sign cooperation treaty.

30 Two-day conference of 28 European states agrees need to halt illegal immigration from East Europe.

November

4– Serbia rejects EC ultimatum as Vukovar bombed; federal army pounds Dubrovnik (6–7); air force intensifies bombing in Croatia (7); EC-brokered peace talks held (13); Serbs capture Vukovar (18); at French-backed talks both sides agree to demilitarization of Dubrovnik (19); 14th cease-fire agreed (23); Croatia agrees to deployment of UN peace-keepers (25); Serbia agrees (28); federal army begins withdrawal from Zagreb (29).

7– In Rome NATO leaders agree new European defence organization built around WEU, agree to establish NACC (8).

22 EC agrees free trade with Hungary, Poland and Czechoslovakia.

26 Poland joins Council of Europe.

December

2– In Yugoslavia EC lifts economic sanctions on Bosnia-Herzegovina, Croatia, Macedonia and Slovenia; federal navy lifts blockade (3); Germany cuts off transport links with Serbia and Montenegro (4); federal army withdrawn from Zagreb (10); Ukraine recognizes Croatian and Slovenian independence (12); UN Security Council votes to send peace-keepers (15); new fighting breaks out in Croatia (20); Germany recognizes Croatian and Slovenian independence (23); fighting continues in Croatia (25–26); 12 UN monitors arrive in Zagreb (26); Karlovac and Osijek shelled (26–29).

5–   Polish premier Jan Krzysztof and government resign; replaced by Jan Olszewski (6); centre-right coalition collapses (12); Olszewski resigns (17); parliament rejects resignation (18); he establishes new government (23).

8–   Romanians approve new constitution; US Secretary of Defense, Dick Cheney, visits (8–10).

9–   At 2-day EC finance meeting in Maastricht agree single currency by 1999; Poland, Hungary and Czechoslovakia sign association accords with EC (16).

MIDDLE EAST

January

7–   PLO chairman Yasser Arafat announces support for Iraq; US Secretary of State Baker holds unsuccessful talks with Iraqi Foreign Minister Tariq Aziz in Geneva (9); UN Secretary-General visits Iraq on final peace mission (13); UN votes unanimously for action against Iraq (14); allies begin *Operation Desert Storm* to liberate Kuwait (16); Iraqi *Scuds* attack Israel (17); *Scuds* attack Saudi Arabia (20); Iraq fires Kuwaiti oil wells (22); Iraq pumps oil into Gulf (25); Iraqi planes escape to Iran (21–).

7–   In Lebanon 4 Belgian hostages held by Abu Nidal PLO group freed; Lebanese Druze leader Walid Jumblatt resigns from unity cabinet (11).

February

6–   Iraq breaks diplomatic relations with coalition members; Saddam offers to negotiate with USSR (12); UN Secretary-General rules out cease-fire before withdrawal (13); Bush dismisses Iraqi offer of conditional withdrawal (15); Iraqi Foreign Minister proposes peace plan in talks with Gorbachev in Moscow (18); Soviet Union unveils peace plan giving Iraq 3 weeks to withdraw (22); Bush dismisses plan (22); allies launch 3-pronged ground attack into Kuwait and Iraq (24); Iraq orders troop withdrawal (25); Security Council agrees no cease-fire until Iraq complies with 12 UN resolutions (26); allies liberate Kuwait City (26) Iraq accepts UN demands for war reparations, declares annexation of Kuwait null and void (27); Bush announces cease-fire (28).

10   Israel lifts curfew imposed on Occupied Territories.

26   Jordan and Iran re-establish diplomatic relations.

March

3–   Iraq agrees terms for permanent cease-fire; first allied prisoners released (4); 8 Arab nations endorse US 4-point peace plan (10); UN agrees to humanitarian food shipments to Iraq (22).

3   Israeli jets fire on PLO Lebanese base; Lebanese rockets fire on Israel (5); Lebanese government orders disarming of all militias (28).

3–   Shi'i insurrection begins in Iraq; Kurds in north attack army HQ in Dukan, fighting spreads to other cities (5); Basra insurrection quelled by army (6); government uses helicopters against Kurds (13); army retakes some northern towns as unrest begins in capital (12); rebels launch attacks in Baghdad (22); US shoots down truce-breaking Iraqi warplanes (20, 22); Saddam Hussein shuffles government (23).

6–   General strike called in Israeli-Occupied Territories; 4 Israelis stabbed in Jerusalem (10); US Secretary of State Baker meets Palestinians (12).

14   Emir of Kuwait returns home; government resigns (20).

April

1–   Iraqi troops advance in north against Kurds; Turkey closes border (3); Iran closes border (7); UK premier Major proposes UN protected enclave, Iran opens borders to refugees (8); EC backs enclave plan (11); remaining US forces in Iraq begin withdrawing to buffer zone along Kuwaiti border (14); Kurds begin peace talks in Baghdad (19); Iraqi army begins withdrawing from north (21); Kurds sign autonomy deal (24); refugees begin returning home (25); UK and US forces expand security zone (28); first refugees enter Zakho (30).

2   British hostage Roger Cooper released in Lebanon.

3   UN Security Council adopts Gulf War cease-fire measure, orders Iraq to destroy nuclear, chemical and biological weapons and pay reparations.

8–   Israel releases Arab prisoners as Baker arrives; Israel agrees in principle to Middle East peace conference (8); retracts agreement (28).

21   PLO begins 3-day meeting in Tunis.

May

1–   Iraq agrees to hold multiparty elections, rejects UN police force in Iraq (6); last US troops leave southern Iraq as US forces expand safe haven in north (7); IAEA team begins assessing Iraqi nuclear weapons capability (15); Security Council approves reparations claim mechanism (20); US and Iraq agree formula to encourage return of Kurdish refugees (22).

10–   Soviet Foreign Minister Bessmertnykh visits Israel; Polish president Walesa visits Israel (20–24); in Tel Aviv, US Defense Secretary Cheney grants Israel $200m in military research aid, announces stockpiling of military equipment in Israel (30).

22   Lebanon signs friendship treaty with Syria.

28   PLO officials meet Syrian president Hafez al-Assad after 8-year rift.

June

2–   Kurds move into Dahuk; UN Security Council Sanctions Committee allows 31 countries to release Iraqi assets (12); allies begin leaving north Iraq (15); UN team enters Iraq to inspect military facilities (22).

3   Israeli air force begins 2-day attack on Palestinian air-base in Lebanon.

5–   Prince Saud al-Faisal, Saudi Arabian foreign minister visits Iran; Austrian President Waldheim begins first western leader visit to Iran in 10 years (9).

26   Kuwait lifts martial law.

July

2–   Lebanese army gains control of Sidon in 2-day operation; *Hizbollah* agrees to integrate into Lebanese army (16).

7   Jordan lifts martial law enforced since 1967 Arab–Israeli war.

14   Foreign Ministers of Egypt, Syria and 6 members of GCC meet in Kuwait to discuss regional defence.

14–   Iraq provides UN with list of nuclear facilities; Iraq fails to meet deadline for disclosure of nuclear weapons programme (25).

August

1–   Israeli premier Yitzhak Shamir accepts invitation to Middle East peace conference; Israel establishes diplomatic relations with Albania (19).

5–   Iraq admits to biological warfare experiments; Turkey attacks PKK in north Iraq (6); Iraqi soldiers enter Kuwait to retrieve weapons (6–7); UN allows Iraq to sell up to $1.6bn of oil for humanitarian expenses (15).

8–   In Lebanon British hostage John McCarthy freed; US hostage Edward Tracy and French hostage Jerome Leyraud freed (11); Lebanese government grants amnesty for General Aoun (27); he flees to France (29).

September

1–   Lebanon and Syria sign security pact; UK hostage Jackie Mann freed (24).

1–   Iraq begins destroying CW; UN inspectors leave Iraq after being blocked
       from inspection of missile sites (13); Iraq agrees to UN helicopter flights
       (16); 6th UN team arrives in Iraq searching for signs of nuclear weapons
       production (22); Iraq fails to meet UN conditions on use of helicopters
       (22); UN inspectors freed after being held in Baghdad for 4 days (29); leave
       with evidence of nuclear production (30).
4   US and Kuwait reach agreement on the outlines of a 10-year security pact.
11–   Israel releases 51 Lebanese prisoners; army kills 3 Palestinians in Golan
       Heights infiltrating from Syria (22).
20–22 Muslim extremists riot in Cairo.
28   PLO agrees to participate in Middle East peace conference.

October
1–   UN ballistic experts fly to Baghdad; *Peshmerga* clash with Iraqi soldiers in
       Sulaymaniyah (5–8); agree a cease-fire (8); allied forces protecting Kurds
       complete withdrawal (10); Turkish troops attack Turkish Kurds in north-
       ern Iraq (11–13); Kurds retaliate (25).
3–   Israel agrees to adopt MTCR rules; restores relations with USSR (18);
       agrees to peace talks (20); Shamir says he will head delegation (23).
21–   In Lebanon US hostage Jesse Turner released.
23   Arab foreign ministers meet in Damascus to coordinate conference
       positions.
30   Middle East peace conference opens in Madrid.

November
4–   Iraq blockades Kurdish towns; *Peshmerga* repel army advance in Kirkuk
       (5); army attacks Kurds in Erbil (25); Massoud Barzani, leader of Kurdish
       Democratic Party leaves for talks in Baghdad (28).
8   Bomb blasts US university in Beirut; UK hostage Terry Waite freed (18).
10   South African President F W de Klerk arrives for 3-day Israeli visit.

December
1–   Israel releases 25 Arab prisoners; US hostages Joseph J Cicippio (2) Alan
       Steen (3) and Terry Anderson freed (4); body of murdered US hostage Lt.-
       Col William Higgins released (22); car bomb kills 30 in Beirut (30).
2   In Syria, Lt.Gen. Hafez al-Assad re-elected president.
4–   Arab delegation arrives for bilateral talks in Washington, but Israel fails to
       appear; talks reconvene after Israel arrives (11–18).
4   Libya arrests 2 men wanted by UK and US over 1988 Lockerbie bombing;
       Arab League backs Libyan refusal to extradite men (5).
9–   Palestinians strike as Israeli army imposes curfew in Occupied Territories
       on *intifada's* 4th anniversary; settlers occupy 6 East Jerusalem homes (12).
15   Czechoslovakian president Vaclav Havel arrives in Egypt for 3-day visit.

ASIA AND AUSTRALASIA

January
2–   Sri Lankan Tamils attack 2 army camps in the north; government ends
       10-day cease-fire (11); Tamils announce cease-fire (15); civilians killed in
       bombing raids by air force (21); Tamils formally abandon cease-fire (25).
24   Papua New Guinea signs peace treaty with secessionists.
30   Indian premier Chandra Shekhar dismisses government of Tamil Nadu
       state and imposes direct rule.

February
5   In Pakistan, general strike protests Indian rule over Kashmir; Prime Minis-
       ter Nawaz Sharif proclaims day as national holiday.
6–   Strike in Tamil Nadu over direct rule from Delhi spreads to neighbouring

states; Kashmiri militants fight soldiers in Srinagar (11).

18 Sri Lankan Tamils kill 44 government soldiers in ambush.

18 North Korea breaks off high level-talks with South Korea.

23– In Thailand military stage successful coup; King Bhumibol Adul Yadej approves military junta (26).

27 Bangladesh National Party wins legislative elections.

March

5– Indian Congress Party leave parliament; parliament dissolved (13).

20 Begum Khalida Zia appointed as Bangladeshi premier.

April

1– In Afghanistan *Mujaheddin* take long-besieged town of Khost; government forces retaliate, firing 4 *Scuds* at city, killing 300 (21).

6– After three days of talks, India and Pakistan sign agreement against airspace violations and for advance troop manoeuvre warnings.

17–19 Gorbachev holds talks with Japanese premier Toshiki Kaifu in Tokyo, fails to resolve Kuril islands dispute.

19–20 US and Vietnam hold talks on US MIA; US announces $1m in aid (25).

23– Prince Norodom Sihanouk's forces accept temporary cease-fire in Cambodia; *Khmer Rouge* accept UN backed cease-fire (26).

23 Military junta in Myanmar force National League for Democracy to drop Aung San Suu Kyi as party leader.

May

1– South Korean students and workers clash with police; police ban rallies; 4th student immolates self as riots spread (8); country-wide demonstrations demand resignation of President Roh Tae-woo (9–19) Premier Ro Jae-bong resigns (22); is replaced by Chung Won-shik (24).

2 Thai government lifts martial law imposed by military on 23 February.

6– Indian army kill 68 Kashmiri separatists; Indian legislative election begins amidst violence (20); former premier Rajiv Ghandi assassinated in Tamil Nadu (21); P. V. Narasimha Rao replaces him as Congress (I) leader (29).

12– Nepalese Congress Party wins legislative elections.

22– Afghan government accepts UN peace plan; President Najibullah offers rebels truce (27); they reject it (28).

June

2– Cambodian premier Hun Sen agrees to Prince Sihanouk as chairman of SNC; *Khmer Rouge* object (3); 3-day peace talks collapse (4); Sihanouk joins SNC (7); factions agree indefinite cease-fire to begin 24 June (23).

11– Sri Lankan Tamils announce readiness to begin peace talks; 10-day curfew lifted in 4 northern districts (24).

11– In India 40 killed in violence in Kashmir; curfew imposed as Indian Congress (I) wins legislative elections (12); P. V. Rao sworn in as premier (21).

12 Former Bangladeshi president Lt. Gen. Ershad sentenced to 10 years.

16– US evacuate Subic Bay and Clark bases on Philippines due to eruption of Mount Pinatubo; US nuclear warheads shipped out (17).

27 Vietnamese premier Do Muoi elected General Secretary of Vietnamese Communist Party at 7th Party Congress.

July

4 UK and China agree deal on construction of Hong Kong airport.

14– Sri Lankan Navy lands on beach near Elephant Pass, beaten back; Tamil Tigers attack Elephant Pass garrison (15); government lifts curfew in north (25); garrison soldiers repulse 2 attacks (28–29).

16–17 Cambodian peace talks held in Beijing and Prince Sihanouk elected unanimously as president of SNC.

19–   Foreign ministers of South-east Asian nations meet in Kuala Lumpur; Japan proposes dialogue on regional security (22).

29–30 Pakistan, Iran and *Mujaheddin* hold peace talks in Islamabad.

August

4–   Sri Lankan army breaks 25-day siege at Elephant Pass; President Premadasa suspends parliament for 1 month (30).

10–   Japanese premier Kaifu begins 4-day visit to China; visits Mongolia for one day (13).

13–   Chinese President Yang Shangkun begins 4-day visit to Mongolia.

27   US and Philippines sign treaty, US agree to use Subic Bay base for 10 years, abandon Clark air base, grant $363-m military aid in 1992.

27   Warring Cambodian factions agree to cut toops by 70%; 5-day peace talks end with only postwar electoral system left undecided (29).

September

2–   Pakistan and India agree cease-fire on Kashmir; army clamps down on United Liberation Front of Assam in Assam (15).

2–   UK premier Major arrives in Beijing for 3-day talks; China and UK sign agreement on Hong Kong airport (3).

9   Vietnamese Foreign Minister Nguyen Manh Cam visits China.

13   US and USSR agree to halt weapon supplies to Afghanistan by end 1991.

15–   Sri Lankan government forces advance on Tamil base in north-east; capture base (26); suspend further offensive operations (27).

16–   Philippine senate votes against extending US use of Subic and Clark bases; President Aquino rejects senate decision (17).

24   At UN South Korean President Roh proposes 3-point peace plan.

October

2   After Supreme Court decision supporting Philippino Senate position, President Aquino gives US 3 years to withdraw from bases.

3–   Japanese foreign minister Ryutaro Hashimoto resigns over stock market and banking scandals; Japan announces $2.5-bn aid to USSR (8).

14   In Myanmar opposition leader Aung San Suu Kyi awarded Nobel Peace Prize.

18–   Cambodian Communist Party endorses multiparty democracy at 2-day congress; peace treaty signed in Paris calling for cease-fire (23).

23   US agrees to withdraw nuclear weapons from South Korea by April 1992.

29   Vietnam and UK sign agreement on forced repatriation of Vietnamese boat people.

November

4–   Imelda Marcos returns to Philippines; US returns Clark air base to Philippines (26).

5–   Vietnamese premier Vo Van Kiet and CP leader Do Muoi begin 5-day visit to China; they sign border and cooperation agreements (7).

5   Kiichi Miyazawa replaces Toshiki Kaifu as Japanese premier.

9   Hong Kong forcibly repatriates 59 Vietnamese boat people.

10–   Prince Sihanouk returns to Cambodia after 13-year exile (14); *Khmer Rouge* delegation returns (17); Sihanouk named president (20); *Khmer Rouge* leader Khieu Samphan attacked by demonstrators, flees to Thailand (27).

11–   Afghan *Mujaheddin* hold talks with USSR, first for 13 years; USSR agrees to end support for Afghan regime (15).

15   Indonesian army kills large numbers of demonstrators in East Timor.

15   US Secretary of State, James Baker, begins 3-day talks in China.

25   Bangladeshi Foreign Minister, Mustafizur Rahman, ends 3-day visit to Myanmar, Myanmar agrees to take back all refugees fleeing to Bangladesh.

December

10–   Troops in Myanmar disperse student rally in support of San Suu Kyi; close universities (11); raid Bangladeshi border area (21); Myanmar and Bangladesh exchange fire in Arakan (24); hold border talks in Maungdaw (31).

12– Chinese premier, Li Peng, begins 5-day visit to India, first since 1960; India and China resume direct trade links (13).

13– North and South Korea sign non-aggression pact in Seoul; President Roh Tae-woo announces all US nuclear weapons removed from ROK (18); N. Korea pledges to allow nuclear inspections (26); agreement reached on draft nuclear weapons ban (31).

17– In Cambodian capital government closes universities as demonstrations continue (23); *Khmer Rouge* leader, Khieu Samphan, returns (30).

20– Australian premier, Bob Hawke, replaced by party colleague Paul Keating; US President Bush arrives for 3-day visit (31).

AFRICA

January

1– Fighting continues in Mogadishu, Somalian capital; President Siad Barre calls for cease-fire (2); ministers and members of Barre's family flee to UAE (7); government resigns (20); Barre flees as rebels take over palace (27); rebels inaugurate Ali Mahdi Mohammed as president (29).

4 Rwandan troops kill 150 rebels in renewed fighting near Ugandan border.

29 In South Africa, Nelson Mandela and Chief Mangosuthu Buthelezi, leader of Zulu Inkatha Freedom Party, pledge end to township violence.

February

12 In South Africa, government and ANC break deadlock on release of political prisoners.

13– Charles Taylor and Prince Yormie Johnson sign Liberian cease-fire agreement at 2-day Togolese meeting; Taylor announces intention to lead interim government, contravening cease-fire agreement (14).

16 At London meeting Commonwealth countries decide to maintain sanctions against South Africa until apartheid dismantled.

March

3– Liberian forces agree to join regional efforts for national peace conference; Sierra Leone sends troops to Liberian border after rebel raids (24).

4– Ethiopian Tigrean rebels claim capture of entire Gojan province.

20 Maghreb nations open first summit since Gulf War in Ras Lanuf, Libya.

22– Curfew and state of emergency imposed in Mali after riots in capital; both lifted after meeting of opposition and government (24); President Gen. Moussa Traoré overthrown by army (26).

April

3– Angolan peace talks resume in Portugal; government leaders and UNITA initial document leading to cease-fire (30).

23– Ethiopian parliament calls for national unity government and cease-fire to end civil war; President Mengistu Haile Mariam appoints Tesfaye Dinka, former foreign minister, as premier and dismisses cabinet (26).

30 Lesotho leader, Maj-Gen Justin Lekhanya, ousted in bloodless army coup.

May

1– UNITA and Angolan government reach peace agreement in Lisbon; Cuban troops complete withdrawal from Angola (25).

3– In South Africa 98 killed in 8-day violence; Winnie Mandela sentenced to 6 years for kidnapping (14); ANC suspends constitutional talks (18).

19– Northern Somalia announces independence; interim government condemns move (27); agrees to participate in talks in Djibouti (29).

21– Mengistu Haile Mariam resigns; rebels attack Asmara (24); government surrenders (27); rebels take capital (28); curfew imposed as Eritreans announce wish to form separate government (29).

26   Sierra Leone recaptures border towns, killing 60 Liberian rebels.

29   In Algeria, demonstrations back strike by Islamic fundamentalists.

June

3–5   OAU meets in Nigeria, signs treaty establishing economic community.

4–   Algerian fire on Muslim fundamentalist demonstrators; President Chadli Benjedid declares state of siege (15); fundamentalists end 2-week protest (7); troops move to Algiers after day of clashes (25); Chadli Benjedid resigns (28); Abbasi Madani, leader of FIS, is arrested (30).

8–9   South African President F. W. de Klerk visits Kenya.

11–   Burkina Faso President Compaore dissolves government; opens talks with opposition (12); transitional government named without premier (16).

17–   South Africa repeals 1950 Population Registration Act; 1913 and 1936 Land Acts and 1966 Group Areas Act repealed (30).

July

1–   In Algeria 700 arrested as army cracks down on anti-Islamic fundamentalists; curfew lifted (16).

5–   In South Africa Nelson Mandela elected president of ANC; International Olympic Committee readmits country (9); Inkatha repay R250,000 to government from secret state funding (24).

12–   Madagascan general strike enters 5th day; 6 opposition ministers installed (22); state of emergency declared (23); 6 opposition leaders arrested (25); premier Ramahatra resigns (28).

14–   Cameroon government bans 6 associations involved in general strike; government begins talks with strikers (24).

16–   Somalian peace talks begin in Djibouti; 6 political groups accept agreement on cease-fire and establishment of provisional government (22).

August

5–   Madagascar extends state of emergency; general strike starts (12); opposition forces seize power (19).

6   Liberian rebel leader Johnson withdraws from interim government.

7–   USSR Deputy Foreign Minister Nikolayenko begins 5-day South African visit; South Africa amnesties political prisoners (16).

27   Togo's National Conference on Democracy elects Kokou Koffigoh as premier as President Gnassinybe Eyadéma leaves capital.

September

2–   Zairean demonstrators converge on Kinshasa; strike tightens (3); France sends 450, and Belgium 500, troops as riots continue (24); President Mobutu and 11 opposition parties agree to form transitional government (29); Etienne Tshisekedi replaces Mulumba Lukoji as premier (30).

5–   Liberian rebels push 20 miles into Sierra Leone; agreement to disarm signed after 2-day summit in Côte d'Ivoire (17).

8–   Violence sweeps South African townships for three days; government, ANC, Inkatha and others sign peace accord (14).

October

2–   Zairean troops loot shops; Belgium and France announce partial withdrawal (4); Mungul Diaka replaces premier Tshisekedi (23); last French troops withdraw as opposition establishes rival government (31).

15   Religious riots take place in Nigerian city, Kano; President Ibrahim Babangida calls state of emergency (16).

23–   Liberian Charles Taylor's forces clash with National Patriotic Front on Sierra Leonese border; at Yamoussoukro summit of Liberian and West African leaders he agrees to surrender his fighters' territory (31).

31   Kenneth Kaunda loses Zambian presidential and legislative elections.
November
1–   Zairean opposition call on army to break ties with President Mobutu Sese Seko as new government sworn in; Belgium withdraws last troops (4); Mobutu signs Sengalese-brokered peace pact (22).
2–   Frederick Chiluba sworn in as Zambian president replacing Kenneth Kaunda; Zambia reopens diplomatic relations with South Africa.
4–   2-day national strike starts in South Africa; all political leaders except PAC agree to hold power-sharing talks (29–30).
18–   Somalian rebels overthrow President Ali Mahdi Mohammed, who flees country; Mogadishu shelled (19–20).
27–   Violence breaks out in Togo after government bans Togolese People's Assembly, loyal to President Eyadéma; troops take over radio and TV stations, overthrow premier Koffigoh and impose curfew (28).
December
1–   In Burkina Faso President Blaise Compaore wins presidential elections; Clement Oumarou Quedraogo, opposition leader, assassinated in capital (9); violence erupts at his funeral (10).
3–   Togolese rebels capture premier Kokou Koffigoh; he and ex-dictator Eyadema agree to form coalition government (4).
13   Iranian President Ali Hashemi Rafsanjani arrives in Sudan for 3-day visit.
20   Inkatha Freedom Party leader, Chief Mangosuthu Buthelezi, boycotts South African constitution talks.

CENTRAL AND LATIN AMERICA

January
7–   Haitian army crushes coup attempt; restores caretaker president to power; party of Father Aristide wins run-off legislative elections (20).
11   Commanders of Colombian Popular Liberation Army (EPL) sign draft peace agreement with Colombian government.
15   Jorge Luis Ochoa, Medellín drug baron, surrenders.
22   Erskine Sandiford re-elected as premier of Barbados.
February
4–   Colombian left-wing guerrillas step up anti-government offensive; car bomb blast in Medellín kills 22 (16).
6–   Jean-Bertrand Aristide inaugurated as Haitian president; Haitian cabinet sworn in (20).
14–   Peruvian cabinet resigns; Carlos Torres replaces Juan Hurtado Miller as premier (15).
March
7–   In El Salvador 3-day truce agreed for national and local elections; ruling ARENA party claims electoral victories (10).
26   Presidents of Argentina, Brazil, Paraguay and Uruguay sign treaty of Asunción, form Southern Cone common market to be known as 'Mercosur', pledge to integrate their economies by 1995.
April
4–   Salvadorean peace talks resume in Mexico; government and FMLN sign agreement on constitutional and political reform (27).
8   Panamanian President Guillermo Endara replaces 5 Christian Democrat ministers with members of his own party, Arnulfista.
May
18   Andean Pact members move further to free-trade zone by signing Act of Caracas in Venezuelan capital.

31   In Colombia rebel Quintin Lame Armed Movement disarms and turns into a political party.

June
3–   Salvadorean peace talks suspended; resume in Mexico (16–24).
13–   Colombian peace talks resume in Venezuela; Pablo Escobar, head of Medellín cocaine cartel surrenders (19).
17   Guatemalan peace talks begin in Mexico.

July
15–18   Presidents of Panama, El Salvador, Nicaragua, Guatemala, Honduras and Costa Rica meet in El Salvador for 3-day summit, agree to eliminate grain trade barriers by end 1991.
20–21   21 Latin American countries, Portugal and Spain meet in Mexico, for first Ibero-American summit, pledge greater economic integration.
26   Peru and US sign $35m military aid and $60m in economic aid agreement, and Peru agrees to use army in drugs war.

August
12   In El Salvador fighting breaks out between troops and FMLN.
14   Haitian government militants force parliament to adjourn and burn down trade union headquarters.
18   Mexico's ruling PRI wins congressional elections.

September
11   Guatemala establishes relations with Belize, ends 400-year dispute.
22   Mexican president Carlos Salinas signs free-trade pact with Chile.
25   Colombian peace talks begin in Caracas.
25   FMLN sign broad agreement with government, includes incorporating themselves into new national police force.
30   Haitian President Aristide arrested in army coup.

October
1–   Salvadorean troops attack FMLN positions; peace talks resume in Mexico (12); clashes continue between FMLN and troops (15–16).
1–   France and US suspend aid to Haiti following coup; ousted president Father Aristide requests OAS help to restore him to power (2); OAS imposes economic sanctions, troops fire on people in capital and seal off palace (7); army installs Joseph Nerette as president (8); Jean-Jacques Honorat replaces Rene Dreval as premier (11); general strike staged (15).

November
15–   Haitian government orders French ambassador Jean-Raphael Dufour to leave; US restarts forced repatriation of Haitian refugees (18); US court puts hold on repatriation (19); 3-day talks between deposed Haitian president Father Aristide and his parliamentary opponents collapse.
16–   In El Salvador FMLN announces unilateral cease-fire; peace talks shattered in weekend clashes (16–17); peace talks resume in Mexico (25).
23   President of Guyana, Desmond Hoyte, announces indefinite postponement of general election; state of emergency declared (28).

December
12   President Hoyte extends Guyanese state of emergency to June 1992.
16   Salvadorean peace talks reconvene at UN in New York.
16–   Haitian police shoot member of parliament and burn down houses on anniversary of free elections; former president Aristide agrees to Rene Theodore as premier (23).
16   People's National Movement wins legislative election in Trinidad and Tobago.

ARMS CONTROL

January

7– 2-week UN Conference on Disarmament concerning chemical weapons begins in New York.

February

11– CFE talks resume in Vienna; talks impose 4-week moratorium over Soviet interpretation of CFE agreement (21).

March

21 CFE talks in Vienna suspended after failure to make significant progress.

27 Last Soviet tanks leave Czechoslovakia.

31 Warsaw Pact military alliance disbanded.

April

9 USSR begins Polish troop withdrawals.

16 CFE summit opens in Vienna.

May

6– US destroys last *Pershing* II missile under terms of 1987 INF Treaty; USSR completes destruction of its SS-20 misssiles (12).

13– Bush announces that US is prepared to destroy all existing stockpiles of CW within 10 years of chemical convention's entry into force, and imposes absolute ban on US use of chemical weapons.

June

3 France proposes global disarmament plan and affirms it will sign NPT.

14 At CFE arms talks USSR pledges to destroy tanks in line with Treaty.

27 South Africa announces intention to sign NPT.

July

8–9 At Paris meeting the 5 permanent members of UN Security Council (China, USSR, France, UK and US) agree to create nuclear-free zone and limit weapons of mass destruction in Middle East.

11–14 Final START talks held in Geneva.

31 Bush and Gorbachev sign START Treaty during Moscow summit.

August

5 Egypt reports submission of proposals to UN on weapons-free zone in Middle East.

September

9 Conference on control of BW opens in Geneva.

27 Bush announces unilateral arms cuts, including destruction of all ground-based short-range missiles and removal of all tactical nuclear weapons.

30 Defence and space talks begin in Geneva.

October

5 Gorbachev announces unilateral reduction of 1,000 short-range nuclear weapons and troop cuts of 700,000, a 1-year moratorium on nuclear tests, and removal of 503 ICBMs from alert status.

18 At 2-day London meeting UN Security Council permanent members adopt proposals limiting arms sales.

24 In Geneva US and USSR end defence and space talks.

November

5 At 'open skies' talks in Geneva USSR agrees to allow overflights of territory to ensure arms-control compliance.

17 China agrees to abide by MTCR.

December

13 Argentinian President, Carlos Menem, and Brazilian counterpart, Fernando Collor de Mello, sign IAEA nuclear safeguards agreement in Vienna.

29 China announces it will sign the NPT.

Glossary

ASEAN	Association of South East Asian Nations	INF	Intermediate-range nuclear forces
ATTU	Atlantic-to-the-Urals	MBT	Main battle tank
APEC	Asia-Pacific Economic Cooperation	MFN	Most-favoured nation
BW	Biological weapons	MINURSO	UN Mission for the Referendum in Western Sahara
CIA	Central Intelligence Agency		
CIS	Commonwealth of Independent States	MIRV	Multiple Independently-Targetable Re-entry Vehicle(s)
CFE	Conventional Forces in Europe	MTCR	Missile Technology Control Regime
CFSP	Common Foreign and Security Policy	NACC	North Atlantic Cooperation Council
Cocom	Coordinating Committee for Multilateral Export Control	NAFTA	North American Free Trade Agreement
COMECON	Council for Mutual Economic Assistance	NATO	North Atlantic Treaty Organisation
CPSU	Communist Party of the Soviet Union	NPT	Nuclear Non-Proliferation Treaty
CSCA	Conference on Security and Cooperation in Asia	OAU	Organisation of African Unity
CSCE	Conference on Security and Cooperation in Europe	OAS	Organization of American States
		OECD	Organisation for Economic Co-operation and Development
CTB	Comprehensive Test Ban		
CW	Chemical Weapons	R&D	Research and Development
CWC	Chemical Weapons Convention	RRC	Rapid Reaction Corps
		RSFSR	Russian Soviet Federated Socialist Republic
EC	European Community		
ECOWAS	Economic Community of West African States	SAARC	South Asian Association of Regional Cooperation
EEA	European Economic Area	SALT	Strategic Arms Limitation Treaty
EFTA	European Free Trade Association		
		SEATO	South East Asian Treaty Organization
EMU	European Monetary Union		
EP	European Parliament	SICBM	Small Intercontinental Ballistic Missile
FPDA	Five Power Defence Arrangement	SII	Structural Impediments Initiative
FTA	Free Trade Accord		
GATT	General Agreement on Tariffs and Trade	SLBM	Submarine-launched ballistic missile(s)
G-7	Group of Seven	START	Strategic Arms Reduction Treaty
HEP	Hydroelectric power		
IAEA	International Atomic Energy Agency	UN	United Nations
		UNAMIC	United Nations Advance Mission in Cambodia
ICBM	Intercontinental ballistic missile(s)		
IMF	International Monetary Fund	UNTAC	United Nations Transitional Authority in Cambodia
		WEU	Western European Union